Speech Communication

A Contemporary Introduction

third edition

Speech Communication

A Contemporary Introduction

third edition

Gordon I. Zimmerman
James L. Owen
David R. Seibert
University of Nevada, Reno

West Publishing Company

St. Paul   *New York*   *Los Angeles*   *San Francisco*

Library of Congress Cataloging-in-Publication Data

Zimmerman, Gordon I.
  Speech communication.

  Bibliography: p.
  Includes index.
  1. Oral communication. I. Owen, James L.
II. Seibert, David R. III. Title.
P95.Z5 1986   001.54′2   85-26561
ISBN 0-314-93529-0

Cover

Robert V. Eckert, Jr./EKM-Nepenthe; Tom Tracy/Photophile; Stan-Pak/International Stock Photography, Ltd.; Pam Hasegawa/Taurus Photos; Peter Russell Clemens/International Stock Photography, Ltd.

Photo Credits

1 Pam Hasegawa, Taurus Photos; **2** Sybil Shelton, Peter Arnold, Inc.; **6** Peter Vandermark, Stock, Boston, Inc.; **9** H. Armstrong Roberts; **15** Jeff Dunn, Stock, Boston, Inc.; **24** Jerry Berndt, Stock, Boston, Inc.; **28** AP/Wide World Photos; **31** Jean-Claude LeJeune, Stock, Boston, Inc.; **33** Jeff Dunn, Stock, Boston, Inc.; **35** Cartoon Copyright Don Dougherty; **42** Drawing by Joseph Farris, © 1984 The New Yorker Magazine, Inc.; **46** Sybil Shelton, Peter Arnold, Inc.; **49** Jerry Howard, Stock Boston, Inc.; **51** Gale Zucker, Stock, Boston, Inc.; **55** Cartoon Copyright Clem Scalzitti; **62** EKM-Nepenthe; **68** Cartoon Copyright Don Dougherty; **69** Jean-Claude LeJeune, Stock, Boston, Inc.; **73** Michael Weisbrot, Stock, Boston, Inc.; **77** Elizabeth Hamlin, Stock, Boston, Inc.; **87** Michael Hayman, Stock, Boston, Inc.; **88** James R. Holland, Stock, Boston, Inc.; **92** AP/Wide World Photos; **98** Bettye Lane, Photo Researchers; **103** Art Stein, Photo Researchers; **108** Frank Siteman, Taurus Photos; **110** Tom Sobolik, Black Star; **112** Art Stein, Photo Researchers; **117** Robert A. Isaacs, Photo Researchers; **119** Drawing by Stan Hunt, © 1984 The New Yorker Magazine, Inc.; **127** Jerry Berndt, Stock, Boston, Inc.; **128** Will McIntyre, Photo Researchers; **133** Elizabeth Crews, Stock, Boston, Inc.; **135** Frank Siteman, Stock, Boston, Inc.; **142** Peter Vandermark, Stock, Boston, Inc.; **145** Christopher Morrow, Stock, Boston, Inc.; **150** Peter Southwick, Stock, Boston, Inc.; **156** Peter Menzel, Stock, Boston, Inc.; **164** Richard Wood, Taurus Photos; **168** H. Armstrong Roberts; **174** Joseph Schuyler, Stock, Boston, Inc.; **178** Tim Davis, Photo Researchers; **180** John Maher, EKM-Nepenthe; **185** Laimute Druskis, Stock, Boston, Inc.; **187** AP/Wide World Photos; **194** Owen Franken, Stock, Boston, Inc.; **203** Peter Russell Clemens, International Stock Photography, Ltd.; **204** David Powers, Stock, Boston, Inc.; **208** Frank Siteman, Stock, Boston, Inc.; **211** Peter Vandermark, Stock, Boston, Inc.; **213** H. Armstrong Roberts; **218** Esaias Baitel, Photo Researchers; **221** Van Bucher, Photo Researchers; **226** Hazel Hankin, Stock, Boston, Inc.; **230** Cliff Moore, Taurus Photos; **233** Rick Smolan, Stock, Boston, Inc.; **238** Peter Menzel, Stock, Boston, Inc.; **246** UPI/Bettmann Newsphotos; **252** Robert George Gaylord, Black Star; **258** Art Stein, Photo Researchers; **260** AP/Wide World Photos; **266** Owen Franken, Stock, Boston, Inc.; **268** Richard Wood, Taurus Photos; **272** AP/Wide World Photos; **274** Owen Franken, Stock, Boston, Inc.; **276** Michael Hayman, Photo Researchers; **278** AP/Wide World Photos

TO: Laura and Ken
Kim
Sara and Robert

Contents

Chapter Two

A Receiver-centered View
of Communication   25

Chapter Three

Verbal Communication: Language   47

Chapter Four

Nonverbal Communication   63

Part Two

Information, Persuasion, and Argument   87

Chapter Five

Informative and Persuasive Speaking   89

Chapter Six

The Nature of Argument   109

Chapter Eight

Speech Development: Composition   143

Chapter Nine

Speech Development: Visual Aids   165

Chapter Ten

Speech Development: Delivery   181

Part Four

Practical Interpersonal Communication   203

Chapter Eleven

One-to-One Communication: The Dyad   205

Chapter Twelve

A Special Dyad: The Interview   219

Chapter Thirteen

Small Group Communication   231

Preface

The purpose of this textbook is to help you improve your understanding and skills in speech communication. The focus is on practical communication needs. Although the text provides an overall perspective on human communication, we have no interest in attempting a definitive statement on speech communication theory and research, nor do we want to encumber a speech fundamentals course with a bulky, all-encompassing overview of the field. We want to help you improve your ability to communicate.

To accomplish this purpose, we have drawn from our three extensive backgrounds in speech fundamentals instruction. This strategy has permitted varied information and frequent feedback on the best approaches for each chapter. As noted in our acknowledgments, we have also been able to profit from numerous reviewers who have provided many insightful suggestions. Additionally, we have had considerable experience with the two prior editions and have received helpful suggestions from our students.

We have patterned the book according to the ways in which many speech instructors actually teach the basic course. We have omitted topics that sometimes appear in basic texts but probably will not help you, the beginning student, achieve the objective of practical speech improvement.

The book has four main parts. Part I, "The Process of Human Communication," provides an overall perspective on the nature of human communication. Basic *concepts* as well as prevalent *misconceptions* are considered, and both *verbal* and *nonverbal* language codes are discussed.

Part II addresses the practical topics of *information, persuasion,* and *argument.* These basic topics are discussed in the context of both public speaking and group activities.

Part III focuses on *practical public speaking.* In separate chapters, we discuss speech development in terms of *basic issues in getting started; speech composition*; use of *visual aids*; and *speech delivery*.

Part IV focuses on *practical interpersonal communication* in dyads and small groups. The material on dyadic communication includes discussion of *interviews*, with special emphasis on the *employment interview*. Small group topics include *decisionmaking, leadership*, and *effective participation*. This final section concludes with a chapter on *listening* and *responding*, emphasizing once again the central role of the receiver in all communication activities.

Each chapter contains study questions and suggested readings. An accompanying *Instructor's Guide* provides teaching strategies and suggested projects and exercises. It also includes sample test questions.

Once more we acknowledge the many speech communication faculty from both two- and four-year colleges who provided incisive prepublication reviews for the first edition. Major reviewers were: William E. Arnold, Arizona State University; Clarence H. Baxter, Jr., Sinclair Community College (Ohio); Gary D'Angelo, University of Washington; H. W. Farwell, University of Southern Colorado; Lucia S. Hawthorne, Morgan State University (Maryland); James A. McCubbin, Bloomsburg State College (Pennsylvania); Donald B. Morlan, Eastern Illinois University; Thomas J. Murray, Eastern Michigan University; James W. Pence, Jr., University of North Carolina; Jim Towns, Stephen F. Austin State University (Texas); and Loretta A. Walker, Utah Technical College.

We are especially grateful for the guidance we received from three communication scholars whose experience with the first edition influenced our revisions for the second edition: Don B. Center of the University of Texas, San Antonio; Harry Hazel, Jr., of Gonzaga University; and Bill Henderson of the University of Northern Iowa. Finally, we wish to thank the six reviewers of our second edition: Deborah Brosioff, New York University; Barbara Curtin, Peirce Junior College (Pennsylvania); Stephen Guempel, Louisiana State University; Ron Hartley, Clarion University (Pennsylvania); Jonathan Hook, University of Texas, San Antonio; and Betty Jo Welch, University of North Carolina. Each supplied us with clear-cut and supportive criticism that we believe has substantially improved the "teachability" of the present volume.

Our gratitude extends to our students and teaching fellows at the University of Nevada, Reno, whose study of the first and second editions resulted in many helpful suggestions for revisions that have been incorporated in this volume. Also, we wish once more to thank Mrs. Betty Ghiglieri for her valuable assistance in preparing the manuscript for the first edition, to Mrs. Merle Owen for her equally valuable assistance in preparing the manuscript for the second edition, and to both Mrs. Owen and Ms. Sara Seibert for their considerable help in preparing the manuscript for the third edition.

Gordon I. Zimmerman
James L. Owen
David R. Seibert

I The Process of Human Communication

Part I explores the process of human communication. In the first chapter, we present a simple model of communication and a set of concepts and principles that offer a practical perspective, based on the notion that receivers are the central element in the communication process. We conclude this chapter with a discussion of prevalent misconceptions about human communication.

Chapter Two elaborates on the receiver-centered point of view and offers a set of concepts and principles for analyzing human beings as

receivers of information. Chapters Three and Four deal with the two major coding systems used by humans in communication, language and nonverbal communication behavior.

These four chapters offer conceptual foundations that form the basis for practical application of informative, persuasive, argumentative, public, and interpersonal communication, all of which are discussed in the remaining parts of the text.

Chapter One

Introduction to Speech Communication

Preview

Most of us spend a major portion of every day communicating with other human beings, initiating messages for the consumption of others, and interpreting messages sent by others. Communication is an activity so commonplace that we tend to take it for granted. Yet it is probably the most demanding and complex behavior that we exhibit. We have the capacity to improve our communication skills continuously throughout our lives. The undertaking is difficult, but if we persevere it can be immensely satisfying. Indeed, the study of communication can be an adventurous exploration into a fascinating frontier—the untapped potential of the human mind.

We begin our study of communication with a discussion of some basic concepts useful in communicating about communication. Chapter One introduces some of these key concepts, which form the basis for further inquiry into the problem of improving communication skills.

Objectives

To equip you with basic terms for thinking and talking about human communication

To encourage you to improve on your own communicative competence

To identify some basic principles of human communication

To discuss some common misconceptions about communication

ONE   Dusk settles around a mountain cabin in which a young man and woman are reading light fiction. The young woman shivers slightly in the draft of cool evening air coming through the open window. Her husband notices her shivering and quietly slips to the window to close it.

A student pilot taxis carefully toward the end of the runway for her first solo flight, acutely aware of the different quality of engine noise in the cockpit now that the instructor is no longer in the right seat. The tower operator's voice, calm and businesslike as always, crackles over the radio: "Cessna Two Three Golf, what are your instructor's directions?" The student replies, "Tahoe Tower, Two Three Golf, I'm supposed to make three takeoffs and landings, two touch-and-goes, and a full stop." The tower operator responds, "Roger, Two Three Golf, report downwind when you're abeam the tower, and good luck."

With slightly sweaty palms and queasy stomach, a college student takes his place behind the lectern, looks around at his classmates, and begins to deliver his speech. After a minute or so, his nervousness subsides as he recognizes signs of attention and interest in the audience.

A Definition of Communication

What do these three incidents have in common? They are all instances of human communication. Moreover, each one exemplifies effective communication—communication that is both productive and satisfying for the individuals involved. The communication is productive in that it helps someone accomplish a task, achieve an objective. It is satisfying because these tasks, when accomplished, help fulfill one or more of the participant's needs.

Communication obviously occurred in two of the three incidents, but you may be wondering about the one in the cabin in which no spoken messages were exchanged. Even this incident demonstrates communication within the broad definition serving our present purposes: *Communication is the process in which persons assign meanings to events and especially to the behavior of other persons.*

Functions of Communication:
Content and Relationship

Presumably you are reading this book because you desire to improve your communication skills. If this is your goal, begin by thinking about the functions and purposes that are served by communication.

As a practical matter, over half the employed citizens of the United States produce nothing but symbolic products—words, numbers, images, and so on for the utilization of others and for the management of other's work. Chances are, you will make your living with your communicative skills. This is obviously the case for journalists, teachers, entertainers, and ministers, but it also holds for managers and supervisors—anyone who must exercise influence over others through the preparation of reports and directives, oral or written.

Your own communicative skills and those of others around you will exert an enormous influence on the way you earn your living—even if you're among the fortunate few who have something to show at the end of a day's work, something you made with your hands.

As social creatures, we also depend on one another to fulfill our needs. This interdependence requires that we cooperate with each other, and cooperation depends on the quality of relationships we establish through communication.

An exhaustive list of communication functions can be divided into two broad categories corresponding to our practical and social needs: content and relationship. First, we communicate to accomplish tasks that are essential to fulfill our needs—to feed and clothe ourselves, to satisfy our curiosity about the environment, and to enjoy being alive. Second, we communicate to establish and maintain relationships with others. Thus, communication has both a content function, which involves exchange of information necessary to accomplish tasks, and a relationship function, which involves the exchange of information about where we stand with others. Of course, communication does not serve either purpose independently of the other: it serves both simultaneously (Watzlawick, Beavin, and Jackson, 1967).

Examine your own communicative behavior in terms of these two broad categories by asking yourself: "How does my behavior help me and others to get the job done?" and "How does my behavior affect the quality of my relationships with other people?" If you earnestly pursue these two questions, you'll be well on the way toward discovering what you must do to improve your communicative performance.

Importance of Communication

If you had not already achieved a considerable degree of competence in communication, you wouldn't be able to read this book. You can read and write and speak well enough to be admitted to college. In fact, you may be thinking that you already know how to communicate and that what you need now is more knowledge to communicate about. However,

the acquisition and sharing of knowledge is so intimately bound up with communication that it's impossible to separate the two. The brilliant nuclear physicist Niels Bohr (1961) saw the relationship between knowing and communicating when he said: "As the goal of science is to augment and order our experience, every analysis of the conditions of human knowledge must rest on considerations of the character and scope of our means of communication."

The practical value of developing and improving our communicative skills and techniques is obvious. Each of us, no matter what our individual goals, must achieve minimal levels of competence in communication just to survive as a free and independent person. Beyond these minimal levels of competence, however, our worth to ourselves, to one another, and to all human civilization is directly linked to our communicative behavior. Do you aspire to a difficult profession? To realize your goal, you must not only master the knowledge needed, but must be able to communicate that you have done so. Do you aspire to become an effective advocate of social change? A good parent? A responsible member in society? These goals are absolutely unattainable without a high level of communicative competence.

None of our technological advances would have occurred without the means to store and exchange information efficiently and rapidly and to cooperate with one another for mutual benefit. No matter which human achievements you deem valuable—NASA's exploration of space, modern medicine, progress toward equal opportunity, or whatever—all have occurred as a direct consequence of exceptionally skillful communication.

Similarly, although not every major problem confronting humans is caused exclusively by a "breakdown in communication," as is often naively assumed, inadequate communication is frequently a contributing factor to personal and social failures. This becomes apparent from any careful interpretation of historical events, such as the Viet Nam War, the Watergate scandal, the Bay of Pigs fiasco, the U-2 incident, Japan's attack on Pearl Harbor, or the mass extermination of European Jews under the Third Reich.

The discovery and implementation of solutions to our problems— indeed, the very recognition of our problems—are based on our willingness and skill in communicating with one another symbolically. Clearly, it is imperative that we acquire a better understanding of how communication works and of what we can do to make it work better.

Elements of the Communication Process

There are six major elements in the process of communication. Each is defined here to aid you in understanding the material covered in later chapters. Figure 1–1 is a simple model of communication in which these six elements are identified.

Sender, Source, or Speaker

The terms sender, source, and speaker are used interchangeably. They refer to an individual whose behavior communicates. It is important to recognize that the spoken message is only a part of the total message sent when persons interact with one another. Thus, it is the sender's behavior that communicates.

FIGURE 1–1

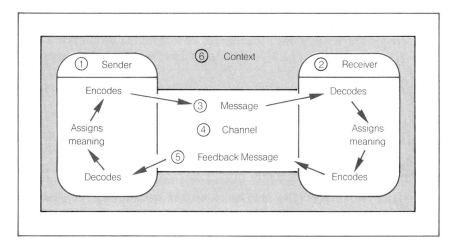

Receiver, Listener, Auditor, or Interpreter

The terms receiver, listener, auditor, and interpreter are also used inter-changeably. They refer to an individual who assigns meaning to the behavior of a sender.

Message

The message is that portion of the sender's behavior to which a receiver assigns meaning. You're accustomed to thinking about a message as something written or spoken. However, messages may take forms other than the shared code of language and speech, and such nonverbal messages contribute much to the meanings assigned by interpreters. Chapter Three introduces the study of nonverbal messages and the kinds of meaning they can stimulate.

Channel

The term channel refers to the medium through which messages are conveyed from senders to receivers. The primary channels of interest are the senses of vision and hearing. Most of the messages we receive are conveyed through patterns of light and sound received through the eyes and ears. As we shall see, however, touch and smell may also be channels in human communication.

Frequently, messages between individuals are mediated by several additional channels, such as electronic media, paint on canvas, or print on a page. Such additional channels permit message transmission between communicators who are separated in space and time. Regardless of the number and nature of media and channels involved, the important thing to remember is that the message received is a product of the sender's behavior.

Feedback

Feedback refers to a message initiated by a receiver in response to a message received, which influences the subsequent behavior of the original sender. Not all responses are feedback. A message is feedback only (1) if it is actually a response to a sender's message that would not have occurred in the absence of the original message, and (2) if it actually influences the original sender's subsequent behavior. Furthermore, feedback may or may not be intentional. For example, if you are giving a speech and someone in the back row is lulled to sleep by your talk, you may or may not notice. If you notice and adjust by raising your voice to awaken the sleeper, you are responding to feedback. If you fail to notice, there has been no feedback.

Context

The term context refers to the situation in which a message is conveyed from sender to receiver. Context includes a number of elements, such as the setting in which the communication occurs, the means of message transmission available, and the various expectations of the senders and receivers. More specifically, a communication context includes such factors as the physical environment, the time of day, the number of people present, their dress, formal and informal rules of conduct for the situation, and even the labels used to describe the situation.

We are all required to communicate in a variety of contexts each day. Each context calls for a different repertoire of communication behaviors and requires sensitivity to the unique demands of the situation. For example, consider the influence of context on the participants' communication behavior in the following five situations:

1. An informal party held outdoors in a public park for twenty-five members of a women's softball team
2. A library tour for a first-year comunication class
3. A formal state dinner in Washington, D.C., for the staff of a foreign embassy
4. A small group of students meeting in the student union coffee shop to prepare for a class presentation
5. That same group's presentation before the class.

The context of a message is crucial to the kind of meaning that will be assigned to it. To illustrate, suppose you encounter two men, one of whom fires a small pistol in the air while the second, who is wearing a black- and white-striped shirt, stops running at the sound of the gunshot. In the context of a football game, these behaviors communicate nothing frightening. In a farmer's field near the state prison, they will produce totally different meanings.

A Definition of Meaning

We said that there are six basic elements in the communication process. To define them, however, we need a seventh term: meaning. When we speak of the meaning of a message, we are referring to some interpreter's response to that message. The distinction between the content and meaning of a message is an essential one because they are not the same thing. When we select words to encode messages, we select ones that we expect will cause our listeners to assign meanings consistent with our intentions. Frequently, a message fails to produce the appropriate response. When this happens, the content of the message has failed to produce the intended meaning.

In general, messages can produce three kinds of meanings (responses) in their interpreters: thinking, feeling, and acting. Morris (1946) has identified three kinds of messages according to the type of meaning responses they produce: designative, appraisive, and prescriptive. *Designative* messages produce thinking responses, which include perceiving, observing, or experiencing objects and events. "This book is printed in black ink" is a designative message because it causes an interpreter to respond on the level of observation—to look at the book and think about whether the message is accurate.

Appraisive messages cause the listener to respond on a feeling level— to evaluate or judge something. "This book is printed with attractive type" is an appraisive message. This message speaks to more than just the observable characteristics of the book because it speaks to someone's feelings about what is attractive and what is not.

Prescriptive messages cause the listener to respond by acting—not just to observe, think, or judge, but to act. "Read this book" is an example of a prescriptive message.

Awareness of these three response categories is useful in helping us prepare messages consistent with our communicative purposes. We send messages designed to stimulate various responses. However, messages do not have automatic effects on their interpreters, partly because interpreters have the capacity to choose how they will respond to a given message. A designative message may stimulate feelings and judgments and may even incite a receiver to action, whereas a prescriptive message may fail to do so. Suppose someone told you, "Your car headlights are on in the parking lot." This is purely a designative message, but one that might cause you to respond with, "Oops, that's no good!" (a feeling response) and might send you scurrying out to turn off the lights (an acting response).

Small children tend to respond only to the literal, explicit content of messages. For example, a father may enter his child's room and announce, "There are clothes and toys scattered all over this room" (designative message), or "This room is a mess!" (appraisive message). If the father's intent is to get the child to pick up, he will frequently have to prescribe, for the child will typically interpret the designative or appraisive message at face value and will fail to recognize and respond to the prescriptive implication in it. In general, the more mature the interpreter, the more likely his or her response to a given message will go beyond the *explicit* content of the message and will reflect what the message implies.

To a large extent, communicative competence involves knowing the receiver's needs with respect to the three kinds of meaning responses— that is, knowing whether, within a given context, the receiver needs a message stimulating him or her to think, feel, act, or do a combination of these things. For example, when the immediate context of communication calls for a rational analysis, as in explaining a mathematical concept, there is a need to stimulate thought. When the context is emotional, as in expressing one's condolences to someone who is grieving, there is a need to stimulate feelings. In a time of grief, it is inappropriate to send messages about the clinical details of death, but highly appropriate to empathize. Finally, when the context requires that the receiver act, there is a demand for prescription. The receiver needs guidance on what to do. When someone is learning to drive a car, fly an airplane, or write a term paper, a lengthy treatise on the theory of internal combustion engines or on linguistic theory will not meet the learner's needs unless it helps him or her perform the acts required to get the job done.

Often a receiver needs a combination of messages—designative, appraisive, and prescriptive. For example, when you go to a physician with a complaint, you are ultimately seeking a prescriptive message: "Do these things and you'll get better." You may also look for messages that describe what is wrong with you: "You've got a common, rarely dangerous, viral infection." You may also want some indication that the doctor empathizes with your discomfort: "It's a miserable bug, but nothing we can't clear up with proper rest and medication." Many communication problems can be avoided if senders are sensitive to the needs and expectations of receivers with respect to designation, appraisal, and prescription.

Much of the material in this book is prescriptive. We intend to tell you what to do to improve your communication skills and to stimulate you to act on the advice. Much of it is also designative, calling on you to observe and think about communication events to understand how they work.

We believe that most people want to know at least some of the theoretical (designative) support for the advice they receive. We, the authors, share some beliefs about human communication—crucial beliefs that have shaped our thinking about communication. They provide the basis for much of the advice we give here. It is appropriate that we share those beliefs with you, so you'll know where we're "coming from."

Communication Theory: Some Basic Principles

All Behavior Communicates

In its broadest sense, the study of communication is the study of what happens when people behave in each other's presence or leave evidence of their behavior where others can find it. If we think of communication as limited to what individuals *intend* to communicate, we overlook some extremely important aspects of the process. For example, the man who lights up a fat cigar in a restaurant may not intend to communicate anything to someone seated at the next table; nonetheless a message is conveyed and a meaning may be assigned. Irrespective of our intentions, our behavior is subject to interpretation by others.

You, as a speaker addressing an audience, may spend a great deal of time and effort polishing the speech, but may fail to influence listeners because you are careless about some of the other messages sent inadvertently during your delivery. If you fidget and shuffle your feet to the point of distraction, if your dress and grooming are inappropriate for the occasion, or if your style of speaking detracts from your credibility, then the meanings assigned to the verbal portion of your behavior may be adversely affected. Remember that a listener has the right and the responsibility to assign meanings to the total behavior of the communicator. You cannot reasonably expect people to just listen to your words and ignore the rest of what you're doing. Listeners, not speakers, decide what is relevant to the assignment of meanings.

This is not to say that all behavior automatically communicates. The point is that any and all behavior may communicate. Behavior that goes unnoticed will not stimulate meaning; behavior that draws attention to itself certainly will.

We Cannot Not Communicate

It is a mistake to believe that by sitting still and keeping silent, we can avoid communicating. When we withdraw from active interaction with others, we are actually communicating a great deal. Passive, silent behavior may stimulate a variety of meanings. At best, silence may lead others to conclude that we are shy or reticent. At worst, it may signify that we are lazy, stupid, incompetent, or indifferent to others. There is even a principle of law that assigns a shared meaning to silence under some circumstances. Silence implies consent. Our silence may be interpreted as indicating our approval of a situation in which we're involved. You may have seen the play or movie *A Man For All Seasons,* a story about Sir Thomas More who was Lord Chancellor of England during the reign of Henry VIII. Henry sought More's approval of his divorce from the queen in order to marry Anne Boleyn, his mistress. More did not approve of the divorce, but chose to remain silent, believing that his silence would give implicit consent and spare him from Henry's wrath, which usually involved the headsman. Henry finally solved the problem by having Sir Thomas beheaded. Your silence may not cost you your head, but you should recognize that it conveys a message and may not produce the meaning you intend.

Messages Do Not Have Meanings

Meanings are assigned by interpreters as responses to messages. It is commonly understood that words have meanings and that the proper meanings of words can be found in the dictionary. This is a serious misconception. Words do not "have" meanings any more than sharp knives "have" cut fingers. Rather, words stimulate receivers to assign meanings. Messages do not convey ideas form one mind to another; they elicit ideas in their interpreters. In short, messages cause meanings but do not carry them.

When someone says that words have meanings, he or she means only that their interpreters are highly likely to assign certain commonly shared meanings to those words. Words communicate accurately only if they elicit the same meanings in both sender and receiver. A college professor once spent many months drafting a manuscript for a new textbook. He gave the manuscript to his secretary with the instruction, "Burn this for me, will you?" He intended for the secretary to photocopy the manuscript, and he was using the office jargon "burn." You guessed it. Months of hard work went up in smoke in the incinerator.

Another unsatisfactory communication occurred in Japan some years ago. A Navy aircraft squadron contracted with a Japanese machine shop to build a nosewheel strut for one of its airplanes. The original strut had developed a tiny, perfectly straight hairline crack at one end. The Americans stressed the importance of replacing the strut with a perfect copy—precisely machined to the dimensions and specifications of the original. When the Americans returned to pick up the new strut, they got exactly what they had requested—a perfect copy of the original strut, including the crack. The Japanese machinists were justifiably proud of their work and announced that the crack had been most difficult to duplicate.

These communication failures were caused by ambiguous or incomplete messages that failed to produce appropriate interpretations in their receivers. They may seem to be extreme examples, but they illustrate common occurrences. You can probably recall incidents from your own experience in which misunderstandings have resulted from the assumption that messages are conveyor belts on which meanings travel intact from mind to mind.

Communication Is a Participative Process

The key words here are process and participate. Let's begin with the notion of process. A process is not a tangible thing, but a pattern of dynamic relationships among things, a patterned sequence of events.

Even the simplest communication between two persons, "Pass the salt," involves a complex chain of events if the receiver complies with the request. Furthermore, it is difficult to determine precisely where and when a given communication event begins and ends. For some purposes, we can say that the preceding event began when person A asked for the salt and ended when person B surrendered the saltshaker. But we cannot account for the event entirely in terms of what happened between the asking and the passing. Both person A and person B drew on past experience to encode and decode the message and to respond appropriately. As another example, consider a person giving a speech. When does the communication between speaker and audience begin? When the speaker takes his or her position behind the lectern? When he or she enters the room? When the person's services as a speaker were initially engaged? When does the communication end? Unless the speaker's message is forgotten the instant he or she stops speaking, audience members may continue to assign meanings to the message months and even years later. Can we really say that the communication process ended at the conclusion of the speech?

How we punctuate or identify critical points in the communication process (such as beginnings and endings) is crucial to our understanding of the process. A small boy once demonstrated precocious wisdom about the communication process:

MOTHER: (Noticing her son's black eye and bruised knuckles after he has been playing with a neighbor's child) Did you and Eric get into a fight?

BOY: Yeah.

MOTHER: Who started it?

BOY: Well, I guess I started with the hitting part, but he started with the talking part.

Another aspect of the communication process is that the various components are constantly undergoing change, which is especially true of the most important components of the process—the communicators themselves. For example, when someone sends a message that is especially important for some receiver, the receiver's orientation toward the sender changes dramatically and vice versa. The sender and receiver experience change as a consequence of the communication between them. Extremely important communication events illustrate this principle: proposals of marriage; disclosures of love and affection; messages that truly inform, persuade, or inspire. Some common and simple messages that produce life-changing consequences for senders and receivers are:

"I love you."

"We find the defendant not guilty, your honor."

"Congratulations . . ."

"We deeply regret to inform you that . . ."

"It is our pleasure to inform you that your application has been approved."

When we say that communication is a process in which senders and receivers participate, we mean that both sender and receiver must participate actively for effective communication to occur. This may seem obvious, but we believe that many individuals tend to view communication as a lopsided process in which senders do most of the work and receivers sit back and soak up the message. It doesn't work that way, or at least when it works that way, it doesn't work very well.

Listening and responding appropriately to the messages of others is demanding work, especially when an opportunity for constructive feedback exists. An actively participating listener assigns meanings to a sender's message on the basis of his or her own previous experiences, both with language and with nonlinguistic perceptual stimuli. Senders rarely express their own meanings as perfect messages—perfect in the sense that they produce the intended meanings for listeners. Productive and satisfying communication does not occur unless listeners work diligently in assigning meanings. It is misleading to think of communication as something done by speakers to listeners, because there is so much room for variation in assigning meanings to a given message and so many many different ways for senders to encode messages reflecting their own meanings. Barnlund (1968) defines communication in two deceptively simple phrases as (1) the process of creating a meaning, and (2) an effort after meaning. Combining the two, we see that communication is a creative effort for both senders and receivers.

We can easily lose sight of this important principle and relax when we think it's someone else's turn to be "on stage." When it's our turn to

deliver a speech, participate in a discussion, or chair a meeting, we usually feel some tension and excitement as the adrenaline begins to flow. When we're not "on," we tend to relax, but if we relax too much, we don't fulfill our obligations in the effort to obtain meaning. Think of it in this way: when you're engaged in the process of communication, try to understand the messages of another human being as if you're always "on."

Myths About Communication

Conventional wisdom about communication is full of fantasy, fiction, and myth. A good way to conclude this introductory chapter is to let you in on some of the things we do not believe about communication, after having told you some of the things we do believe.

Communication Is Good

Contrary to popular opinion, we, the authors, do not subscribe to the view that communication is inherently good. Neither do we believe it is bad. We view communication as essentially neutral, that is, as a general object of judgment. Far too often, naive advocates of communication claim that it has unwarranted curative powers for all kinds of personal and social ills. Communication breakdowns, failures, and barriers are frequently blamed for problems in which communication is a major cause rather than a cure. The movie *Cool Hand Luke* depicts two men engaged in a violent fight while an onlooker smugly proclaims, "What we have here is a failure to communicate." Nonsense. What we have in the fight is communication in its most primitive and brutally direct form—two men engaged not only in a physical contest but in a rhetorical, symbolic act as well, the extended meaning of which is far more important than the immediate victory itself.

Not wishing to belabor the point, let it suffice to say that most fights, wars, neuroses, psychoses, depressions, recessions, frauds, and other catastrophes under human control have communicative acts—usually an exchange of words—as both a root cause and an ultimate remedy. Communication is much like fire in that it is a marvelous benefactor and a formidable foe.

Communication Is Technique

Much communication is instrumental—that is, it is deliberate, intentional, and is aimed at producing a desired response in some person or persons. One of the main reasons to study communication is to develop and refine technical skills toward producing a desired response. Although a view of communication as technique has utility in skills training, it can narrow your vision of the process of human communication to the point of folly, by overemphasizing the behavior of senders and neglecting receivers and contexts as critical elements of the process. Communication viewed purely as the mastery of technique leads to the kind of paradoxical vision that says, "Communication skill is 99 percent sincerity, and once you've learned to fake that you've got it made."

Persuasion Is Bad

The persuasion myth is closely related to the previous one. Persuasion is communication with a purpose; the communicator intends to affect someone's responses in some predetermined way. The term has come to be associated with the selling of products, many of them useless; the selling of political candidates, many of them inept; and the selling of ideologies, many of them destructive. Persuasion has come to be associated with deception, manipulation, dishonesty, and self-interest. It is seldom seen as communication that is altruistic, where the benefits to the receiver are as great or greater than those to the sender. This outlook is unfortunate because persuasion is ethically and morally neutral, a kind of communication that can be put to good or bad ends, using both good and bad means. The view that persuasion is something bad is just as dangerous as the view that communication is something good. Your view of persuasion should not be colored by the image of the shyster-lawyer or the dishonest used-car salesperson. Persuasion is also the tool of physicians in their efforts to heal, ministers in their work to comfort the afflicted, and teachers in their process to instruct.

Honesty Is Always the Best Policy

This one is a product of the 1960s with its enormous investment in the exploration of inner space—the self, the individual, in intimate relationship with others. One of the things explored at length in the human relations movement was the effect of violating the rules, customs, formalities (although most of them were unwritten and informal) that used to be known as "good manners." One such unwritten rule was that half-truths and "white lies" often lubricate human relationships far better than the truth, the whole truth, and nothing but the truth, especially when the truth involves judgments of one another.

The advancement of honesty led to all sorts of jarring encounters. Cheery greetings in the hallway, "Hi, how are you this morning?" were met with, "Lousy, if you really want to know, but you probably really don't give a damn anyway and were just performing a meaningless social ritual." Insensitive communication became socially acceptable, justified in the name of giving "feedback." Subordinates felt freer to communicate honest appraisals of the performance of their superiors, often with career-changing consequences. Students did likewise with teachers. Spouses confessed with increasing frequency to marital infidelities, thereby unburdening themselves of guilt feelings and often losing their partner as well. Self-disclosure (revelation to another of personal facts that would not normally be known unless voluntarily disclosed) among relatively new acquaintances became common practice, often to the surprise and chagrin of persons only interested in polite conversation. They suddenly found themselves in the role of confessor, confidant, and therapist for a relative stranger eager to "let it all hang out."

Selectivity in communication is a critical aspect of communicative competence and skill. Knowing what is appropriate to say to a given person in a given circumstance is a matter calling for ethical and aesthetic judgment guided by empathy and sensitivity to the needs and feelings of others. Selectivity implies that too much of a good thing, even of honesty, is *too* much.

Content Is All that Matters

The "content is all that matters" myth about communication is a favorite among task-oriented, nose-to-the-grindstone individuals whose view of communication is simply to get the work of the world done as quickly and as efficiently as possible. People who subscribe to this view are likely to lack sensitivity and skill in sending and receiving cues about relationships between themselves and others, or to demonstrate little sense of what is appropriate in terms of form and style in composing and transmitting messages for various occasions. For example, suppose you received an invitation to a party at the home of a prominent individual in your community. The invitation states that you are to be a guest of honor, one among many individuals being honored for a community service you have performed. The invitation takes the form of an original letter, signed by the host. Such a letter, by virtue of its form as well as of its content, honors you doubly, and is likely both to receive your prompt attention and to make you feel important for your efforts. Now consider receiving precisely the same information content contained in the letter by alternative means:

- a telephone message from the host's secretary
- a photocopy of a form letter addressing all invitees in general
- an announcement appearing in the newspaper

Would you feel the same way about this invitation under all four circumstances? Perhaps you would, but we doubt it.

In a sense, the *form* of a message *is content*, because it elicits meanings that are often equally important to the literal message content itself. This point of view is also frequently used to justify or excuse sloppy, careless, undisciplined work, ranging from poorly typed papers to monotonously delivered speeches. The sender assumes that as long as the necessary information is available to some recipient, his or her obligations have been met. This is a grievous error because a poorly prepared and delivered message often has a self-cancelling effect, damaging the credibility and attractiveness of the sender and thereby rendering the message less salient and effective.

Communication is a multilevel process, with several messages traveling simultaneously much of the time. The form of a message is a second message, one that says something about the first, which is the literal content. A term often used for this is *metacommunication,* or communication about communication. The care evidenced in preparation and delivery of a message can say you "cared enough to send the very best," or it can say that you "cared so little because you didn't even bother to spell the recipient's name correctly."

An overemphasis on content at the expense of form also suggests a lack of understanding of style in communication. Style is a matter of aesthetic or artistic judgment—a set of characteristics of a message that gives it a special flavor or tone. There are so many different elements of style in written and spoken messages that a complete list is impractical here, but consider just a few of the stylistic alternatives available to the human communicator:

Whether or not to use sensory imagery or vivid terms

Whether or not to use humor

Whether or not to use irony

Whether or not to use figurative language

Whether or not to be clear and specific

Whether or not to use special vocabulary

Whether or not to use complex sentences

Persons who win acclaim as exceptionally good communicators are masters of style. Conversely, terse, efficient, and accurate-information senders are frequently seen as dull and uninteresting, because they fail to make listeners see the value of their messages. When General Douglas MacArthur retreated from Corregidor early in World War II, he made a pledge to his men and to the citizens of the Philippines he left behind saying, "I shall return." This potent phrase is well remembered. Would they enjoy such a place in history had he merely said, "I'll be back"?

Unfortunately, a good many skilled communicators understand the power of form and style, and use that power to achieve their ends at the expense of substance. This is particularly true of communication campaigns aimed at large numbers of people for purposes from winning elections, to selling products, to soliciting donations for charitable or religious organizations. *Propaganda* is a term commonly used to denote one-sided communication designed to produce a very specific and pragmatic outcome—to narrow rather than broaden the receivers' perceptions of alternatives and choices. By its nature, propaganda appeals to the less rational side of human nature, because the communicator uses evidence and reason selectively at the expense of accuracy and completeness.

Although we urge you, as students, to devote your energy to developing communication skills involving the use of form and style, we certainly do not encourage you to do so at the expense of content. Attention to content means accuracy and completeness in reporting facts, logic in reasoning from those facts, and thoroughness in disclosing your sources of information, your purposes, and the underlying values that motivate you to undertake communication with your chosen listeners.

The Sender and the Message Are the Central Elements in Communication

You recall that the communication process involves six basic elements: sender, receiver, message, channel, feedback, context. Stop reading for a moment, and consider which of these elements is the most important in communication and which is the next most important.

If you think you've just been asked a silly question, you're right. In any complex system or process in which all the elements are interdependent, no one element is more important than the others. The question we asked is analogous to asking which side of a rectangle, its length or its width, contributes more to its area. However, in the context of a course such as this one in which the objective is to improve communication skills, there is often relatively more emphasis placed on two of these elements than on the other four. More specifically, we believe that the sender and the message are often viewed as more important than the others. When the sender is seen as most prominent or important, we call this a sender-centered view of communication.

The Sender-centered View of Communication   A sender-centered view of communication sees the sender as the most important element of the process. It's not too surprising that senders get a lot of attention. In a public speaking situation, the speaker "has the floor," meaning that some group of individuals has sufficient interest in what the speaker has to say to remain silent and listen for a while. Often, the speaker is someone with special skill, authority, knowledge, or whatever that accounts for the interest of the audience.

The sender-centered view emphasizes the motives and behavior of the sender of a message and assigns meaning to the sender's message in those terms. There's nothing wrong with this view, per se, *except when it is the predominant view of the sender.* You've probably seen the following statement about communication on bulletin boards, for example:

I Know That You Believe You
Understand What
You Think I Said, But
I Am Not Sure
You Realize That What You Heard
Is Not
What I Meant.

Is the sender of this message terribly preoccupied with his or her *own* meanings and intentions to the point that he or she takes insufficient account of the needs, motives, intentions, and other relevant characteristics of listeners? It is easy to lose sight of the simple fact that a receiver cannot "hear what we mean," but only what we say.

An extremely sender-centered view is that of an individual who expects others to understand, on the basis of very little information, what he or she thinks and wants. Such a person is easily frustrated in efforts to communicate, and does not enjoy the work involved in communicating for its own sake.

The Message-centered View of Communication One whose view of communication is message-centered places major importance on the mere existence of messages, often attributing to them power that is almost magical. We see many examples of a message-centered view in our society. For example, we invest a lot of authority in the fine print of a written contract in our business dealings. We record and store messages at an astronomical rate, even claiming solemnly that the explosion of printed information in our libraries and databases constitutes an explosion of "knowledge," despite little evidence that most individuals are any more familiar with the contents of these sources than they have ever been.

The message-centered person may say, "I hate to say I told you so," but probably doesn't at all object to reminding listeners of a previous communication that was presumably unheeded.

The message-centered view has some frightening implications. In instructing juries, taking pleas, questioning prospective jurors, and communicating the many other procedures necessary to due process of law, some judges in our law courts become more concerned about "getting the right words into the record" (the trial transcript) than with making sure that the persons in the courtroom actually understand what is going on. Similarly, teachers become preoccupied with "covering the material"—uttering the words form the lecture notes—rather than with whether or not the students are able to assimilate the information presented. Citizens become complacent about the protections afforded by the words in the U.S. Constitution, not realizing that those words have no power apart from the daily exercise and vigorous pursuit of our rights which, like muscles, soon wither and die if unused.

The Receiver-centered View of Communication The receiver-centered view of communication is a pragmatic one in which the receiver is seen as the most critical element in the communication process because it is the receiver who ultimately assigns the meaning to communication events. Communication between people is productive and satisfying to the extent that *meanings are shared.* Shared meanings result from the intentions of the sender being captured in a message that produces mutual understanding in the receiver. The effective functioning of the message depends upon the experience and skill of the receiver in interpreting messages. It is therefore critically important to view the receiver as the central element in the communication process if you are to understand the outcomes of communicative acts.

Summary

As the text progresses, we develop these principles further. For now, understand that our purposes are to help you become more effective communicators, more conscious of the ethical and moral dimensions of communicative acts, and more able to recognize and reconcile the natural tension that exists between pragmatic and ethical objectives in human communication.

As you continue reading, refer back to these ideas from time to time to help you organize your thinking about the communication process.

We've introduced a simple model of communication and defined its elements: sender, receiver, message, channel, feedback, context, and meaning. We've said that all behavior communicates and that we cannot not communicate. We've said that messages do not have meanings but rather serve to stimulate them in receivers, and that meanings are the responses of receivers to messages. We have characterized the communication process as participative, and identified a number of myths about communication that we believe are prevalent today.

Questions

1. Why do our attempts to avoid communicating frequently communicate things we do not intend?

2. What are your greatest strengths and weaknesses as a communicator? What kinds of feedback have led you to these conclusions?

3. What are some of the communication skills demanded of you in connection with your current activities? What kinds of new demands do you anticipate ten years from now? Twenty years from now?

4. Suppose you were asked by your instructor: "Would you rather be graded in this class on the basis of what you *really know* about the subject, or on what you are able to communicate about what you know?" Consider this question in light of what you know about communication, and offer a reply to the instructor's question.

5. Do you agree with what we've said about communication myths? Why or why not?

Suggested Readings

BARNLUND, D. C. (1962). Toward a meaning-centered philosophy of communication. *Journal of Communication, 12,* 197–211.

DE VITO, J. A. (1981). *Communication concepts and processes* (3rd ed.). Englewood Cliffs, N.J.: Prentice-Hall.

GERBNER, G. (1972). Communication and the social environment. *Scientific American, 227,* 152–160.

GOLDMARK, P. C. (1972). Communication and the community. *Scientific American, 227,* 143–150.

MILLER, G. (1969). *The psychology of communication.* Baltimore: Penguin.

Chapter Two

A Receiver-centered View of Communication

Preview

In Chapter One, we propose that communication should be viewed from a receiver-centered perspective. In this chapter, we suggest some concepts and principles we've found useful for analyzing receivers.

We begin by defining the concepts of beliefs, values, and attitudes, as characteristics of receivers that are essentially verbal in nature and have a direct bearing on how they behave. We move to a discussion of receivers' beliefs about themselves and of how such beliefs relate to communication.

Next, we discuss some principles of motivation relevant to the formation of beliefs, values, and attitudes. We believe these principles are generally true of human beings, and have strong implications for both their communicative behavior as senders and for their susceptibility to influence by communication from others.

Objectives

To elaborate on receiver-centered view of communication

To offer some basic concepts and principles for analysis of receivers

To suggest some motivational principles useful in understanding how receivers assign meaning in communication

To identify some of the similarities and differences between people that affect communication

TWO   This chapter focuses on human beings as information-processing systems, "consumers" of information if you will, although we caution you not to make too literal an interpretation of the term "consumer."

Adopting a receiver-centered perspective of human communication requires naming of parts—identifying some characteristics of human communicators that are useful in describing, explaining, and predicting their behavior. We have found the following set of concepts useful for this purpose.

Communication and Motivation— Causes and Consequences

There are many ways to talk about human behavior and motivation—why persons do what they do. Similarly, there are many ways to discuss the role of communication in human behavior—how an individual's own communicative behavior influences other forms of activity, and how information communicated by others influences behavior. We proceed on the rather commonsense assumptions that behavior is influenced by beliefs, values, and attitudes, which in turn are influenced by communication.

Definitions—Beliefs, Values, Attitudes, Behavior

Beliefs

Beliefs are intrapersonal statements, that is, basic units of what we commonly call "thinking." Unexpressed beliefs are private intrapersonal statements about reality as each of us perceives it. When expressed publicly in speech or writing, they are called *opinions.* Just as a sentence represents a relationship between subject and object, beliefs represent *perceived relationships* between subjects or between a subject and one or more of its attributes. Each of our beliefs is characterized by a degree of confidence in its truth—the probability we assign to its accuracy. Virtually any idea that can be expressed as a declarative statement beginning with "I believe that . . ." is a belief.

As defined here, even those things that we "know for certain" are beliefs, as are those things that we accept tentatively with varying degrees of assurance. All these statements are expressions of beliefs:

The sun rises in the East and sets in the West.

God exists.

Every action is accompanied by a reaction equal in force and opposite in direction.

All behavior communicates.

Murder is wrong.

John will be late for our luncheon.

A study by the Los Angeles City Planning Commission aptly illustrates the differences in our individual beliefs. Members of the commission asked people from various ethic and economic groups to draw a map of the city. Each individual was asked to include as much detail as possible. Study findings showed the following:

Upper class residents from Westwood had an extensive knowledge of the city, including the location of such features as beaches, airports, universities and museums. But, Black residents of Avalon (near Watts) perceived L.A. as consisting only of the inner city with a few main streets. Maps made by Hispanic residents of Boyle Heights contained, in addition to their own neighborhood, only City Hall, Union Station and the bus terminal. Both poor Blacks and Hispanic citizens were aware that the city is, in fact, larger than their own neighborhoods, but depicted other areas only with empty circles (Newsweek, March 15, 1976).

Each individual develops not only a set of beliefs or "mental map" of the city in which he or she lives but an entire cultural perspective made up of beliefs that pertain to a multitude of other events. Beliefs pertain to what we *see* and how we draw boundaries around what we see. Our mental maps vary in completeness and incompleteness, in accuracy and distortion, and in the extent to which they are shared or not shared by others in our environment. Just as our mental maps of a city largely determine the ways in which we will use a city, our mental maps of self, of others, and of the world around us provide the basis for the ways in which we communicate with ourselves and others and for how the world communicates with us.

The ways our unique concepts directly influence communication are illustrated by the experiences of an American social worker assigned to a Peruvian village. Studies had shown that contaminated drinking water was the source of many of the villagers' diseases, and the social worker was training the Peruvian women to boil water as one means of reducing illness in the village. An extensive effort to communicate this "simple" information about the benefits of boiling the water affected the behavior of only a handful of the women! Why did the communication fail? Attempts to answer this question led to several discoveries. First, the Pe-

ruvian women had no concept for "bacteria," nor could they imagine how something invisible could be harmful. Furthermore, the villagers believed that "warm" was for the sick and "cold" for the healthy. Accordingly, their customs dictated that they serve cold water to the healthy and warm to the ill. To boil water for a healthy person was to contradict beliefs well established in village traditions (Rogers and Shoemaker, 1971). Thus, the failure in communication was traced to differences in the beliefs held by the social worker and the villagers; that is, the villagers had no concept for "bacteria" and the social worker did not share their belief that "warm" was only for the sick.

The study of intercultural communication reveals many differences in the beliefs we hold. For example, our concept that a cow is something to eat is abhorrent in India where cows are sacred. Although these great differences in beliefs are clearly apparent across cultures, they are sometimes less perceptible within a single culture, perhaps partly because we frequently stress our similarities while avoiding our great individual differences. These differences exist and contribute to many communication failures.

Values

Values are beliefs that are evaluative or judgmental in nature, such as, "Murder is wrong." When expressed verbally, they include value terms, such as *good, bad, right, wrong, just, unjust, pleasant, unpleasant, important, unimportant.* Thus, values are beliefs that reflect our *feelings.*

Most individuals have a relatively small number of basic, or *central,* values, perhaps as few as ten or twenty, but these basic values form a core of judgmental beliefs that may form the basis of thousands of other beliefs. For example, if you have a basic value that might be called "reverence for all living creatures," this value will bear directly on many related beliefs, ranging from beliefs about weapons and war to beliefs about pesticides and pollution.

Your central values are enormously important, because they are significant in the way you define yourself and hold yourself in esteem. Rokeach (1968) has identified thirty-six values that are predominant in U.S. culture, half of which are instrumental values (preferred ways of behaving), and half of which are terminal values (goals worth achieving). *Honest, obedient,* and *logical* are examples of the instrumental values, whereas *salvation, a world at peace,* and *family security* are examples of terminal values. How you order these values in terms of importance is an indication of their centrality for you. Bear in mind that beliefs, such as, "The world is not at peace," are beliefs about fact, not about value. "A world at peace is very important," is a value belief.

Attitudes

Attitudes are belief systems—clusters of fact and value beliefs relevant to some common object of judgment called an *attitude object.* Values included within the cluster determine the favorability of the attitude object. These systems of belief may be thought of as general likes and dislikes that serve as predispositions to behave in somewhat consistent and predictable ways toward their objects. Virtually anything that can be named can be an attitude object—material objects, ideas, or events.

For example, consider *public speaking* as an attitude object. An individual holding a favorable attitude about public speaking is one whose beliefs about this activity, taken together, are consistent with the individual's basic values, goals, and objectives. Such an individual might typically hold the following beliefs:

"I believe that public speaking helps my career" (fact belief).

"I believe that my career makes a worthwhile contribution to society" (value belief).

"I enjoy speaking to an audience" (value belief).

"I believe that public speaking gets me social recognition" (fact belief).

"Social recognition is a goal worth achieving" (value belief).

This is obviously not an exhaustive list of an individual's beliefs that are relevant to public speaking as an attitude object. Each one implies the existence of other beliefs about related objects and issues, such as career objectives, relationships with people, and so on. Nonetheless, this small list of representative beliefs suggests a consistent attitude toward public speaking that would predispose the individual to engage in the activity.

Now consider the individual who is afraid of public speaking (unfortunately, a fear that is shared by a good many persons). It is likely that such an individual will subscribe to beliefs consistent with this fear:

"I believe that public speaking makes me very nervous" (fact belief).

"I dislike being nervous" (value belief).

"I believe that public speaking exposes me to ridicule and rejection" (fact belief).

"I believe that ridicule and rejection are unbearable" (value belief).

Such a cluster of beliefs constitutes an unfavorable attitude toward public speaking, predisposing the individual to avoid it.

A person's beliefs, both factual and evaluative, can cluster in limitless combinations to form attitudes, and the number of attitudes that may form is enormous. Each individual's system of attitudes is unique, because the combination of beliefs that comprises it is a product of individual experience. It is also clear that each individual's conception of what is *relevant* to a given object or topic is likely to differ from anyone else's conception of relevance.

Behavior

Broadly defined, behavior is anything a person does that is observable by someone else. The unit of behavior is the *act*. Beliefs, attitudes, and values held by an individual are not observable to others; behaviors are. We cannot see, hear, feel, taste, or smell the beliefs, values, and attitudes of others, but we can infer their existence from the way people behave. Do you believe that littering is wrong? If so, there's no way for anyone else to know it unless you act to disclose your belief, either by saying so or by taking pains not to litter. Whether you state your belief as an opinion or go out of your way to deposit trash in trash containers, you are behaving in a way that indicates your beliefs.

Attributing beliefs, attitudes, and values on the basis of indirect evidence often results in errors. For example, it is absurd to conclude that all military personnel like killing or have favorable attitudes toward war simply because they have chosen to serve in the armed forces. Some persons who hate public speaking do it anyway, choosing the least undesirable of two unattractive alternatives, such as losing a job. Too, direct statements of belief are not always reliable indicators of what people actually think and feel. People lie, even to themselves. The only way to draw reliable inferences about what a person believes is to observe him or her over a period of time long enough to determine whether the individual's verbalized opinions are consistent with his or her behavior with respect to the beliefs in question.

Origins

No one is born with beliefs, values, and attitudes. These are part and parcel of our human capacity to represent our experience symbolically, using language and speech as our tools. Our beliefs, values, and attitudes do not begin to take shape until we acquire verbal skills. Nor are we born with the behavioral repertoire of a mature adult. These behaviors are acquired in the process of maturation and are profoundly influenced by our interactions with other people in symbolic communication.

From a developmental point of view, we can see communication as the process whereby we develop repertoires of beliefs, values, attitudes, and behaviors as a consequence of our unique histories of interaction within a social community. Communicative behavior is essentially social behavior. Although our basic capacity for communication can be attributed to our unique genetic history, the particular form and scope of a person's communication can be attributed to historical influences on his or her language communities. It is no accident that people who grow up in an English-speaking community speak English, whereas individuals who are raised in a Hispanic community speak Spanish. The effects of the language community upon the individual go far beyond vocabulary and grammar, determining what we see, how we feel about what we see, and how we are likely to respond to the world around us.

A speaker's language behavior itself evolves from a considerable amount of social interaction and instruction. Children imitate the language of their parents and others in their immediate environment. The child is encouraged to use language, is provided with models, is corrected when mistakes are made, and is rewarded when he or she gets it right. After the community is successful at getting the child to generate a lot of talk, the next problem is to get the child to curb talk and keep quiet! The child must learn to distinguish between those occasions where certain forms of talk are encouraged and those where talk is discouraged. With increasing age and maturity, the silent, *intrapersonal* talk we call thinking refines

our beliefs, values, and attitudes, but it is important to recognize that these things originate in social interaction.

It seems obvious that a person's behavior is motivated by his or her beliefs, values, and attitudes. Less obvious but just as reasonable is the proposition that our beliefs are consequences of our habitual behavior (Bem, 1970, 54). For example, consider once again our public speaking example. Have you ever known anyone who never makes public speeches but truly believes that it is an enjoyable and important activity? Probably not. Many, if not most, persons are initially frightened about public speaking and develop favorable beliefs about it only after they have given some speeches and have discovered some form of personal satisfaction in doing so. The behavior occurs *prior* to the formation of favorable beliefs about the topic. A little reflection about some of your own favorite activities and how they came to be favorites will reinforce this point.

Beliefs About Self

These concepts give us a way of addressing two fundamental issues that bear on human communicative behavior—what do we know about the similarities among people, and what do we know about their differences that account for the way they respond to communication? One way of getting a handle on these issues is to acknowledge that *what people believe about themselves* is a powerful determinant of how they respond to their environments. Put another way, a person's *self-concept*—beliefs that a person holds that virtually define for the self who he or she is—is the key to understanding that person's communicative behavior, as a receiver of information and as a sender. Let's postulate, then, one critically important similarity among people: everybody has a self-concept, and each person's is unique and different from everyone else's. For example, some of the crucial beliefs in (David's) self-concept include that I am Becky's husband, father of Sara and Robert, teacher, avid water-skier and windsurfer, and someone who enjoys making people laugh. These are ego-involving elements for me, in the sense that they are central to the way I define myself and are inextricably tied to my central value beliefs about what is worth doing and what goals are worth achieving. Notice that items relating to family life, career, and leisure activity are included. Many individuals would have corresponding beliefs about themselves in the first two areas but would not regard leisure pursuits as definitive of themselves as I do. The main point here is that the *content* of people's self-defining beliefs is quite variable—unique to each individual—and is the key to understanding the uniqueness of each individual's responses to information communicated by others.

Communication and Self-Concept

Think of yourself as a receiver of information. In fact, that is precisely what you have been doing most of your life—receiving information from your environment, some of which takes the form of spoken messages

initiated by others specifically for you. It is this information from your environment that has caused you to develop your potentials in specified ways, and the verbal information has been especially crucial to your development.

As we learn language and speech in the first two years of life, we acquire not just a means of communicating with others, but a means of communicating with ourselves as well. One's self becomes a subject of communication, a topic about which humans exhibit enormous curiosity that can be satisfied only through communicative behavior. Consider for a moment how you know what you know about yourself. Your first reaction is probably to see this as another silly question. Obviously because you have spent so much time with yourself, you are in a better position than anyone else to know yourself well. Much of the information you receive about yourself is observable only to you: it is private, a part of your inner experience. However, much of the information you receive about yourself is also accessible to others—readily available to anyone who takes the time to observe. For example, you alone know what it *feels* like to throw a ball, solve a math problem, or see the humor in something, but others can see your overt actions, and so can you. You observe yourself throwing, catching, laughing, and getting the same number as the bank does on your account statement on occasion. Thus, a part of what you know about yourself is based on the same kind of information you use to know about others, and vice versa.

Now consider for a moment how *accurate* your knowledge about yourself may be. The accuracy of a person's self-knowledge is not guaranteed any more than the accuracy of any other topic. We humans have a remarkable capacity to be wrong when it comes to basic facts about ourselves. Moreover, the less accurate our knowledge about ourselves, the less we are able to function as effectively at work, at play, and in our relationships with others.

Communication plays a critical role in the acquisition of self-knowledge and in the accuracy of that knowledge. One of the most interesting features of being human is that we are alone among living creatures in our ability to talk to ourselves about ourselves. Our language gives us the power to verbalize about our own nature, to go beyond the raw experience of living and talk about that experience, both silently and aloud. The talk becomes raw experience itself, and we can then talk about the talk. Believe us when we tell you this! Many scholars believe that this feature is not incidental or trivial, but a crucial aspect of our humanness, and that which sets us apart from all other living creatures with whom we share the earth.

The reasoning runs something like this. Because we are able to represent ourselves with the symbols of language, we acquire a system of beliefs about who we are and what is true and good about us as individuals, typified by such statements to ourselves about ourselves as:

"I'm no good at math."

"I'm attractive, but not beautiful in the classic sense."

"I may not be the brightest person in the world, but I work hard."

"Face it, old buddy. Your feet are too long, your nose is too big, you get nervous on dates, and you can't carry a tune either."

Statements such as these probably start out as tentative hypotheses about ourselves based on our own observations and feedback from others. If we make these silent statements to ourselves enough times, there's a good chance we'll come to believe them whether they are accurate or not. How do we check for accuracy?

Many communication theorists believe that knowledge about the self is tested in the same way we test other kinds of knowledge—by social consensus. When we are uncertain about some facts relating to our environment, we usually turn to others whom we trust as reasonable, credible people, and ask for corroboration of our perceptions. "Do you see what I see or what I think I see?" is the healthy response to many uncertainties. When a person discloses his or her perceptions of self to another, and when these perceptions contain information that would not normally be known to the other unless shared voluntarily by the person, the responses of the other serve as a check on the accuracy of the perceptions. Thus, *self-disclosure*—the sharing of information about the self that is not directly available to the other—is the mechanism by which we validate our beliefs about ourselves. These beliefs are called our self-concept and have important implications for all of our behavior. The beliefs that a person holds about himself or herself are powerful predictors of the person's behavior, especially of the communicative behavior. They serve as a kind of filter or screen through which information from the environment is sifted and sorted, and sometimes distorted, in systematic fashion. They influence the kinds of decisions and choices the person will make regarding exposure to new experiences, establishment of friendships, career planning, and information-seeking and information-avoiding. For example, if you are a person of strong religious conviction, you are likely to define yourself in terms of your religious beliefs, which are in turn likely to influence how you will spend your time, with whom, whom you will marry, and so on.

"Earl, I'm very fond of you, but I simply cannot continue this relationship until I know where your head is at!"

We assume that human beings make behavioral choices as a result of the resolution of internal conflict among competing motives. Let's turn now to a discussion of some general propositions about those motives and their effects on communication, beliefs, and behavior.

Motives—Rational and Otherwise

Human psychology is not yet an exact science and perhaps never will be. We simply do not understand enough about the workings of the human mind to make accurate predictions about what we will do under all circumstances. Because we do not fully understand why we do what we do, it isn't possible to set forth hard and fast principles of communication that completely describe and explain how we are influenced by information in our environments. Nonetheless, careful and systematic observation of human behavior has led to some tentative conclusions in this area. We'll offer some general principles of human information-processing. Some of these are rooted in the logical, rational side of human nature, and some of them are extrarational and extralogical, that is, outside the domain of purely rational processes.

Psychological Economy

We tend to form beliefs, attitudes, and values in such a way as to minimize the psychological effort involved in doing so. Given the choice between laborious and difficult psychological processing of information and simpler, more efficient processes of decision making, we tend to favor the latter. This tendency means, on the one hand, that we are inclined toward intellectual and emotional laziness at times—toward reaching snap decisions when careful thinking is in order, toward stereotyping others when we should look further for individual differences, toward making black or white judgments when there are many shades of gray. On the other hand, this tendency implies that we have a natural inclination toward energy conservation in our thinking. For example, a good theory should include the minimum number of concepts, terms, and principles necessary to satisfactorily account for the phenomenon to which it applies. It should not include any excess baggage in terms of units of thought that don't really add anything to the explanations required. Thus, there are both beneficial and detrimental aspects to this principle of "least psychological effort."

During the student strike at San Francisco State College in 1968, militant speakers kept repeating, "If you're not part of the solution, you're part of the problem." The effectiveness of such a slogan as persuasive rhetoric, and as a polarizing tactic, is illustrative of the principle of psychological economy.

Belief Systems

We tend to adjust our beliefs, especially our simultaneously expressed beliefs (opinions), to make them consistent with one another. Logical consistency among beliefs means that the individual attempts to resolve apparent logical contradictions among related beliefs as he or she becomes aware of such contradictions, and perhaps even in the absence of conscious awareness (McGuire, 1960).

The principle of belief consistency has been stated formally in many ways in the literature of attitude change and persuasion. Generally, the principle involves two types of consistency: purely logical consistency and what is sometimes called "psycho-logical" consistency. Psycho-logic refers to quasi-logical reasoning that does not conform to the rules of formal logic. What appears reasonable in psycho-logic is therefore logically invalid in the formal sense. The term is attributable to Abelson and Rosenberg (1958) and is used in a broader and looser sense by Bem (1970).

Unlike Mr. Spock of "Star Trek," typical humans do not order their related beliefs into precisely logical belief systems. Their attempts to maintain apparent logical consistency often result in somewhat bizarre and idiosyncratic reasoning, more psycho-logical than logical. Consider the following exchange:

A: I'm against killing. I don't think it's ever justifiable to take another person's life.

B: OK, but suppose you had had an opportunity to take Hitler's life back in the thirties after you discovered some of
the atrocities he had committed, thereby preventing him
from murdering millions more.

A: Yeah. I see what you mean. But guys like Hitler are a special
case in my book. I don't really consider them human.

This kind of Alice-in-Wonderland reasoning involves an apparent change
of meaning for the term human, which takes place as if by magic in mid
discussion. It is a common ploy invoked when purely logical consistency
is challenged. To maintain the appearance of logical consistency, person A invokes a psycho-logical prerogative, which might be stated: "It is
OK to redefine a term in the middle of a line of reasoning in order to
maintain apparent logical consistency."

There seem to be many common psycho-logical rules governing what
individuals will accept as "reasonable" if not altogether logical. Frequently
encountered logical fallacies suggest dozens of such rules of extrarational
logic. One of the implications of psycho-logical consistency is that we
tend to generalize our judgments in nonlogical, if not altogether illogical,
ways. Advertising appeal takes advantage of this tendency. For example,
popular sports stars are retained to endorse products ranging from panty
hose to coffee makers on television. The strategy here is to induce us to
transfer our favorable evaluations of the sports figures to the products
they endorse. Advertisers assume that if we like Joe Namath, and if Joe
Namath likes a particular brand of panty hose, we will experience a
psychological pressure toward consistency that requires us to find the
same brand of panty hose preferable. A further assumption is that we
will pay more attention to a well-known celebrity than to an unknown
commercial narrator; therefore, we'll experience more pressure to accept
and comply with messages we listen to closely than with messages we
give only cursory attention. These pressures are not necessarily predi-
cated on logic and reasoning; they may be, but they may also rest on
absurd violations of sound reasoning.

Beliefs and Behavior

On reflection, you will realize that most of us occasionally act in ways
that are inconsistent with our professed opinions. We call it hypocrisy
when the other person's actions don't fit with his or her words. For
example, most people would probably agree that overeating, smoking,
drinking, and failing to get adequate exercise are unhealthy practices; yet
many of these same people continue to overeat, tip a few too many,
and lead sedentary lives. When confronted with the discrepancies between their opinions and their actions, people typically experience some
degree of uneasiness or psychological discomfort. When pressed, they
will frequently "rationalize" their actions, offering somewhat bizarre jus-
tifications to show that, after all, they are not being inconsistent. Ration-
alization is simply finding reasons that justify a decision or an act after
the fact. The tendency to rationalize is most pronounced when individuals

are called to account for apparent discrepancies between their actions and their beliefs.

Festinger (1957) has coined the term cognitive dissonance for the feeling of psychological discomfort that results when an individual recognizes a discrepancy between opinions and behavior or between opinions that seem to contradict each other, either logically or psycho-logically. For example, those who voted for Richard Nixon probably experienced cognitive dissonance over the Watergate disclosures, knowing that their voting behavior was inconsistent with their beliefs about appropriate conduct for politicians. Cigarette smokers who value their health yet believe that smoking is harmful would also experience cognitive dissonance. According to Festinger, the arousal of cognitive dissonance is at the root of all efforts to bring beliefs, attitudes, opinions, values, and behaviors into harmony with one another. Cognitive dissonance is uncomfortable and causes us to do psychological work. It is like a motivational itch that requires scratching. When we experience dissonance, we take steps to reduce or eliminate it. The principle of "least psychological effort" determines the way in which we go about reducing the dissonance. Whatever is easiest for us to change, we change. Sometimes it is easier to change a troublesome belief or attitude, sometimes a behavior. For example, if it is more difficult for you to quit smoking than to change your nagging belief that it is harmful to smoke, you are likely to find ways of eliminating the belief that to smoke is ultimately more harmful than to quit. Changing the troublesome belief often involves some circuitous reasoning, such as, "I know that smoking is harmful to my health, but it takes time for the harmful effects to happen. I'll quit later, before the damage is irreversible. Besides, nervous tension is also harmful, and right now I'm under a lot of pressure and smoking helps me relax. It's going to take a lot of effort to quit, and right now I just haven't got the energy to devote to stopping." Here the problem belief is not really eliminated, but the introduction of a time perspective helps to reduce the dissonance temporarily, as does the introduction of some rationalizations.

Most of us at one time or another have announced New Year's resolutions to change some behavior that has been causing us to experience dissonance. Making the dissonance public is tantamount to confessing an inconsistency, thereby subjecting oneself to public ostracism unless the offending behavior is changed. For some individuals, such resolutions are an effective way of helping to motivate the change. For others, ritual declarations of intent, such as New Year's resolutions, seem to melt away with the winter snow. The next principle may help explain why.

Tolerance of Inconsistency

People differ in the extent to which they can tolerate and react to apparent inconsistencies among their beliefs and behaviors. Some individuals are openly embarrassed and humiliated when caught in self-contradiction. Others seem to enjoy publicly acclaiming their incongruities. Disclosure of seeming inconsistencies is an effective device for attracting attention to oneself. After a confrontation between members of the American Nazi party and students in a speech class at San Francisco State University, one young woman secured an invitation to speak to the class by identifying herself—in all seriousness—as a black, Jewish, pacifist Nazi, and a member of the clergy to boot.

Some individuals finding themselves exposed as inconsistent will resort to elaborate rhetorical rationalizations to justify their conflicting views and actions. Others will merely acknowledge the inconsistency with a broad grin, a wink, and perhaps a reference to Emerson's often quoted remark: "A foolish consistency is the hobgoblin of little minds, adored by little statesmen and philosophers and divines."

Wishful Thinking

We tend to let our values, wishes, hopes, and aspirations interfere with our judgments of fact. Often called wishful thinking, this principle simply means that we sometimes tend to believe what we wish were true in spite of hard evidence to the contrary. Wishful thinking is illustrated in many kinds of peculiar reasoning, ranging from the commission of common logical fallacies to outright denials of facts so obvious as to cast doubts on the sanity of the wishful individual. McGuire (1960) has found experimental evidence of wishful thinking through experiments with formal deductive reasoning.

Wishful thinking is not just the reasoning of fools. Many of the noblest human achievements are attributable to an individual's persistent faith against overwhelming evidence. Goals that reasonable people have deemed unreachable have been accomplished. Anne Sullivan's work in helping Helen Keller acquire the gift of speech is an example. Recent advances in the treatment of cancer offer another vindication of raw hope in the face of doomsday logic. Many physicians now believe that cancer patients all to frequently die largely because they, their loved ones, and their physicians give up hope of the possibility of cure because of gloomy statistics from previous cases. There is a major persuasive campaign underway in the medical community to convince people, and their doctors, that cancer is in many instances completely curable and that the cure is frequently contingent on the patient's belief about the disease and the course of treatment prescribed.

Selective Exposure

We tend to protect and defend against contradiction and disconfirmation of beliefs with which we've grown comfortable. This principle is manifested in the information-seeking and -avoiding behavior of individuals. We do not seek after new information indiscriminately; rather, we are selective in our attention to sources of new information. We read some newspapers and magazines while ignoring others. We listen to certain radio stations, watch particular television programs, and avoid others. We affiliate with some people and not others. Even though we may affiliate with a fairly large number of people for different purposes, we do not communicate with all of them about the same subjects.

Not all of this selectivity is motivated by a desire, conscious or unconscious, to protect and defend our cherished beliefs against attack. But common sense and a substantial number of research findings indicate that some of our selectivity is so motivated. Several studies of communicator choice—our preferential choices of other persons with whom to interact—indicate that we tend to seek out others whose beliefs and attitudes are similar to our own. One explanation is that others similar to us do not threaten us with exposure to contrary views, which would generate discomfort and require us to do psychological work.

This principle is consistent with the principle of "least psychological effort." Imagine what it would be like to place yourself in a perpetual state of intellectual and emotional turmoil by actively seeking out information contrary to any and all of your convictions. An ancient Greek paradox is applicable here. There was once a wise old philosopher who taught the importance of skepticism—the persistent tendency to doubt the truth of one's beliefs. One day, as he walked in the garden with his protégé, the old scholar slipped and fell, becoming stuck headfirst in a mud hole. The student suddenly found himself in a state of motivational paralysis, unable to act to save his teacher. He had immersed himself so deeply in skepticism that he couldn't decide whether it was worthwhile to extricate the old man to learn more about skepticism.

A certain amount of skepticism is a necessary condition for intellectual development, and natural consequences of skepticism in a healthy mind are inquisitiveness, curiosity, and the active pursuit of new information. Without skepticism, an individual can be exceptionally gullible, ripe prey for any new idea that comes along, or exceptionally dogmatic, closed to any outside influence that might threaten his or her petrified views. In the other extreme, skepticism robs an individual of a sense of purpose and meaning by stripping him or her of basic convictions of fact and value on which to predicate behavior.

The Priority of Needs

Although we all share similar needs at the level of basic survival, we differ in the higher order needs that become operative once lower order needs are satisfied. Maslow (1954) argues that human needs form a hierarchy, illustrated as follows:

Self-actualization needs

Self-esteem needs

Belongingness and love needs

Safety needs

Physiological needs

Physiological needs are basic needs for sustenance and protection from the elements. *Safety needs* relate to protection from threats, such as war, pestilence, disease, and unlawful behavior. *Belongingness and love needs* are needs for affection, friendship, and acceptance by others. *Self-esteem needs* are exemplified by need for self-respect and the respect of others, a sense of competency and accomplishment, and recognition of one's worth in the social environment. Finally, *self-actualization* refers to your need to realize your full potential in life, to "be all that you can be," as the Army recruiter promises.

Maslow argues that higher-order needs do not become operative for an individual until lower-order needs are fulfilled. In affluent cultures such as ours, many individuals seek gratification at the higher levels. They are well fed, clothed, and sheltered. They are safe in their homes and communities. They enjoy the love of intimates and the companionship of friends. They are confident of their worth as workers, citizens, and parents. Finally, they enjoy considerable choice in creating their own advanced needs and in finding ways of fulfilling them, unlike persons whose total daily output is required to eke out a meager subsistence.

Clearly, how far an individual has progressed through this hierarchy affects the values that individual will deem important, and because those central values are self-defining characteristics, the individual's concept of self is affected as well.

Implications—Interpersonal Differences and Influence

Interpersonal Differences   Ultimately, what necessitates and powers communication as a social phenomenon are the differences between senders and receivers, or more precisely, the differences that senders and receivers perceive to exist between them. These differences are variations in the content of beliefs, values, attitudes, and patterns of behavior. They are what makes the world both an interesting and a dangerous place to live.

The receiver-centered view of communication demands that a communicator place as much or more importance on his or her *receiver's perceptions of these differences as on his or her own.* This is an essential point of departure in initiating communication with another person.

Furthermore, this initial communication goal should perhaps more frequently be acknowledged as an ultimate communication goal—to consider the chief end of human interaction to be understanding of interpersonal differences, rather than their elimination. Too often, we believe that the difference between people are viewed by communicators as something to be eliminated or rejected rather than to be understood and accepted.

Influence   Communication influences beliefs, values, attitudes, and behavior. By influence, we mean that they can be not only changed, but shaped, and reinforced. With respect to beliefs, some are more susceptible to influence and some are less so. As a general rule, inconsequential beliefs about facts are easily influenced, as are inconsequential value

"*Good God! He's giving the
white-collar voters' speech to the blue collars.*"

Drawing by Joseph Farris; © 1984 The New Yorker Magazine, Inc.

beliefs. More difficult to influence or change are value beliefs that are
central to a person's belief system—central in the sense that they have
implications for many other beliefs, and play a major role in how a person
defines himself or herself.

When we undertake to influence another person through communication, our efforts will be futile unless we understand enough about the
beliefs held by that person to tell us what we're up against. We must
understand what beliefs the person holds, and how strongly, in order to
inhibit or facilitate the influence we wish to accomplish.

Consider, for example, someone trying to teach someone else how to
use a personal computer (PC). If the prospective student already believes
that a personal computer is a potentially useful tool to be learned quickly
and painlessly, then the teacher's task is simple. If, on the other hand,
the student doesn't know how to type, doesn't like to type, is afraid of
machines, and has trouble reading and following directions, then the
prospect of learning how to use a PC is formidable, and the teacher has
a problem. What a person believes about his or her own needs, abilities,
and interests is a crucial determinant of his or her readiness to learn—
even about things that might turn out to be totally absorbing, entertaining,
and useful.

Now consider an even more difficult influential attempt—someone trying to persuade a friend to stop smoking or abusing drugs, or to change his or her mind on a significant policy issue, such as abortion or capital punishment or euthanasia. Issues such as these involve a person's central values, and no influential attempt has any chance of success unless it is based on a solid understanding of the content of these important beliefs. For example, suppose you wished to persuade me that capital punishment should be abolished. If I already agree, you might as well not waste the effort, unless you think it is advantageous to reinforce my beliefs on the matter or unless you are merely interested in disclosing your own views to me. If you know that I don't agree, it's important that you find out why if you're going to affect me as you wish. You might present evidence showing, for example, that capital punishment does not serve to deter crime. You could spend a great deal of time and energy on this issue alone, only to discover ultimately that either (a) I don't believe that deterrence is necessary to justify capital punishment, or (b) I agree with you that it has no deterrent value but support it anyway, perhaps because society benefits in other ways from avenging heinous crimes.

We do not influence others by drowning them in a sea of information. Whatever the nature of the attempted influence, be it teaching, counseling, informing, advising, persuading, coercing, haranguing, nagging, or heckling, it is certainly going to be inefficient and almost definitely ineffective unless it is aimed at the relevant beliefs held by the receiver—what he or she believes about self and environment. Thus, the central skill to be developed in communication is sensitivity to others, enabling us to see the world from the other's perspective, from the inside out.

Summary

The key to understanding and skill in human communication is a receiver-centered perspective that acknowledges receivers to be the ones who assign meanings. Explaining and predicting how receivers do so depends on a knowledge of the similarities and differences among them.

We believe that the concepts of *beliefs, values,* and *attitudes* are useful in discussing these similarities and differences. Especially important are beliefs a person holds about himself or herself, because these beliefs—the self-concept—directly affect how the person responds to all kinds of information from the environment.

We have identified some principles of motivation based on the concepts of beliefs, values, and attitudes that have a direct bearing on how these factors influence communication and behavior. Included are the principles dealing with *psychological economy, belief consistency, wishful thinking, selective exposure,* and the *priority of human needs.* The principles we've chosen are some that have direct consequences on how receptive people are to information, how they process that information, and how it affects their behavior.

Communication that enables us to understand and perhaps to change the differences between ourselves and our fellow humans is implied by a receiver-centered view. The understanding is essential both to the acceptance of others and to changing them. The central communication skill, then, is the ability to see the world from another's point of view.

Questions

1. What is a belief? An attitude? A value?

2. How do beliefs, values, and attitudes influence behavior, and how does behavior influence beliefs, attitudes, and values?

3. What are some of the differences among people that influence how receptive they are to information and how they respond to information they receive?

4. In what ways do you see yourself as a unique individual, different from anyone else? In what ways do you see yourself as similar to others?

5. How have your beliefs about yourself influenced your conduct?

Suggested Readings

BEM, D. J. (1970). *Beliefs, attitudes, and human affairs.* Belmont, Calif.: Brooks/Cole.

BOORSTIN, D. J. (1962). *The image.* New York: Atheneum.

CATANIA, A. C. (1979). *Learning.* Englewood Cliffs, N.J.: Prentice-Hall.

CRONKHITE, G. (1976). *Communication and awareness.* Menlo Park, Calif.: Cummings.

DANCE, F. E. X., AND C. LARSON (1976). *The functions of human communication.* New York: Holt, Rinehart and Winston.

MASLOW, A. (1954). *Motivation and personality.* New York: Harper & Row.

POLANYI, M. (1958). *Personal knowledge.* Chicago: University of Chicago Press.

ROKEACH, M. (1968). *Beliefs, attitudes, and values.* San Francisco: Jossey-Bass.

WILMOT, W. W., AND J. R. WENBURG. (1974). *Communication involvement: Personal perspectives.* New York: Wiley.

ZIMBARDO, P. G., E. EBBESEN, AND C. MASLACH. (1977). *Influencing attitudes and changing behavior* (2nd ed). Reading, Mass.: Addison-Wesley.

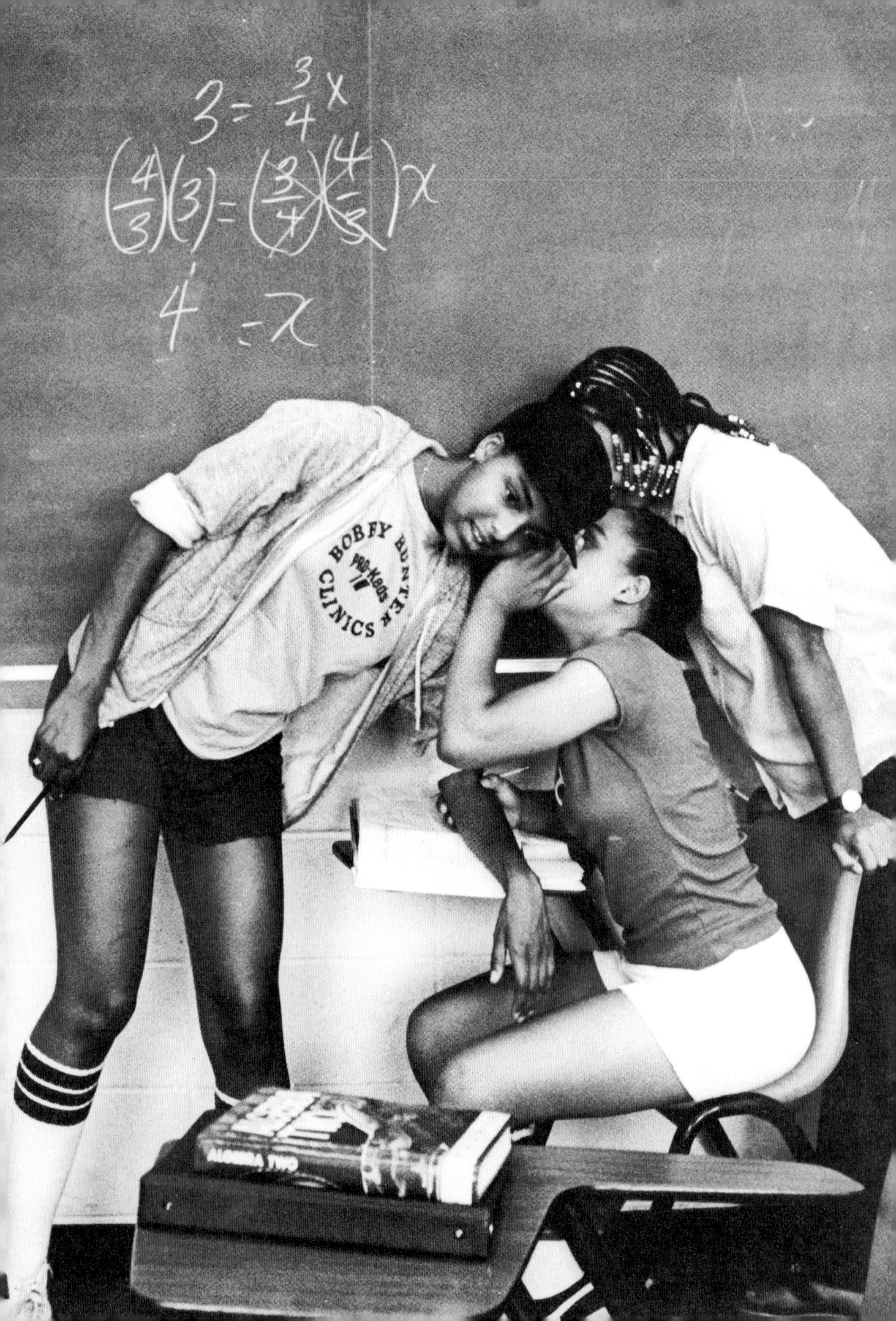
CLINICS
ALGEBRA TWO

Chapter Three

Verbal Communication: Language

Preview

This chapter and the next deal with the codes of communication, verbal and nonverbal. Verbal codes are the spoken and written languages of humans. Nonverbal codes, the topic of the following chapter, are signs other than written and spoken words, such as gestures, clothing, and the ways people arrange themselves in space.

The materials selected for presentation by no means constitute a comprehensive or definitive statement about these two kinds of codes. We have limited our selection to concepts that have practical value and application in the development of communication skills. Our intent is to stimulate your thinking about some choices available to you in your efforts to communicate. Verbal and nonverbal codes afford us an incredibly sophisticated toolbox for communication. Let's rummage around in it for awhile.

In this chapter on language, we'll examine some of the different ways in which scholars look at language and how language relates to communication behavior. We'll discuss the way language affects perceptions of reality. Human language is compared to other systems of signs, which are stimuli that represent, or "point to," things other than themselves. Concepts are presented for analyzing language in terms of grammatical rules (syntactics), definitional rules (semantics), and usage rules (pragmatics). Finally, some of the ways that language usage varies are discussed in order to expand your awareness of the communication choices available to you in the rich storehouse of linguistic tools.

Objectives

To briefly discuss the nature of human language as a system of signs

To show how language influences perception

To present some concepts useful in understanding language behavior

To identify language variables that give us choices for the effective use of language

THREE   During the first two years of a normal person's life, a learning miracle occurs; the person learns to speak. The acquisition of language behavior is perhaps the most complex intellectual and motor achievement of our life, but something we take for granted because it is such a normal part of the toddler's development.

No one knows how human languages began, nor how they evolved. Dozens of theories have been proposed, some of them by brilliant and respected scholars, but none have widespread acceptance. So baffling is the problem of the origins of language that it is not even considered a respectable scholarly pursuit by many learned individuals.

Whatever the origins of language, it is clearly the thing that sets humans apart from all other creatures on earth in two important respects. The first is that language gives us a highly developed and sophisticated means of communication, enabling us to store and transmit information rapidly and efficiently for a variety of purposes. The second, less obvious consequence of language is that it gives us a means of redefining and refining our conceptions of reality. Because language permits us to deal with representations of reality, it affords us the means to travel in time and space without ever leaving our chair. Try this: make a list of places you know something about but have never been to, persons who have communicated with you whom you've never met, and things you believe not because you observed the evidence directly, but because someone credible informed you.

Verbal Codes—Language

There are thousands of different languages in the world, and it is only fairly recently that more than a few dozen have become written languages. Many remain spoken languages only for their users, although a good many that fall into this category have been transcribed into some sort of written form by linguistic scholars.

For many years, the work of such scholars focused on the structural differences among human languages—differences such as whether adjectives precede nouns as they do in English or follow them as they do in French or Spanish. More recently, following the lead of Noam Chomsky

(1957), linguists have sought to discover the basic similarities among all human languages. Chomsky, some thirty years ago, argued that the differences among languages are only superficial characteristics of surface features, and that at a deeper level, there exists structural similarities corresponding to standard features of the human nervous system—the "hardware" common to us all. Chomsky advanced the theory that humans have "linguistic competence," a capacity to use language, which is genetically endowed and produces deeper level structural similarities among all human languages.

Linguists and other language scholars—grammarians, etymologists, lexicographers, semanticists, and so on—are interested primarily in describing the characteristics of the language codes themselves. The results of these descriptions are extremely useful—dictionaries full of definitions, which are rules commonly accepted among a linguistic community for the use of words: grammars that specify the commonly accepted rules for putting words together to form phrases and sentences; historical accounts that give the derivations of modern words; and descriptions that offer the sometimes subtle differences in connotative meanings elicited by words that are denotative synonyms.

It is far beyond the scope of this text to deal with what is known about language in depth. However, because human communication relies so heavily on the verbal codes we call languages, our understanding of the

one is ultimately based on our understanding of the other. We will therefore limit ourselves to an admittedly cursory treatment of this fascinating
subject, offering but a few concepts and principles that we believe are
especially useful to any student working on improving oral communication skills in his or her native tongue.

One of the most important things to understand about language is that
it is human behavior. When the primitive grunts of stone-age men and
women began to evolve into the sophisticated symbol systems we use
today, there were no grammarians around to give instruction in proper
speech. The *rules* of language are descriptions of patterns of linguistic
behavior, rather than prescriptions about the rightness or correctness of
certain forms and patterns. Without the uniformity and standardization
reflected in these patterns, language would not function as it does in
communication. At the same time, languages do not evolve and grow
unless we humans experiment with our language behavior, giving rise
to new rules and sometimes breaking old ones.

The important thing about language rules is not the rules for their own
sake, but the extent to which the rules serve the needs of sender and
receivers in the act of communication. Adherence to the rules of grammar
and spelling is primarily *metacommunicative* in nature in many situations—saying something above and beyond the literal content of a message exchanged that may dramatically influence the overall interpretation
of the message. For example, consider a situation in which a college
class is asked to take careful notes on a lecture. A student blurts out, "I
don't got no pencil. Could you borrow me one?" No one whose native
tongue is English has any trouble interpreting the literal meaning of this
utterance, so the basic requirements of clarity of content have been met.
But classmates and instructor's perceptions of this student's preparedness
for his role as a college student are likely to be affected far more significantly by his speech than by his lack of a pencil.

Linguistic Determinism:
Language Influences Perception

An intriguing notion about language that stands in rather stark contrast
to Chomsky's ideas is the concept of linguistic determinism. Advanced
by two individuals named Edward Sapir and Benjamin Lee Whorf (1956),
who reached the same conclusion independently, linguistic determinism
holds that the particular language we speak profoundly affects the way
in which we experience our environment—our very perceptions of reality.
Furthermore, languages differ from one another in the way they "map
onto" reality. English is a language in which the most frequently appearing
part of speech is the noun—a word representing a person, place, or
thing. Thus, English is an object-oriented language, which characterizes
as "things" or objects a number of "things" that are not objects in any
physical sense at all. For example, abstract nouns, such as *love, de-
mocracy,* and even *communication,* do not refer to physical objects at
all, but rather to processes that take place or to patterns of activity in the

ways persons relate to one another. Thus, these common English nouns might better be verbs, because verbs are parts of speech that signify action, movement, and change. Indeed, some human languages represent most "things" by verbs rather than by nouns, and are thus process-oriented languages rather than object-oriented.

Another way that a particular language can influence our experience has to do with the way in which discriminations are handled within the language. An often cited example is that English has but one word for snow, but many adjective modifiers to describe different kinds of snow, such as *powder* snow, *corn* snow, *spring* snow, *crusty* snow, and so on. Eskimos have different words signifying snow for each of these conditions. Differences such as these show how our environments shape our language. To be functional, language must reflect useful discriminations we make in perceiving the environment. For someone living in snow, these discriminations are a matter of survival.

Language as a System of Signs

Human language is a system of signs. Signs are a special class of stimuli that represent something above and beyond themselves, and produce responses that are not attributable to their own properties alone, but to the properties of things they represent. As a special class of stimuli, signs produce responses in their interpreters on at least two levels. All stimuli exert the first kind of influence, impinging on the individual as a pattern of sound, light, pressure, and so forth, and producing responses directly attributable to the physical properties of the stimulus.

A sign produces a second kind of response, attributable in part to the interpreter's association between the sign and other stimuli that need not be immediately present. A sign response, then, depends upon what the interpreter brings with him or her to the encounter with the sign, a function of memory of one kind or another.

The associations between a sign and the stimuli it represents may be either innate (biologically determined) or learned. An example of a biologically determined sign is the chemical marker trail left by a scout ant, which directs other ants to the location of food (much to our annoyance during the summertime). An example of a learned sign is any word in any human language.

Symbols

Symbols are a subclass of signs. Symbols are learned rather than being innate, are associated arbitrarily with their referents, and are capable of being reproduced by their interpreters. The words in human languages are symbols, being purely arbitrary and exhibiting no necessary connections to the things they represent. If this were not so, then every human language would use the same words and would be structured in the same way. Instead, we have literally thousands of different ways to represent any one thing or class of things in our environment. Even within a particular language, many words often exist to signify the same thing.

Representational stimuli that are not arbitrary—do exhibit a necessary connection with the things they represent—are called signals. For example, a sore throat may be a *signal* of an infection, but the relationship between the soreness and its cause is hardly arbitrary. Signals often represent things of which they are a part, or a consequence, as thunder signifies a storm. Symbols, on the other hand, are merely associated with their referents by human decree.

Morris (1946) offers two tests to determine whether a representational stimulus is a symbol. It is a symbol if it (a) is reproducible by its interpreters, and (b) has an arbitrary relationship to its referent, thus any other stimulus can substitute for it. All words meet these tests.

Subdisciplines of Language Study: Semantics, Syntactics, Pragmatics

Semantics

Semantics, commonly understood to refer to the study of the "meanings of words," is more appropriately described as the study of the relationships between words and the "things" they represent. In Chapter One, we point out that meanings are not properties of words, but rather are the responses of interpreters to words. Semantics, then, is the study of the predictability of responses when interpreters are stimulated by certain words and combinations of words. Put another way, semantics is about what "things" are likely to be represented by what words, by virtue of the response patterns of interpreters.

Syntactics

Syntactics refers to the study of the relationships among words when they are put together to form larger units of discourse, such as phrases, sentences, paragraphs, and so on. The rules and conventions of grammar are syntactic rules. As we have already mentioned, syntactic rules should be regarded as predominantly *descriptive* rather than *prescriptive*. They are descriptions of conventional usage rather than prescriptions of "correct" language behavior. However, *conventional usage can facilitate effective communication,* whereas deviation can be perilous, and we would prescribe conformity to conventional rules for most purposes. Consider the following utterances, each of which are difficult to interpret because of departures from syntactic conventions:

Throw the horse over the fence some hay.

Flying airplanes can be dangerous.

Brothers and sisters have I none, but this man's father is my father's son. (In this example, what is the relationship between the speaker and "this man"?)

These examples illustrate that syntactics and semantics do not operate independently. The way words are arranged provides clues to what the sender is talking about, or sometimes fails to provide enough clues. Frequently, speech is less problematic than writing because vocal cues can be used to eliminate ambiguity. Can you change the senses of the first two examples above by saying them aloud in different ways?

Pragmatics

Pragmatics refers to relationships between words and their interpreters, and is concerned primarily with the effects of language on people. Pragmatics deals with how the act of speaking and arranging words works in practice, which often differs from expectations based purely on semantic or syntactic rules. For example, numerous organizations have recently acknowledged the need for more understandable messages used in formal communication with lay persons. Insurance companies try to rewrite policies, judges revise jury instructions, and sometimes even professors clean up their lecture notes. A pragmatic approach to this process dictates that the revisions actually be tried out on their intended interpreters to see how they actually respond to them, rather than be based on editing principles grounded in semantic and syntactic considerations.

Variety in Language

The biblical account of the Tower of Babel explains the diversity in human language as God's intervention to prevent completion of a tower that would enable humans to explore heaven. According to the legend, this was God's way of limiting human knowledge. Whether we subscribe to this explanation or not, the varieties of language do produce some significant communication problems for us, but also some fascinating and enriching features.

One of the wonderful things about words is that they are a renewable resource—they can be used over and over again. Moreover, they afford an infinitely variable way of encoding messages for communication. No matter what it is you want to say, there are many ways to say it, each retaining the essential, literal content you need, but each having subtly different implications for interpretation. For example, suppose you have been trying to persuade a friend to change in some way, without success. Your friend's resistance to influence is "steadfast." Or is it "resolute?" "Insistent" might be more accurate, or perhaps something stronger—"stubborn?" What the heck, if he or she is too "pigheaded" to take your advice, it's his or her problem anyway.

Denotation Versus Connotation

Words that are synonyms at the literal level are said to *denote,* or refer to, the same thing. Rarely do such synonyms have the same *connotations,* however, which are suggestions or implications associated with the words above and beyond their literal intepretations. Charles Osgood (1957), a psychologist interested in semantics, developed a technique called the *semantic differential* to measure the connotative meanings we

assign to words. Osgood's method asked people to rate "concepts" (words) using seven-interval scales bounded by adjective antonyms, such as:

Good ____:____:____:____:____:____:____ **Bad**
Strong ____:____:____:____:____:____:____ **Weak**
Active ____:____:____:____:____:____:____ **Passive**

Osgood found that these three scales were particularly apt descriptors of how connotative meanings are assigned. He concluded that these were the most significant dimensions of connotative meaning, and called them the evaluation dimension, the potency dimension, and the activity dimension. When we wish to be deliberate about connotation, our selection of words to characterize someone or something can be guided by these three dimensions. Consider the differences suggested to you in terms of evaluation, potency, and activity by the following alternatives:

Public official *versus* bureaucrat

Teacher *versus* professor

Student *versus* scholar

Woman *versus* lady

Error *versus* mistake

Fat *versus* portly

Steal *versus* swipe

Lusty *versus* sexy

Abstract Versus Concrete Language

Abstraction is the elimination of details. Words vary in terms of their degree of abstraction, depending on the specificity of the thing they represent. For example, we might order the following set of terms from more to less abstract:

MORE ABSTRACT
System of signs
System of symbols
Languages
Romance Languages
French
LESS ABSTRACT

The level of abstraction used by a speaker effectively limits the number and variety of probable responses produced in an interpreter. "System of signs," for example, might cause you to think of anything from the chemical trails of ants at your picnic to highway markers, whereas "French" narrows the options to something much more specific. All verbal symbols are abstract to some degree, because they only represent something else and are not that something. Semanticist S. I. Hayakawa (1964) likens words to *maps,* and the things words represent to their corresponding *territories.* He cautions us to remember that the map is not the same thing as the territory, nor does it represent all the details of the territory.

Selecting words at an appropriate level of abstraction for communication is much like choosing a proper map. Too many details (too low a level of abstraction) may clutter up the field, distract the interpreter, and make navigation difficult. Too few, or the wrong details, may make navigation impossible.

Descriptive Versus Prescriptive Usage

Recall from Chapter One's discussion of meaning that Morris (1946) has identified three basic kinds of messages—designative, appraisive, and prescriptive—that produce thinking, feeling, and acting responses respectively. These message types might also be termed description, evaluation, and prescription.

Many communication objectives can be accomplished with one or the other of these types of messages. Recall the example from Chapter One of merely describing for someone the fact that his car lights have been left on. There's usually no need to tell him to turn them off, or that it's not a good thing to leave them on and run down the battery. This is understood by most drivers. But sometimes it is more efficient to match the message to the objective and explicitly evaluate or prescribe for the receiver, especially when the desired response on the part of the receiver is a well-defined and structured sequence of behavior the receiver needs to learn. For example, learning to operate a complex machine, such as a computer, or to perform a sporting maneuver, such as sailing a windsurfer or slalom skiing, is facilitated by simple prescriptions. "Bend your knees!" or "Tuck your fanny!" gets straight to the point, whereas a descriptive analysis of the dynamics of the body's center of gravity on performance may not.

Interestingly, studies in persuasion have shown that description is sometimes preferable to explicit prescription, even when the sender wishes to produce a very specific behavioral response. This seems paradoxical, but is based on the notion that people are sometimes influenced more if left to draw their own conclusions from a set of facts than if they are subjected to too much interpretation by another. When the credibility of the communicator is low, and when the topic is one of great significance for the identity of the receiver, this seems to be the case.

Choosing between descriptive and prescriptive message forms is related to choosing between more neutral, predominantly denotative terms, or more loaded, connotatively potent terms. Prescription implies evaluation, and of course, appraisal *is* evaluation.

Similarly, the descriptive-prescriptive distinction is related to levels of abstraction, and somewhat paradoxically at that! Telling someone to, "Tuck your fanny!" is abstract in the sense that it leaves out a lot of details about the reasons for the act, but is concrete in the sense that it tells the receiver what to do about those reasons. Thus, the abstractness or concreteness of a given message is not an absolute matter, but is relative to the communication objectives of particular situations.

Redundancy   All human languages, as they are spoken naturally, are approximately 50 percent redundant. This means that all the information required for accurate interpretation is available in roughly half of the cues conveyed. To illustrate:

The English language is about 50 percent redundant. = English is half redundant.

Or even

E gli h is h lf r d nd t.

Given time, a native speaker could easily decode the last message, but not without some effort, and many nuances of meaning are lost when redundancy is decreased. Redundancy functions to give interpreters time to process the information in ordinary speech. Written messages need be far less redundant because readers can go at their own pace, and can backtrack if they get confused. Even written messages can become excessively nonredundant and difficult to interpret, however. For example, publications in scholarly journals are often difficult to interpret, even for experts in the field, because they have been edited to minimize redundancy in order to reduce publication costs. Maintaining an appropriate level of redundancy, both for the communication task at hand and for the skills and interests of receivers, is a critical communication objective.

Literal Versus Figurative Language

Hayakawa's map-territory analogy is an example of figurative language. A word is not literally a map, but the map analogy is useful to illustrate some of the more important principles of language. There are many different kinds of metaphors, or figures of speech, available to help communicators. When used appropriately to the communication task at hand, they are powerful tools. When mismatched to the task or mixed up, they can be either engaging incongruities or ludicrous blunders, as in:

> The candidate tested the political waters by throwing his hat into the ring as a trial balloon.
>
> Play with fire and you'll wind up in deep water.
>
> This accomplishment caused the company to soar to new depths of creativity.
>
> The ship of state is in danger of tipping over into the abyss.

Figurative language is powerful because it facilitates the understanding of a new idea by comparing it to an old one. The resulting association, often perceived as artistic or clever in its own right, serves as an aid to memory. The effectiveness of some of history's greatest orators is attributable to their skill with figurative language. The legendary Daniel Webster, whose oratorical skill is celebrated in Stephen Vincent Benet's epic poem *The Devil and Daniel Webster,* is perhaps the most noteworthy example. More recently, Presidents Kennedy and Reagan have won acclaim for rhetorical performances in which figurative language plays a prominent role.

Standard Versus Nonstandard Language

Standard language is language spoken in a person's language community that does not draw attention to itself within that context. Texans, New Yorkers, and Vermonters all speak English, but with noticeable differences in dialect, syntactic customs, word usage, idioms, stylistic habits, and so on. Black Americans have certain distinctive patterns of speech that do not correspond to regional differences, as do various other ethnic groups that have maintained their cultural cohesiveness. Sometimes, these differences are perceived as errors or as improper use of language. Recognizing this, many Americans have developed fluency in several different "standard" patterns of speech, and adapt their behavior to the particular persons they are with.

Various professions are identified with nonstandard language behavior. Many have a highly sophisticated and useful vocabulary—the jargon of the trade—that spills over and affects the speech habits of members outside the professional context. Too, in-group slang and cant frequently serve to identify individuals as members of valued groups, and ordinary standard speech may even bring on derision and ridicule under certain circumstances, especially among young teenagers.

Unfortunately, some nonstandard language behavior is linked to handicaps, such as hearing loss or neurological damage caused by stroke or injury to the brain. Speech and hearing disorders take a terrible toll in human suffering and are among the most misunderstood and debilitating handicaps to be endured. Hearing loss, for example, is frequently misperceived as a lack of intelligence, with devastating effects on the lives of the impaired. Where nonstandard language behavior might be linked to such handicaps, special sensitivity and extra effort in communication is in order on the part of the unimpaired parties.

Improved Verbal Communication

Our advice with respect to verbal communication is simple in principle and complex in practice.

1. Learn to interpret, and perhaps to speak, the language(s) of those with whom you wish to communicate. This may well mean that you should become familiar with more than one standard for your native tongue.
2. Learn to use the variables of language to advantage—levels of abstraction, redundancy, connotative meanings, figurative devices, and so forth. Don't be reluctant to add tools to your toolbox. They're free, except for the investment of your time.
3. Adapt your language behavior to the persons you are with, both as a sender and as a receiver of messages.
4. Adapt your language behavior to the communication goals and tasks you wish to accomplish.
5. Keep an open mind about the language behavior of others, recognizing that some of the differences in language behavior are subject to faulty interpretation.

Summary

If you are interested in improving communication skills, you can benefit from an understanding of language. Although it is not absolutely necessary to have a grasp of language theory to be a skilled user of language, linguistic theory helps you understand the factors affecting those skills and can suggest choices to further enlarge the communication toolbox. A world-class skier need not understand the physics of skiing, but those that do have an advantage.

Language is behavior, guided but not determined by rules that have their origins in ordinary usage. These rules can be categorized in terms of semantics, syntactics, and pragmatics, which are interdependent in producing meaningful communication through language. Language is behavior of a special kind, involving a highly developed system of signs, which are stimuli that "point to" or represent things other than themselves. The language we speak affects the way in which we experience reality, and not just the way in which we report it.

Language affords us a rich variety of choices because of some of its features—connotation, abstraction, redundancy, figurativeness, and nonstandard usage. It is a renewable resource that is constantly evolving, enabling us each day to say something about a newly discovered reality that has never been said before.

Questions

1. How does language affect perception?

2. How do the following concepts relate to one another?
   signs   symbols
   signals   language

3. Describe the following features of language, giving examples.
   Denotation and connotation
   Abstract and concrete terminology
   Redundancy
   Standard and nonstandard usage

4. Why is the often repeated statement, "That's merely a matter of semantics," often an oversimplification?

5. What factors might influence your decision to use figurative language to illustrate a point?

6. Did you solve the riddle about, "This man's father is my father's son," on page 53? Can you explain what it is about the language of the riddle that makes it difficult to interpret?

Suggested Readings

CHURCH, J. (1961). *Language and the discovery of reality.* New York: Vintage.

DE VITO, J. A. (1981). Language and verbal messages. In *Communication concepts and processes* (3rd ed.). Englewood Cliffs, N.J.: Prentice-Hall, 59–67.

HAYAKAWA, S. I. (1964). *Language in thought and action.* New York: Harcourt Brace.

SEBEOK, T. A., AND R. ROSENTHAL (Eds.) (1981). *The Clever Hans phenomenon: Communication with horses, whales, apes, and people.* In *Annals of the New York Academy of Sciences* (Vol. 364). New York: New York Academy of Sciences.

Chapter Four

Nonverbal Communication

Preview

When most people think about communication, they think of speaking with words; when they think about a speech class, they envision students trying to improve their verbal abilities. Although the verbal message continues to be the focus of courses in speech communication, we must recognize that we are constantly sending and receiving many messages that are not expressed in words. These messages are nonverbal. They prompt us to develop significant meanings and responses for our perception of the behavior of the environment around us.

Words interact with nonverbal messages so intricately that we really cannot understand the communication process without also knowing one of the crucial components of that process—the message that is truly "beyond words." You are better off if you develop a good awareness of the nonverbal dimension of communication before practicing the kinds of verbal skills we discuss in later chapters.

Objectives

To identify many different kinds of nonverbal factors that affect the communication process

To enhance the development of skills in perceiving and interpreting nonverbal cues in our environment

To increase awareness of our personal nonverbal messages

FOUR A candidate for U.S. senator had to make a decision. His campaign was well financed and had a good staff, but he had no experience in public affairs and was not well known. Though he was an attractive man, he was a marginal public speaker and had little grasp of the intricacies of public issues. What should be his campaign strategy? The candidate and his staff decided on a media campaign. There would be no mass rallies, no public speeches at high schools or service clubs, no difficult question-and-answer sessions. Instead, most voters would learn of the candidate through television, radio, and newspapers. They would see him in thirty-second or one-minute television spots, in full-page newspaper ads, or on large posters or billboards with color photographs of his handsome face. They would see him shaking hands with senior citizens, schoolchildren, factory workers, leaders of minority groups, and famous politicians. They would watch the family man as he romped with his happy children and chatted with his pretty wife at their tasteful suburban home. They would read a personality profile in a news magazine and see old photos of the candidate in his military uniform and as a janitor working his way through law school. The evening news would report on his appearance at a local shopping center, public barbecue, or sports event. Makeup experts, fashion coordinators, photographers, and other consultants would ensure that the candidate's hair was always neatly trimmed, his clothes carefully tailored, his face well tanned. The candidate would appear smooth, confident, relaxed, congenial, trustworthy, and competent. And he would be elected.

A young executive replaced the retiring branch manager of a large insurance company. On arriving at her new assignment, she saw a discouraging situation. Productivity in this branch had consistently been the lowest in the company. Absenteeism and employee turnover were high. Most employees sat a gray desks arranged in rows and faced the same direction, with the supervisor watching from behind. A time clock welcomed the workers to the drab, barren offices. Talking was permitted only in relation to specific job duties. The noise of typewriters and photocopy machines was monotonous. The floor, walls, and windows were dirty. In general, the office complex was a depressing place to be. The new executive began to make changes. Employee committees were asked to suggest changes in the working environment. Partitions were installed and desks rearranged to provide semiprivacy for smaller work teams. Plants, curtains, carpeting, and attractive furniture were purchased. Quiet recorded music was piped to all offices, and the lighting was improved. Rooms were repainted. An extra janitor was hired. In sectors where employees met the public, a dress code was established. Coffee corners were set up for casual employee conversation. The time clocks were removed, and area supervisors were asked to keep informal records of employee attendance. A permanent employee committee was established to develop ideas for improving the work operations and environment on a continuous basis. The branch office became a pleasant place to be. Absenteeism declined, and morale improved. Within a year, office productivity had increased to offset the cost of the changes.

Professor Bland is a brilliant mathematician. Several books and scholarly papers have made him a nationally respected scholar. With his students and colleagues, however, his reputation is quite different. He speaks in a rapid, high-pitched, often stammering whine, and his gestures are nervous and repetitious. As he lectures, he rarely looks at the students; as people talk to him, he looks to either side and never establishes direct eye contact. He paces back and forth. Professor Bland sighs and frowns whenever a student seeks clarification of lecture material. When people talk to him in his office, he often glances at his watch as they are explaining their problems. He interrupts others in midsentence and often impatiently and abruptly changes the subject. He bathes infrequently, his hair is disheveled, and his clothing mismatched, wrinkled, and usually dirty. When greeting colleagues, his handshake is limp and brief. He has much to contribute to his field. His words are carefully chosen and sometimes beautifully arranged; his ideas are profound. Yet nobody can stand to be around him. People avoid Professor Bland like the plague.

What is happening here? What do these three examples have in common? Obviously, they all involve human communication, but we believe that their most significant messages are conveyed by *nonverbal* communication—by means other than words. In the first case, the candidate depended not on verbal messages concerning the issues, but on public impressions of his "image" as revealed through visual appeals. In the second, the executive did not verbally command or even request improved employee performance; rather, she changed the nonverbal environment so that it began to say something different: "This is a good, comfortable place to work, and we are glad you are here." In the third example, a man with enormous intellectual and verbal competence failed to recognize his nonverbal behaviors and characteristics, negating the potential productivity of his interpersonal encounters.

Nonverbal is a term that describes "all communication events which transcend spoken or written words" (Knapp, 1972, 20). In Chapter One, we draw an important distinction between behavior that we perceive and behavior that goes unnoticed. In this chapter, we emphasize that nonverbal communication includes only the events, behaviors, and characteristics *that we perceive and give meaning to.* It is difficult to know precisely when a communication event begins and ends, particularly when the event consists of nonverbal behavior. When does a gesture or facial expression begin? When do we first notice the nonverbal environment—the room, furniture, space, background noise? When do we stop noticing a person's clothing, grooming, or posture? In practice, we can define and understand nonverbal communication only in general terms, because it is virtually impossible to know precisely the specific boundaries of behavior we perceive.

Types of Nonverbal Communication

What are the behaviors and features—the messages—of nonverbal communication? Several different nonverbal events usually interact to form the perceived message. Thus, although we suggest several categories of nonverbal communication, discussed next, each category inevitably overlaps one or more of the others.

Physical Features of the Human Body

A perhaps regrettable trait of human beings is that we develop important meanings from a person's physical features. A tall man with slender waist, muscled torso, and square shoulders may appear confident, strong, and attractive. If he is too big and too muscular, however, we may think him muscle-bound and simpleminded. A short, thin man with stooped shoulders may suggest a timid, unassertive person, though we may also guess him to be intelligent. A woman with the so-called hourglass figure may be viewed as sexier and less intelligent than one with straighter lines. Facial features of both men and women—eyes, nose, mouth, and shape—prompt immediate judgments of pretty, ugly, plain, handsome, funny, or sexy. Thinness and fatness are characteristics that we almost always notice in others and use as an index of attractiveness. Hair style (or baldness) is also important. If you ever look at a personal photograph taken several years ago, your hairstyle may be the first thing you notice.

The tendency to take nonverbal meanings from physical features can be insidious, cruel, and dangerous. Brown- and black-skinned people have suffered for hundreds of years because of the unfavorable meanings given their racial characteristics. Yet ironically among Caucasians, a deep tan may seem more attractive than a pale skin that may suggest weakness and anemia. The absence of typical bodily features also creates meaning, often with unfortunate overtones. Missing or shrunken limbs from amputation or birth defects, blindness, and paralysis may prompt a variety of responses from the receiver, most of them emotional reactions to characteristics that should not affect communicative transactions but often do.

There is evidence (Knapp, 1972, 63–79) that the meanings we associate with physical features significantly influence our judgments of credibility, intelligence, attitudes, dating and marriage decisions, personality, and ability. Sadly enough, many of these same features are elements over which a person has very little control. Still, we diet, exercise, lift weights, use cosmetics, groom, and even undergo plastic surgery in attempts to change our physical features and encourage positive responses from others to the nonverbal messages conveyed by our appearance.

Bodily Movement and Posture

Closely related to our physical features are bodily movement and posture. We use the term *kinesics* to denote the broad category of observable physical motion that communicates—that is, to which people give meaning. The three types of observable physical motion discussed here are facial, gestural, and postural. Note, however, that although we can categorize types of bodily movement, *they are all closely linked. It is usually difficult to determine which discrete portion of the total movement or position is essential to our interpreting a particular meaning. Furthermore, physical movement and features interact in conveying a total bodily message.*

Facial Expression   In general, the face provides crucial nonverbal cues in communication. In phone conversations, for example, the absence of facial expression significantly decreases the number of cues that the listener can receive and interpret. Facial expression may also be the most precise indicator of a person's inner feelings. For example, we can usually interpret another's happiness, anger, fear, sadness, surprise, pain, or affection simply by observing his or her facial movement. Facial expression can also be quite ambiguous, however, giving a variety of possible interpretations. For example, judges try to appear totally passive as they listen to courtroom testimony, even though they undoubtedly feel surprise, disagreement, happiness, boredom, anger, concern, or enthusiasm. Of course, jury members *take meaning* from this passive expression; they do interpret the judge's mood, though probably less accurately than if he or she expressed more active facial movement. An example of a misleading expression might be that of the celebrity who smiles whenever in the public eye. This so-called painted-on smile may deceive the observer, though some of us claim to be experts at detecting phoniness.

Notice how closely facial *movement* interacts with facial *features*. A smile or frown (movement) on a round, chubby face (features) may suggest a different meaning than a similar smile or frown on a narrow, gaunt face. Obviously, both movement and features interact as we receive and interpret these nonverbal messages.

The focal point of facial communication is the eyes, usually the most expressive part of the face. Eye contact is obviously a key signal in our communication with one another. *Length of gaze,* the duration of uninterrupted eye contact, can suggest a number of messages. For example, if your eyes and a stranger's meet for only a second or two, you both may receive the message, "I see you, you are unfamiliar, and I do not wish to interact with you." If the gaze last considerably longer, the message may be, "I've seen you somewhere before," or "You look interesting and I'd like to meet you." Courting behavior, flirting, and other romantic interaction depend on the skillful use of eye contact. The avoidance of eye contact can be equally communicative: "I don't like you so I'll pretend not to notice you," or "I want this conversation to end so I'll look away," or "I am shy and self-conscious," or "I'm thinking about something else." Of course, eye contact *alone* cannot give the receiver a reliable indication of another person's thoughts, feelings, or truthfulness. But these non-verbal cues are crucial to the understanding of the total facial message.

Gestures   In speech communication, we most often think of gestures as arm-and-hand movements. However, gestures also include a wide range of behaviors, such as shrugging the shoulders, cocking the head to one side, kicking a leg, swishing the hips, or tapping the toes.

Gestures may simply add emphasis to audible messages, as when a speaker uses a chopping motion of the hand every time he or she stresses a word with the voice; or gestures may convey more elaborate meanings to different observers, depending on the context of the message. The following nonverbal gestures, for example, are open to a variety of inter-pretations:

a step backward

a step forward

arms outstretched, palms up as if pushing

arms partially forward, palms down

one arm partially extended, hand and index finger shaking

arms folded, one foot tapping

fists clenched, arms down

fists clenched, arms partially forward

one arm outstretched, sweeping from one side to the other

one leg swinging, as if kicking at the dirt

arms close to body, hands folded

None of these gestures has inherent meaning. Message content depends largely on context—a gesture is perceived and interpreted by *unique human beings* in *unique situations.*

Posture   Posture is defined roughly as body position and stance. We can describe different postures as formal, relaxed, rigid, defensive, aggressive, suggestive, sexy, slouched, awkward, and the like. Not only is a specific posture important nonverbally, but postural shifts can also be revealing. Notice what happens, for example, when a military officer approaches a group of recruits in casual conversation or when a person whom we consider an enemy moves too close. Like many other species, human beings do a great deal of deliberate posturing that conveys to others our attitudes, intentions, and roles.

A special type of physical communication is *sign language,* the specific and identifiable movements of fingers, hands, and arms to denote letters, words, or phrases. Used for communication by and with the deaf and mute, this form of message is not nonverbal at all because sign gestures are as uniform and unambiguous as actual written verbal messages. Sign language can instead be thought of as a different form of verbal communication.

Vocal Inflection

The human voice is an instrument for uttering language symbols, or words, in the primary form of verbal communication—speech. The voice

is also part of the nonverbal arena, however. We use it to give special forms and patterns of inflection to verbal sounds. Communication scholars often use the term *paralanguage* to describe the vocal (audible) cues that accompany spoken language. *Paralanguage* does not refer to words themselves, but rather to everything that we can hear about the *way* in which words are spoken. Paralanguage or vocal inflection becomes nonverbal *communication* when we perceive the sound and assign meaning to it.

Emphasis, loudness, and force are all terms that refer to an important element of vocal inflection—increased volume. A change in volume usually signals a change of meaning. Consider, for example, the sentence, *I want you to go.* If the *I* is emphasized, the meaning might be, "I don't care if *John* wants you to stay; *I* want you to go." If *want* is accented, the sentence may mean, "I'm not *ordering* you to go, but I *want* you to go." If *you* gets the stress, it may mean, "I know *John* offered to run the errand, but I want *you* to go." Using force on all the words with special emphasis on *go* may indicate anger: *"I want you to GO?"* Variables other than volume that may affect the meaning of the verbal message are *pitch* (highs and lows of the voice or tones), *rate* of speech (fast, moderate, slow), and voice *quality* (raspy, nasal, hoarse, gravelly, breathy).

Some vocalizations do not modify verbal symbols but are rather discrete sound units. Laughing, crying, burping, hiccupping, grunting, sighing, audible yawning, swallowing, coughing, moaning, loud inhaling or exhaling, and throat-clearing all may suggest significant meanings. We may clear our throat to get someone's attention, grunt to imply agreement, or breathe deeply to show impatience or exhaustion. Some utterances like *oh-oh, um, ah-HA, er, a-a-a-ah, o-o-o-oh, oo-oo-ooh,* or *uh-huh* are often used in lieu of actual words or even whole sentences. For example, on the proverbial "morning after," a slow, pained groan may be the only vocal cue necessary to describe one's condition.

The *pause* is usually classed as an element of vocal inflection. Whether silent or audible (*er, uh, um*), the pause may connote indecision, reluctance, confusion, or a variety of potential meanings. Pauses may also simply be habitual and mean nothing at all to most listeners. For an example of a meaningful pause, suppose you ask a friend for a loan of ten dollars. A quick, "Well, sure!" may imply that he has no reluctance to grant you the loan. But a hesitant, "Well, uh. . .sure," may suggest quite another meaning.

As with bodily movement, all specific characteristics of a particular inflection pattern will interact to modify the spoken language. We do not usually take meaning solely from, say, the speed of delivery; instead, we take it from a combination of speed, loudness, pauses, and changing pitch levels. Interacting vocal cues are among the most subtle and complex elements of speech. In fact, paralinguistic meanings are often the last and most difficult phase of learning a second language. Notice, for example, how many jokes in English depend to some extent on vocal inflection. People for whom English is a second language may laugh politely, but chances are that they do not completely appreciate the humor. And even for native speakers, we sometimes say, "You just don't know how to tell a joke," meaning that the speaker has not mastered the intricate vocal shadings that are the source of the humor.

Touch and Smell

Human beings assign meanings to touching behavior (*tactile* communication) and to odors (*olfactory* communication). Both are primitive forms of messages that each of us experiences from birth. Most of us receive significantly less information through touching and smelling than through seeing and hearing, but some tactile and olfactory messages can still be crucially important.

Among Americans, touching is generally less acceptable than in other cultures around the world. Touching is usually confined to close interpersonal relationships, as between family members, lovers, or close friends. Formal or impersonal touching includes handshakes, pats on the back, or kisses on the cheek. Touching that goes beyond these societal conventions carries significant communicative implications. For example, men touching men, other than in a simple handshake, is taboo to some people, a suggestion of homosexuality. A nudge or shove may indicate hostility and prompt a fight. A kiss or a hug that lasts longer than usual may stir romantic interests or rumors (in observers).

We know that the meaning interpreted from tactile messages depends partly on the amount of physical contact—how long, how much pressure, how frequent—and partly on the regions of the body that are touched. Touch can be a fairly accurate indicator of emotional messages, such as anger, love, affection, sympathy, and happiness. It is perhaps regrettable that in our culture we rarely get close enough to people to permit the richness of tactile communication to develop.

Olfactory messages, or communication through smell, may also be much less common in America than elsewhere. Body odor is given a negative connotation, so we bathe every day and cover our bodies with perfumes and deodorants, brush our teeth and use mouthwashes, buy breath-freshening candies, use scented hair sprays, and wear clothing that has been deodorized. But the perfumed smells that replace natural body scent nevertheless may be given meanings, such as sexy, pretty, nauseating, offensive, or pleasant.

Artificial scents in our environment also tend to reduce our sensitivity to olfactory communication. We try to eliminate natural household odors with perfumed sprays and exhaust fans. We clean our rugs and furniture. We substitute fresh foods with processed, canned, and frozen products almost devoid of natural odor. We even try to deodorize our pets. Some smells in our environment are clearly offensive, but the increasing standardization of smells through commercial products may be depriving us of meaningful nonverbal information.

We receive many messages through our senses of touch and smell—messages subject to different interpretation by different people. What nonverbal messages might be suggested by the situations below?

While talking to another person, you notice an offensive odor.

Just before you are introduced to give a speech, the person sitting next to you reaches over and squeezes your arm.

A new business acquaintance shakes your hand with a strong and almost painful grip.

You observe two women walking arm in arm along the sidewalk.

Your partner on a first date kisses you lightly on your ear.

Waiting for dinner at a friend's home, you smell something burning.

Object Language

The preceding nonverbal cues are associated with a communicator's bodily characteristics and personal behavior. *Object language,* on the other hand, involves the physical things in our environment—things we see and use—that become nonverbal cues.

Perhaps the most relevant communicative objects are *artifacts,* clothing, jewelry, and other accessories that we use to present and describe ourselves to others. Artifacts help define who we are and whom we want to associate with. The owner of a sporty, colorful, stylish, flowing wardrobe might have little in common with the wearer of tight, straight, formal, plain clothing. The man who wears traditional jewelry—wedding ring, wristwatch, key chain, cufflinks, and tie clasp—might feel uncomfortable around a man with one earring, several rings, necklace, beaded belt, and sequined shirt.

Artifacts have another important function, however. They also suggest our moods and our behaviors. The following situations, for example, call for different types of clothing consistent with the participants' emotions and activities:

business conference

tennis match

funeral

family picnic

cocktail party

rock concert

Army Reserve meeting

intramural softball game

That we would dress according to what we expect to be doing seems obvious. Less obvious but intriguing is the proposition that our clothing might actually influence how we behave and how we feel. Do artifacts ever *cause* us to do certain things? It seems that they do. For example, people who have been in law enforcement, the military, or on athletic teams have noted that they interact differently with others when they put on their uniforms. Certainly, others who take meanings from those artifacts behave differently, too.

Other objects, like cars, houses, furniture, art, food, and sundry consumer goods, may convey meaning. *Status symbols* are nothing more than objects to which we expect the perceiver to assign favorable meanings. We like to surround ourselves with objects that not only make us comfortable but also communicate nonverbally. The leather-jacketed mo-

torcyclist, the blue-jeaned and sandaled owner of a Volkswagen van, and the business-suited Cadillac owner are all sending messages through object language.

Some argue that we should not evaluate or relate to each other on the basis of physical features or objects, that we should always try to perceive and understand the "real person" underneath. Such an argument is well meaning but, we believe, unrealistic. People inevitably take meaning from objects in their environment. More important, however, is the question, "What is the 'real' person?" Isn't he or she in part the one who *selects* the artifacts, who *buys* products, who lives in the environment that he has helped create? From this perspective, object language is not a facade that hides a person, but instead a fairly consistent indication of the way that person wants to be perceived.

Space

The distances between ourselves and others, as well as the space around us, frequently become important nonverbal messages. The term *prox-emics* (think of *proximity*) is used to describe our perception and use of personal and social space for communication. One key dimension is the *distance between people*. We all have a kind of personal territory, and like other animals, we can sense invasions of that personal space and can seek to defend it.

A noted researcher in nonverbal communication, Edward Hall (1959), categorizes and defines four spatial relationships between communicators. He also discusses *close* and *far* phases in each category, suggesting that such variations depend on the relative intimacy between communicators. *Intimate distance* occurs from the actual touching to about eighteen inches apart; sensory awareness of the other person is very high. *Personal distance,* about eighteen inches to four feet, is the typical space for conversation between people who are personally acquainted. *Social distance* (four to twelve feet) suggests a more impersonal relationship as in everyday work activities. Business offices are typically set up to conform to social distance. *Public distance* (twelve feet to the limits of hearing or seeing) gives participants the option of attending to or ignoring the messages of others, and sensory input is minimal. No close interpersonal contact or recognition is expected. Public speeches are examples of the use of public distance. A crowded environment, like a packed elevator or bus, can also modify the boundaries of each distance category.

Size of space also communicates. A large office, an expansive backyard, a roomy car, or a massive lecture hall will prompt different meanings than their opposites. Both in our homes and in most organizations, we can accurately assess the rank or status of people simply by the amount of space they control and by how private that controlled space is.

In addition to distance and size, the *flexibility* of environmental space may be important. Hall identifies and defines three types of space according to their relative flexibility and the messages they may impart. *Fixed-feature space* has permanent features that tend to dictate how much of the space should be used. For example, we do not take a bath in the kitchen or prepare meals in the bathroom. We do not conduct a public meeting in a small office or hold an interview in an auditorium. The inflexible features of particular settings usually prompt us to create meanings and decide appropriate behavior for each setting. In *semifixed-feature space,* objects such as furniture may occasionally be moved to alter the nonverbal environment. Anyone who has ever rearranged a living room or office knows how that exercise may change not only our moods but also the typical ways in which we behave and interact with others in the altered space. The third category is *informal space,* which deals *not* with physical objects but with the way in which we *use* the space around us while we interact. The messages suggested by the distance between communicators, discussed previously, are examples of how we communicate by means of informal space.

Whether our environment is fixed or flexible, it will frequently affect our communication behavior. Sommer (1969) explores in depth the impact of spatial factors on communication, noting that these factors tend to promote or discourage close communicative interaction, depending on the communicators and the setting—for example, small groups and informal encounters in classrooms, in offices, and even in homes. As with other forms of nonverbal communication, spatial messages are interpreted by the perceiver who answers the question, "How am I expected to behave in this environment?"

Time

The dimension of time has at least two nonverbal connotations in communication. First, time as *a specific point on the clock* carries significant meaning. For example, we may notice when someone is late for an appointment and may begin thinking of possible reasons: "It's 1:30 and Jane isn't here yet; I hope nothing's wrong." We may notice that it is noon and suddenly become hungry. We may be pleased to get a friendly phone call in the early evening but may be irate if it comes at 2:00 A.M. We may begin to equate a person's punctuality with dependability, tardiness with irresponsibility. Americans tend to be preoccupied with clock time; our personal and institutional lives depend on timepieces to "tell" us when to begin and end most of our everyday activities.

A second way of thinking about time is *duration,* or time span. Closely related to clock time, and often measured by it, time span may suggest potent messages. "You haven't written in three weeks; that means you don't love me anymore!" "You've been swimming for over an hour; you must be getting cold." "How long has she been lecturing? Seems like forever!" "He grabbed my hand and held it for the longest time. I wonder what he was trying to tell me?" "There hasn't been a major earthquake in this area for over thirty years." A situation or a behavior is not only communicative in itself, but also significant in terms of the length of time involved.

Silence

As if nonverbal communication were not complex enough, merely the *absence* of audible messages also may carry meaning. Silence may also be called *tacit* communication. When a person who could communicate orally chooses to remain silent, either briefly or for some time, that choice has message content we may interpret.

Jensen (1973) suggests five communicative functions of silence. First, it may serve as a *linkage* between people. Moments of silence shared between two people may suggest an invisible bond of trust and compatibility. Silence may also suggest the *absence* of a linkage, however, as when one fails to respond to a spoken message from another.

Second, silence serves an *affective* function in that it has impact on our emotional interaction. For example, "holding our tongues" during a violent argument may prevent even greater anger, whereas giving someone the "silent treatment" may cause increased hostility.

Third is the *revelational* function, which can either reveal or keep something hidden. If we remain silent in response to questions, we hide explicit information. For instance, if we ask, "How was your day?" and get no response, we do not receive explicit information. On the other hand, we may then think, "I'll bet she's upset from a rough day; I won't bother her." Not revealing some information was the basis for developing another message. Silence may also reveal personal traits, such as moodiness, shyness, thoughtfulness, hostility, arrogance, or any number of other characteristics.

A fourth function is *judgmental.* We use silence to suggest good or bad, agreement or dissent. For example, some argue that not speaking out against social evils is implied agreement with those conditions. We use the "silence implies consent" premise in our daily lives, as when we say, "If no one objects, I'll go ahead and do it." Silence may also show a negative judgment, as when a teacher or parent glares silently at an unruly child.

Finally, silence serves an *activating* function. It can move us to do or think certain things that might not occur if we talk. The familiar phrase, "Let's stop talking and start working," implies that silence may better activate physical effort than continued oral communication. The person who says, "Let's take a breather," and is met by silence from the others may be prompted to continue working!

General Characteristics of Nonverbal Communication

We have seen that nonverbal aspects of communication take many forms having tremendous complexity, variety, and communicative significance. Nonverbal communication also has a number of general characteristics that apply to the variety of individual elements discussed previously.

Nonverbal communication is usually interdependent with verbal interaction. As we speak and listen, we observe cues in other people and in the environment. For example, the comment, "I'm really tired today!" may be accompanied by sagging shoulders, sad facial expression, and a slow, quiet vocal inflection that reinforce and amplify the verbal message. Similarly, the comment, "I like you; you're fun to be with," can best be interpreted in the context of a face-to-face awareness of the other person's behavior. Hence, when we study nonverbal communication— how specific personal and environmental cues affect meaning—we must remember that such a process can be truly understood only when we appreciate interrelationships among all messages, verbal and nonverbal.

Nonverbal messages are frequently more significant than verbal messages; that is, we may give considerably more attention to nonverbal cues. From his experimental studies, Mehrabian (1968) suggests that the "total impact" of a message is derived from 7 percent verbal cues, 38 percent vocal cues, and 55 percent facial cues. Percentages vary, of course, and with the close interrelationship between verbal and nonverbal cues, we can probably never know precisely how much of the meaning we create in a given situation is based on nonverbal factors. In any case, we should never underestimate the relevance of nonverbal messages, even though the initiator of a message may place the greatest emphasis on the spoken or written words.

We cannot avoid nonverbal communication. In Chapter One we say that we cannot *not* communicate. If we are being heard, seen, smelled, or touched, or if our absence or silence is noticed by others, meanings will be created. Communication occurs whether we like it or not. For example, suppose Jane decides, "Every time I meet with the group, I always say the wrong thing, start arguments, or put my foot in my mouth. So today I'll just keep silent and try to listen pleasantly to the others." In other words, Jane tries not to communicate. For an hour, she makes no verbal input. After the meeting, some group members chat. "What was bothering Jane today?" "She was really in a foul mood, wasn't she?" "If

she isn't willing to participate, I wish she wouldn't come." "She's so arrogant, so aloof; does she think she's better than the rest of us?" "I think her feelings were hurt. I argued against her last time, and now she's pouting." Obviously, group members were receiving and interpreting many messages from Jane. And if she decided not to attend the next meeting, even more "messages" would be created.

Nonverbal communication is especially potent and accurate at the subjective or emotional level. When we want to communicate logical, factual information, we usually rely on verbal or mathematical symbols. "Population increased 21 percent over the past ten years with the largest growth in metropolitan areas." But the expression of emotional information is frequently nonverbal—through behaviors that suggest happiness, sadness, anger, moodiness, fear, confusion, love, melancholy, contentment, enthusiasm, boredom, disgust, frustrations, and so on across the spectrum of human emotions. Davitz (1964, 178) reports studies showing that emotional meanings could be communicated accurately with several different types of nonverbal behaviors or media. Our accuracy in interpreting the emotional condition of another person probably improves if the nonverbal behavior is *involuntary*—if the person "sending" the cues is unaware of his or her behavior and has no conscious strategy for projecting a particular look or image. Because we emit some involuntary cues no matter how hard we try to control them, it is difficult to deceive others about our true feelings.

Nonverbal factors define relationships between people. Our clothing, offices, homes, physical traits, animation, and vocal patterns tell others who we are. Others interpret our cues and use them to determine how they should interact with us. How do we know when to begin a conversation with a stranger? To avoid antagonizing someone who appears upset? To treat certain people with formality and respect? To terminate a conversation? To touch another person? Chances are that the elaborate meanings involved in most interpersonal relationships evolve primarily from nonverbal cues. Without those cues, we would drift more uncertainly in a trial-and-error process of determining how we should behave.

Nonverbal Cues and Communication Problems

If we can observe, categorize, and explain nonverbal behavior, why do we still have problems with interpreting the messages of others? Why is it still so difficult to establish shared meanings between people if nonverbal factors are such a rich source of information? The answers to these questions lie in the nature of nonverbal cues themselves, particularly in their susceptibility to widely varying interpretations and in their potency at the emotional level. These characteristics and their implications are explored next.

Low Reliability of Meanings

One key problem with nonverbal messages is *the low reliability of their meanings*. Similar nonverbal behaviors or characteristics, when perceived at different times and by different people, frequently result in widely varied meanings. We selectively perceive some portions of the nonverbal environment and behaviors and filter out other parts. Also, we attribute great significance to some cues and very little to others. Only rarely will a nonverbal message elicit identical responses from different observers. True, certain kinds of messages have high reliability. Facial and vocal cues usually prompt accurate assessments of a person's emotional condition. A room with desk, filing cabinets, calculator, conference table and chairs, typewriter, and clerical supplies obviously suggests "business office" to most people. Nodding the head means *yes* and gesturing toward a door means *you go first*. But despite the clarity of these simple messages, unreliability is a frequent problem.

Interdependence of Diverse Cues

Perhaps the greatest source of poor reliability of some messages is the interdependence of many diverse cues. In an earlier section, we tried to identify specific cues, but we also cautioned that such cues are rarely perceived in isolation. For example, we don't just see a head nod but also a facial expression, body posture, and clothing that may intervene to present a total message that we interpret. How, then, can we say we "know what it means" when a person smiles? What if he or she is also extending a hand? Backing away from us? If the situation involves a formal reception, and the smiling face greets one person after another, what does the smile mean then?

The fact is that although we try to codify nonverbal cues and even catalog pictures of typical nonverbal behaviors, we will never have a nonverbal dictionary like we use for verbal symbols. A dictionary might suggest two meanings for the word *orange:* a color and a type of citrus fruit. Every time we see or hear *orange* we ascribe one of those two meanings. But what meaning do we ascribe to the property of orangeness, like a room with orange walls and furniture or orange clothing? And what do we think of when we see oranges on a tree? What is the inherent nonverbal meaning of orange? How do we *respond* to it? We cannot write down in a dictionary, "Whenever you see an orange-colored room, you will think warm and pleasant thoughts." The intricate complexity of cues, the unique situation, and the unique person account for the unreliability and inconsistency of interpretations.

Unnoticed Nonverbal Cues

Communication problems also may result from a *failure to notice nonverbal cues.* We might call this tendency *out-of-awareness*—events occur, situations exist that we do not perceive. One person might say, "Did you see how nervous John got when he saw Margaret?" Another responds, "No, he seemed relaxed to me." In truth, some people are naturally more skillful than others at picking up subtle cues and processing them meaningfully. Those who do notice cues in others may be blinded to their own nonverbal messages. In verbal communication, we know what we write and speak, and we are generally confident that we know what we mean by a particular set of words. But nonverbal behavior is so subtle and unconscious that we may not stop to think about the messages we may be sending. If communication problems occur when people interpret the *same set* of *verbal* symbols, think of the potential for error when, due to missed cues, we interpret *different* sets of *nonverbal* events.

Nonverbal-Verbal Contradictions

Nonverbal messages may contradict verbal messages. One person at a formal party, for example, may greet another with, "It's good to see you," whereas facial expression, formal distance, and vocal inflection seem to say, "For the sake of decorum I'll be cordial with you, but I really don't like you very much." Another example is the teacher who announces: "I hope we can develop rapport with each other. Let's avoid the formalities and be on a first-name basis. Come talk to me about any problems you may have and think of me as a friend." For the students, however, there are continual reminders of the teacher's rank and status: the grading

system; the assignments and deadlines; the formal classroom arrangement; the teacher's formal clothing; the difference in age, formal language,
and precise inflections; and the teacher's traditional office arrangement.
The verbal communication says, "I want to be your friend." The nonverbal
message is, "I am much different from you."

Which message—verbal or nonverbal—do we judge more credible?
No definitive answer is possible. We suspect, however, that in most
situations the quantity and clarity of nonverbal cues, combined with past
experiences in which people have used verbal messages to manipulate
or mislead, may tip the balance in favor of the nonverbal. Of course,
nonverbal cues can mislead as well—witness people who use cosmetic
techniques to hide their true age or who show off fancy cars to give the
appearance of wealth. Too, in many situations, verbal messages may
carry the intended meaning. The communication breakdown occurs when
the receiver of contradictory messages selects the wrong cues as being
the most accurate.

Individual Differences

Accurate interpretation of a given individual's nonverbal behavior depends upon the extent to which you are familiar with the individual. The
better you know someone, the more likely it is that you accurately interpret that person's nonverbal cues. Be skeptical about the widely held
belief that some nonverbal behaviors exhibited nondeliberately have inherent or intrinsic meanings; they don't. Simplistic notions about specific
facial, gestural, or postural cues can lead to trouble. Don't assume, for
example, that just because a member of the opposite sex has his or her
legs crossed toward you, you are sexually attractive to the person. Look
for the totality of cues being exhibited—in context—and bear in mind
that individuals vary considerably in their nonverbal behavior just as they
do in their verbal behavior. In assigning meaning to nonverbal cues, treat
each individual as the unique person he or she is.

One thing that can improve your accuracy in interpreting nonverbal
cues is to look for *changes* in a person's nonverbal behavior. Changes
in routine patterns of behavior are reliable signals that something is going
on. For example, a person's pattern of gazing (eye contact) might change
during testimony in court. Ironically, and contrary to popular notions
about the meaning of eye contact, a sudden shift *toward* steady eye
contact *might* provide a clue to the fact that the witness has just begun
to conceal the truth.

Intercultural Variations

The generally accepted meanings of many nonverbal cues are determined
by a *culture*—a group of people who share common geographical, racial,
religious, or social heritage. An *intercultural event* is an interpersonal
transaction between two or more people of different cultural backgrounds. *Differences between cultures* can cause communication problems.

The most obvious problem in intercultural events is language. When we are unaware of the other person's verbal symbol system, we may rely on rough gestures or sign language, an imperfect system that limits our communication potential. Even if a person of one culture has learned the language of the other, his or her speech may suffer from a heavy accent and limited vocabulary.

Most intercultural events in this country involve a shared language— English. Yet we still encounter problems because the subculture of an individual teaches specific "meanings" of various nonverbal events. White middle-class Americans, for example, take positive meaning from direct eye contact. A black child, on the other hand, may have been taught that to look an adult in the eye shows disrespect. Suppose that boy is scolded by a white teacher and looks at the floor. The teacher demands, "Look at me, Tommy, when I'm talking to you! Show me respect!" Tommy continues to look down, not daring to violate the norms his parents taught him. The teacher becomes even angrier at Tommy's impudence. Each is acting "out-of-awareness" of the nonverbal meanings of the other.

Within a culture, like "general American," there are many subcultures, special variations caused by an assertion of ethnic heritage or religious background or even special lifestyle. Thus, in North America we encounter such ethnic subcultures as Afro-American (black), American Indian (native American), Mexican American (Chicano), or Asian American (Chinese, Japanese, Vietnamese, Korean, and other groups once termed *oriental*). Pockets of European cultural identity in this country include the Jewish community, Italian Americans, Polish Americans, Irish Americans, and French Canadians. Even religious, social, and political groupings can take on subcultural characteristics—for example, the environmentalists, the feminists, the drug culture, the counterculture, the "anti-Nuke" groups, the New Left and other antiwar groups of the 1960s, and the "establishment" organized around business and government.

Although this continent is blessed with rich cultural diversity, the implications for nonverbal communication are significant. Review again the many categories of nonverbal factors. In each may be several potential communication problems due to special cultural interpretations. Depending on a person's cultural background, what might be the "meaning" of the following events?

A young black male walks with a rhythmic strut past a white policeman; the young man wears sunglasses, high-heeled shoes, and a brightly colored hat.

A Mexican American with a heavily accented English speech and a college degree walks into the office of a midwestern executive to apply for a job as a computer analyst.

A student of Navajo descent wears a tribal headband and beads to his graduation exercises at a suburban high school.

A woman wearing jeans, T-shirt, sandals, sunglasses, and no makeup walks into the Sunday services of a suburban Protestant church.

A black man and white woman stroll across campus holding hands.

Two young men stroll across campus holding hands.

A Chinese American woman with a slight accent is promoted to vice-president in a large stock brokerage company.

These and other communication events with nonverbal cues are troublesome because our personal reality, imposed on us by our subculture, determines the meanings we assign to what we perceive. This problem, combined with other barriers—low reliability, failure to notice cues, and verbal-nonverbal inconsistency—are obstacles to developing shared meanings.

Improved Nonverbal Communication

Nonverbal information can both clarify and confuse; it can be a blessing or a curse. What can be done to improve nonverbal communication events? The complexity and spontaneity of such events suggest that we shall never be totally accurate in sending, receiving, and interpreting cues. As outlined next, however, there are several ways in which we can improve our handling of nonverbal cues.

1. Look for cues. Seek them out. We miss some messages simply because we are not observant enough. A theater professor once had his students spend several hours in a bus station watching people so that their stage interpretations could be more varied and fluent. The students watched for body posture, mannerisms, conversational styles, facial expressions, and clothing. On a more informal basis, individuals can train themselves to really *see* the people and the environment for the first time.
2. Tell others about your reception of nonverbal cues and the meanings you are forming. "I noticed that you seemed uncomfortable when I mentioned the new proposal. You shifted nervously and you were frowning." For many people, it may be the first time they realize that others notice their nonverbal behavior.
3. Seek verbal feedback, especially when you think your nonverbal cues may be ambiguous or contradictory. Feedback that we receive naturally may be incomplete, haphazard, and confusing. We should seek it more actively. "Did you think I appeared angry with the group?" "Do you think my office encourages free and open communication?" Some feedback, of course, is not too reliable. Others don't always level with us; they tell us what they think we want to hear. So feedback from several sources may be necessary to clarify nonverbal messages.
4. Even without feedback, try to increase awareness of personal nonverbal cues. We are not suggesting that you stand in front of a mirror and practice a winning smile. Rather, we believe that before, during, and following a communicative transaction, you should become consciously involved in interpreting your personal messages. What information do you hope to initiate with your appearance and behavior? How are you behaving at the moment? How did others respond to your nonverbal cues? What might you change in future encounters?
5. Do some personal analysis of how you typically interpret nonverbal messages. We really cannot be confident about understanding others

until we first understand ourselves and the way in which we interpret information. How do you tend to stereotype particular types of clothing? Bodily features? Certain cultural groups? Do you react positively or negatively to certain kinds of behavior? In what ways do movies and television dramas condition you to read cues? In what ways has your background determined how you will respond to silent messages?

In conclusion, return again to the three examples that introduced this chapter. The political candidate, the executive, and the professor are all intimately involved with nonverbal messages. If you can now analyze those events in depth, then you will have taken an important step toward improving your communication skills.

Summary

We have explored the varied communication events that transcend the spoken or written word. Nonverbal messages may originate from several sources: bodily features, including shape and skin color; bodily movement and posture (kinesics), especially facial expression and eye contact; vocal inflection or paralanguage; communication by touch (tactile) and smell (olfactory); object language, like clothing and other consumer goods; spatial communication through interpersonal distances and room characteristics; time; and silence.

Despite the variety of nonverbal cues, together they have some common features. Nonverbal communication is interdependent with verbal messages but occurs more frequently. It cannot be avoided: we cannot *not* communicate. Nonverbal communication is especially accurate at the subjective or emotional level. Most importantly, it is instrumental in defining our relationships with other people.

Important problems exist in our ability to perceive and interpret nonverbal messages. Either we do not notice important cues or those cues are unreliable and contradictory. Because we all ascribe meaning according to our cultural backgrounds, intercultural nonverbal transactions can be especially difficult. The best solutions to nonverbal communication breakdowns are to increase awareness of nonverbal cues, both in ourselves and others, and to use verbal interaction more actively to check and supplement nonverbal messages.

Questions

1. What do the following terms have to do with nonverbal communication: *kinesics, proxemics, paralanguage, tactile,* and *olfactory?*

2. Why is the statement, "Meanings are in people, not in messages," especially appropriate in reference to nonverbal communication?

3. What is meant by the *interdependence* of verbal and nonverbal stimuli? Why must we use caution when we study specific verbal or nonverbal messages?

4. What are some of the barriers to shared meaning in the area of nonverbal communication?

5. How can we improve nonverbal communication, both as initiators and perceivers of cues?

Suggested Readings

ARDREY, R. (1966). *The territorial imperative.* New York: Atheneum.

BIRDWHISTELL, R. L. (1970). *Kinesics and context.* Philadelphia: University of Pennsylvania Press.

HALL, E. T. (1959). *The silent language.* Garden City, N.Y.: Doubleday.

————. (1969). *The hidden dimension.* Garden City, N.Y.: Doubleday.

HARRISON, R. P. (1974). *Beyond words: An introduction to nonverbal communication.* Englewood Cliffs, N.J.: Prentice-Hall.

KNAPP, M. L. (1978). *Nonverbal communication in human interactions.* (2nd ed.). Englewood Cliffs, N.J.: Prentice-Hall.

MEHRABIAN, A. (1981). *Silent messages.* Belmont, Calif.: Wadsworth.

SOMMER, R. (1969). *Personal space.* Englewood Cliffs, N.J.: Prentice-Hall.

II Information, Persuasion, and Argument

Speech communication events can be described in terms of their *structure* (public speaking, dyads, and small groups) and in terms of their *functions* (activities common to all structural formats).

Informative and *persuasive* speaking constitute the basic functions of most communication events, and these functions are common to all communication formats. Information serves as the basis for *understanding* and *effective action,* but it is primarily through persuasion that we influence each other's *beliefs* and *values* and *encourage a "preferred" course of action.*

The language of information is essentially *descriptive.* In informative speaking, we employ descriptions in an attempt to characterize the ways things *are.* By contrast, the language of persuasion is also *evaluative* and *prescriptive.* Through persuasion, we try to influence the ways that we think things *should be.*

In both informative and persuasive speaking, we encounter inevitable questions about the accuracy of our so-called "facts," or the appropriateness of underlying beliefs and values. Accordingly, in both informative and persuasive speaking, it is usually necessary to develop and support our point of view through the use of logical argument. In Chapter Five, we consider the various types of speech communication and then focuses on basic issues related to informative and persuasive speaking. Chapter Six addresses the basic processes of logical argument. An understanding of these fundamental topics should enhance your ability to perform effectively in a wide variety of communication settings.

Chapter Five

Informative and Persuasive Speaking

Preview

The focus of this chapter is on informative and persuasive speaking because we achieve most of our communication goals by employing either of these two forms. Through informative speaking, we try to characterize the way things are; through persuasive speaking we try to influence the way that we think things should be. Information provides understanding and preparation for effective action. Persuasion provides a means by which we can influence a listener's beliefs and values, and gain support for a specific policy or course of action.

Objectives

To identify basic types of speech communication

To describe basic features of informative and persuasive speaking

To compare and contrast informative and persuasive speaking

To consider the nature of speaker responsibility and credibility

FIVE   A speech communication event can be viewed as a "holistic" activity in which a variety of processes occur simultaneously. A single communication activity can serve to *inform,* to *persuade,* to provide *ceremony,* and to *entertain.* On a specific occasion, however, a speaker is likely to focus in a relatively singular direction. For example, an educator usually focuses on informative speeches in order to share knowledge; a politician frequently concentrates on persuasive speaking in order to win votes; in the celebration of an important historical event, a speaker provides a traditional message as part of a social ceremony; on other social occasions, a speaker's predominant motivation is to entertain. Because of these different interests, it is useful to distinguish among the different "types" of speech events, while at the same time recognizing that they may "overlap" in important ways.

Basic Types of Speech Communication

Consistent with a receiver-centered perspective, the general "types" of speech communication can be defined in terms of their effects upon a listener:

Informative communication helps the listener make contact with a particular state of affairs. Information provides *awareness, understanding,* and preparation for *effective action.*

Persuasive communication encourages the listener to take a specific position with regard to a particular state of affairs. Persuasion can produce one or more of the following listener responses: (1) *belief* in the speaker's characterization of a particular topic; (2) *evaluation* (acceptance or rejection) of a particular event or policy; or (3) *motivation* to engage in a particular course of action.

Ceremonial communication employs traditional messages in order to provide the listener with a familiar and socially meaningful experience. Ceremonial messages form an integral part of a wide variety of social events, including the exchange of "greetings"; the introduction of a speaker; the presentation or acceptance of gifts and awards; traditional ceremonies surrounding birth, graduation, marriage, and death; and ceremonies unique to particular organizations or institutions.

Entertaining communication employs a variety of "human interest" messages and provides the listener with a pleasant or humorous experience, or one which is novel, suspenseful, stimulating, or provocative. Ceremonial messages tend to be traditional in character, but entertaining messages are often the product of originality and creativity.

Ceremonial and entertaining speech communication show a considerable amount of variation among individuals and institutions, and we have not attempted to deal with them in depth. Instead, the remainder of this chapter focuses primarily on the basic aspects of informative and persuasive speaking. Virtually all occasions for speech communication involve the key processes of information *exchange* and interpersonal *influence.*

Informative and persuasive speaking can be discussed as relatively unique activities, or as events that "overlap" in important ways. In the following discussions, both approaches are employed. Firstly, unique aspects of informative and persuasive speaking are separately considered. Then, each is examined in terms of specific issues common to both. The chapter concludes with a discussion of receiver-centered informative and persuasive speaking.

Informative Speaking

A speech event is classified as informative if its primary effect is to help the listener make contact with a particular state of affairs and if it provides listener awareness, understanding, and preparation for effective action. Informative speaking stops short of explicit attempts to motivate listener acceptance of the information or adoption of a course of action based upon it. By way of contrast, a speech event is classified as persuasive if its primary effect is to motivate a belief, an evaluation, or a specific course of action.

Metaphorically speaking, information can be viewed as a kind of "flashlight" that serves to illuminate certain aspects of our universe. Through information, we are brought into contact with our world, including contact with the behavior of others as well as with our own.

Having information has practical implications. When we *know* about conditions around us, we are able to take effective action in relation to them. For example, when we know that water from a particular source is polluted, we can avoid contact with it. When we know that certain kinds of nourishment will contribute to our health and well-being, we can adjust our eating habits accordingly. When we know that an automobile can be made safer through the installation of "airbags," we can begin to investigate the possibility of their use.

In most cases, an informative speaker focuses on relatively *new* information in order to increase the listener's knowledge about some aspect of our world. However, the speaker's information can be familiar or unfamiliar to the listener.

The speaker may wish to convey familiar information when the essential purpose is to review and reinforce what the audience already

knows. For example, a club president may review information that pertains to a particular issue before she asks the membership for a vote on that issue. In some cases, a speaker may wish to review familiar information as a means of preparing the audience for the new information about to be introduced. Clearly, however, the presentation of familiar information is appropriate only for specific purposes, and most informative speakers will emphasize new material that will expand the listener's knowledge and awareness.

A distinction can also be made between informative and persuasive speaking in terms of the "tone" of the language employed. Informative language is basically *descriptive* in nature, whereas persuasive language is also *evaluative* and *prescriptive*.

Through the use of shared descriptive terms, the informative speaker is able to characterize the nature of the subject matter. These descriptive terms point to *structural* features (what something looks like or how it is organized); or *functional* features (how something works or what it will do). For example, you might provide information about a new word processor by describing the size and weight of its various components and the ways in which they are interconnected (its structure). Or you might describe the kinds of software it will utilize and the tasks it will perform (its function). See Table 5–1 for a sample of the wide range of descriptions you can generate.

Information and Level of Difficulty

Informative speaking is a relatively simple task as long as you employ commonly shared terms and address familiar topics. Many informative tasks only require relatively simple directions, instructions, or demon-

TABLE 5–1

A Selective Sample of
Different Types of Descriptive Statements

Directions:	Descriptions of how to put something together or of how to get somewhere.
Instructions:	Descriptions of how to behave or of how to do something.
Examples:	Descriptions of a representative event of condition.
Illustrations:	Descriptions in the form of visual diagrams, charts, and so forth.
Definitions:	Descriptions of what a word means or of how it is to be used.
Relationships:	Descriptions of patterns; how one thing precedes another, or how they co-occur.
Rules:	Descriptions of appropriate behavior in a particular setting, or description of guidelines for appropriate behavior.
Explanations:	Descriptions that account for the occurrence of an event; depending on your point of view, these descriptions can be "casual" or "correlational."
Interpretations:	Descriptions of an event in the language of a particular concept or theory.
Problem:	Description of specific conditions that you then classify as a "problem."
Solutions:	Descriptions of specific measures to be taken in an attempt to solve a problem.

strations. More advanced topics, however, may require considerable research and expertise as well as a specialized vocabulary. Advanced topics may also include difficult concepts that require detailed descriptions, or complex relationships that can only be captured in well-prepared visual charts or diagrams. Informative speaking also becomes more difficult when you are called upon to provide a neat and articulate *summary* of the pertinent facts relative to a particular issue, or when the task is one of *interpreting* the significance of certain facts in terms of their implications or the consequences they produce.

An informative speech designed to clarify a "concept" or a "theoretical perspective" is an example of a highly challenging form of informative speaking. This type of information involves far more than the simple organization and transmission of relatively unequivocal facts. Yet, this information can be extremely helpful to the listener. It can provide new ways of looking at "what is going on." New concepts or perspectives can free the listener from the boundaries of "provincialism," or "limited perspective taking."

Information and Objectivity

It is tempting to assume that informative speaking provides us with "objective" descriptions of the "realities" around us. To some extent, however, we are all embedded in our own particular culture, and part of that culture includes the conceptual orientations we adopt and the language we use. Descriptions based on a particular conceptual orientation are called *interpretations*. Suppose, for example, that you have adopted the perspective that a behavioral response produces various forms of positive reinforcement, negative reinforcement, or punishment. Once this perspective is adopted—consciously or unconsciously—your "descriptions" can be guided by it. That is, you begin to see and interpret specific cases of reinforcing consequences. Without this particular frame of reference, you might observe the same set of events but might describe them in very different terms—that is, in terms consistent with a very different frame of reference.

It is also the case that listeners are less than "objective" or "neutral" in their interpretation of speaker messages. A listener can respond only in terms of his or her own learning history, including his or her own conceptual orientations and ways of assigning meanings to speaker messages.

Information in the Form of Inferences

Although we rely heavily on descriptive statements that pertain to things we can observe when we speak informatively, we can also point to the likely implications of our observations—through the process of drawing *inferences*. For example, you may observe the height of a tree at two different points in time, and based on its increased height on the latter date, you may infer "growth." Inferences of this sort carry considerable integrity in the sense that they are closely connected to reliable observations. However, inferences can also be lacking in integrity in the sense that they are only based on partial or inconclusive observations. In any case, all inferences are *conclusions* arrived at through a line of reasoning.

Clearly then, even when we attempt to stay within the strict boundaries of informative speaking—and try to avoid persuasive overtones—our performance usually includes a variety of messages that function as "subtle persuaders." Persuasive influence of some sort of another is an inherent part of all human interaction; only potatoes and carrots can maintain a position of total objectivity!

Persuasive Speaking

Persuasive speaking not only provides information but also employs a variety of persuasive appeals designed to gain a specific belief, evaluation, or action. Persuasive speaking can serve to *reinforce* and thereby strengthen current beliefs, values, and behaviors, or it can be designed to *change* them.

A politician's speech to his or her party members may be designed to reinforce and strengthen the party's point of view on some political issue. A church leader's presentation to the congregation may be designed to reinforce and strengthen particular beliefs already held by the members of that congregation. In both examples, the central purpose is to maintain and strengthen the status quo.

Other persuasive speeches are designed to change some aspect of the status quo. If a Democratic candidate is speaking to an audience composed mainly of registered Republicans, he or she may design a persuasive speech to change audience voting behavior. If a church leader is dissatisfied with certain behaviors of some congregation members, the minister may develop a message designed to encourage a *change* in those behaviors.

Persuasive Appeals

The term *persuasion* is usually employed with reference to relatively "mild" forms of interpersonal influence. Persuasive appeals include (1) the character or reputation of the speaker, (2) emotional appeals directed at listener sentiment, and (3) rational appeals, encompassing arguments and evidence.

Speakers establish a reputation from their credentials or accomplishments or through listeners' positive association with them. In general, we are more open to a speaker's influence to the extent that we hold him or her in high regard. Emotional appeals can take the form of well-selected anecdotes or of extended examples that set the tone for further messages. Situational pomp and ceremony can be employed to generate excitement or interest. When a listener is emotionally prepared for certain types of messages, he or she may respond more favorably toward them. Clearly, however, emotional appeals need to be selected with care and should be appropriate in terms of the occasion.

Rational appeals motivate a preferred course of action by (1) pointing to the *desirable consequences* that should follow that action or (2) by pointing to the *undesirable consequences* that can be avoided through that action. When the speaker motivates by pointing to desirable consequences, the persuasive appeals might be referred to as "requests," "recommendations," "advice," "pleas," or "calls," depending on the strength of the appeal. When the speaker tries to motivate action by pointing to the undesirable consequences to be avoided, the appeal can be referred to as a "warning."

Sometimes the speaker tries to motivate listener action by pointing to certain types of positive consequences that would be *provided by the speaker*. We might refer to this tactic as a "promise" or a "guarantee." If speaker-provided consequences are conditional on appropriate listener behavior, the appeal might be referred to as a "deal" or a "bargain."

In the context of speech communication, the term "persuasion" is not usually employed with reference to stronger forms of interpersonal influence, such as "demands," "threats," or "intimidation." Tactics like these go beyond persuasion by suggesting that a lack of listener compliance will result in some from of *punishing* consequences. Also, responsible persuasion does not depend on distortion or deceit. Responsible persuasion is a relatively mild form of interpersonal influence, and one that both presumes and protects listener integrity.

Information in Persuasive Speaking

As noted earlier, you can distinguish between different types of speech events in terms of their major focus; however, a single speech may achieve a variety of goals. In the development of a persuasive speech, for example, the speaker provides a considerable amount of information. It can even be argued that a persuasive speech achieves its special status from the types of information provided and from the ways that information is organized in order to produce changes in listener's beliefs, values, or behaviors. For example, a typical persuasive format consists of identifying a *problem* prior to advocating a *solution.* Important aspects of the problem are typically developed by providing a history of the problem, the dimensions or magnitude of the problem, or the specific consequences of the problem. In effect, each of these aspects of problem development amounts to a "mini" informative speech about specific conditions that characterize a problem.

In approaching a proposed solution to the problem, a speaker is likely to outline the major features of the solution, including the personnel or materials needed and their cost. Here, the details of a proposed solution may be viewed as another "mini" informative speech. Finally, the speaker may promote the adoption of his or her solution through information about the likely benefits to be derived relative to their costs.

In brief then, each aspect of a persuasive speech can be viewed as an information type message. However, the overall effect is clearly persuasive when viewed in terms of the information selected and the manner in which that information is organized and presented. The speech becomes persuasive (1) to the extent that it includes an implicit or explicit call for listener belief, evaluation, or a course of action and (2) to the extent that the speaker employs persuasive appeals in the pursuit of these goals.

Basic Issues Common to Informative and Persuasive Speaking

Although it is important to be able to distinguish between the basic processes of informative and persuasive speaking, effective participation in interpersonal and public speech settings requires more. You must also be able to think clearly about the basic issues that underlie message development and about how they function in the context of informative and persuasive speaking. In the following section, these basic factors are identified and discussed in terms of *topics, issues, propositions, arguments,* and *evidence.*

Topics

The topic pertains to the general nature of a speaker's subject matter. For example, a speaker's topic might be nuclear weapons, tax simplification or abortion. A single topic can be approached in virtually limitless numbers of ways, and can provide the basis for either informative or persuasive speaking (for examples, see Table 5–2). A major task therefore is to *limit* a topic to a specific purpose so that it is manageable in terms of your time and energy, and suitable in terms of the constraints imposed by a particular occasion. A common mistake is to presume that a topic must be "covered" in a particular way. In reality, however, a speaker should always maintain a position of control. By limiting your objectives, you can exercise control over the materials required, and can

TABLE 5–2

Representative Sample of Informative and Persuasive Speech Topics

Informative Speech Topics	Persuasive Speech Topics
1. Five new advances in home computers	1. Why you should (should not) buy a home computer
2. How to play hockey	2. Why you should (should not) support your local hockey team
3. Three ways to save on your income tax	3. Why tax laws should (should not) be made simpler
4. The major stages of prenatal development	4. Why abortion should (should not) be a matter of individual choice
5. The major requirements for a balanced vegetarian diet	5. Why we should (should not) become a vegetarian
6. The relationship between professional boxing and serious head injuries	6. Why professional boxers should (should not) be required to wear protective headgear
7. Major events that produced the American Civil War	7. Why the American Civil War was (was not) justified
8. Classical American jazz: What it is and is not	8. Why Louis Armstrong was (was not) our best jazz artist
9. Typical features of a Van Gogh painting	9. Why the federal government should (should not) help support public art galleries
10. How to construct a valid IQ test	10. Why IQ tests should (should not) be administered by our public schools

adapt them to agreed-upon time limits and to the needs of a particular audience.

Issues

An issue pertains to a specific aspect of a general topic; a single issue can be clearly articulated in the form of a *question.* For example, "Would an all-out nuclear war produce a nuclear winter?" or, "Could a computer malfunction cause a nuclear war?" You can see that each of these issues addresses a different aspect of the general topic, "nuclear war."

In the context of informative speaking, it is important to select issues in terms of their relevance to audience interests and needs. In the context of persuasive speaking, focus on pivotal issues that must be resolved in order to gain audience acceptance and support.

There are three basic types of issues: (1) questions of *fact*, (2) questions of *value*, and (3) questions of *policy*. These types parallel the three types of *propositions* described in the following section.

Propositions

Propositions pertain to the types of statements that we can make about our topic or subject matter. There are three types of propositions—fact, value, and policy—and each is defined in terms of its means of verification.

Proposition of Fact   A proposition of fact is a statement about some *observable* feature of ourselves, others, or the world around us. It is a statement that can be confirmed or disconfirmed through observation. For example, the statement, "Bill weighs 205 pounds," is a *factual type* of statement because (1) it pertains to an observable event and (2) the "truth" or accuracy of the statement is verifiable (with the help of a scale) through observation. If the scale reads 205 pounds, then the statement is a correct statement of fact. If the scale reads something else, it is an incorrect statement of fact, but it is still a *factual type* of statement.

When used in this context, the word *fact* does not necessarily impart truth or accuracy to a statement. Rather, it indicates only that the statement can be verified by observation. "There is a unicorn in the garden" is a proposition of fact even though it is untrue. It is a proposition of fact because we could check its accuracy by looking in the garden. Scientific theories are arguments involving statements of fact, because the truth of a theoretical statement is verified through observation.

We can distinguish between (1) informative speaking designed to *describe, summarize,* or *interpret* our observations and (2) persuasive speaking designed to *win belief* for our characterization of those observations. That is, when dealing with relatively simple and familiar issues, our informative exchanges are relatively straightforward and unproblematical. However, where the accuracy of factual statements are in question, a speaker may be required to adopt the posture of an *advocate* and develop a series of persuasive messages in support of their accuracy. For example, you might seek more than the mere understanding of a particular economic theory and its rational implications. You might want to convince us of the accuracy of that theory or provide reasons why we should accept the theory as a reasonable explanation of current economic activity.

Proposition of Value   A proposition of value is a statement about personal preferences. A value statement reflects someone's position regarding what is good or bad, right or wrong, just or unjust, beautiful or ugly. To say that cigarette smoking causes cancer is to state a proposition of fact. By way of contrast, a statement that cigarette smoking is *bad* is a proposition of value.

In a limited sense at least, we "confirm" a value statement by simply declaring our personal point of view. Usually, however, we also appeal to other individuals or groups who share that view. Sometimes we try to confirm a value statement through an appeal to an "authority." For example, we might refer to an art critic who shares our evaluation of a painting or a sculpture. But an art critic—like any other authority—is necessarily a biased person with credentials. A particular authority may have special training, experience, or may hold a particular position of power, and for one or more of these reasons we may be influenced by his or her opinions. In any case, however, an authority can do no more than state a preference or provide a recommendation in the light of his or her background and current status.

Sometimes we also try to confirm a value statement through an appeal to majority opinion. But members of a majority are no more than collections of individuals, each of whom can only express his or her personal preference. We might also add, "The majority opinion of today is often the minority opinion of tomorrow"—and vice versa.

On occasion, confusion arises between value statements and factual statements about our values. There are, of course, many factual questions that can be raised about our values: "Do most people prefer 'Classic' Coca Cola, the new and sweeter Coca Cola, or Pepsi Cola?" Or, "Which advertising appeals are most influential in changing our preferences for a particular cola?" These are factual type questions that, presumably, can be answered through the kinds of observations made possible by modern methods of social science research.

Accordingly, we can also distinguish between (1) informative speaking designed to provide information *about* people's values and (2) persuasive speaking designed to *advocate adoption* of a particular value. In an American history class, for example, an instructor might lecture about the essential values held by the framers of the Constitution. He or she might show how particular values in 1776 were translated into specific elements in the Constitution. A contemporary opinion survey might reveal information about contemporary values or shifts in values, and this data could easily provide the basis for an informative speech. By way of contrast, a salesperson might try to gain a positive evaluation of his or her product or service; a politician might try to promote a favorable evaluation of his or her political party; an educator might encourage a more positive evaluation of our schools.

Proposition of Policy   A proposition of policy is a call for action. Any statement that advocates a particular course of action is a proposition of policy. It is helpful to remember that a policy type of statement always includes an implicit or explicit use of the term *should*. For example, "Cigarette smoking *should* be banned in public restaurants."

Propositions of policy are "verified" or "confirmed" through an *implicit* or *explicit* appeal to relevant facts and relevant human values. For example, in an attempt to gain support for the policy to ban smoking in public restaurants, you can present explicit factual statements about the observed detrimental effects of secondhand smoke on nonsmokers. Here, presumably, you would include references to specific scientific studies that provide evidence concerning the accuracy of these statements.

In this type of speech, there is also an *implied* appeal to the audience's values; that is, to good health and a longer life. These commonly held values in the context of this particular speech do not require explicit treatment. In some policy speeches, however, it may be useful to make *explicit* references to relevant values and their relation to your proposed course of action. For example, we frequently encounter speakers who remind us of basic values reflected in the Constitution or Bill of Rights, then they proceed by showing us how a particular policy is consistent with the fundamental values. Also, a speaker might encourage specific types of behavior by showing us how they are consistent with respected social or religious principles.

Finally then, we can also distinguish between (1) an informative speech designed to provide information *about* a particular policy and (2) a persuasive speech designed to *advocate* the *adoption* of a policy. For example, you could describe those conditions that lead to a specific policy proposal; you could describe the actual details of that proposal; or you could speculate about the acceptability or popularity of the proposal or its likely consequences. Political journalists frequently provide these types of information about proposed or existing governmental policies, while trying to maintain a position of relative objectivity at the same time. By way of contrast, you might advocate the adoption of a particular policy. In its ideal form, democratically governed institutions allow for individual influence and policy change by providing opportunities for persuasive speaking in open debate and through some form of participative decision making.

Briefly then, there are three basic types of propositions and each is verified or confirmed through a unique type of appeal. Propositions of fact gain support through an appeal to observation. Propositions of value gain support through an appeal to an individual's personal interest, to majority opinion, or to respected authorities or standards. A proposition of policy is a call for action and is supported through an appeal to both facts and values that encourage a specific course of action.

Arguments

In the speech communication discipline, the term "argument" is employed in two different but related ways. First, it may refer to a *reason* you should believe something, value something, or why you should take a specific action. In this case, the argument (or reason) is stated with the implicit or explicit use of the word "because." For example, you might claim that a particular automobile should be purchased "because it represents the latest in stylistic features" or "because it has incorporated the latest technological advances."

Second, the term argument is employed with reference to *a line of inductive* or *deductive reasoning.* Inductive reasoning moves from a series of specific observations to a general conclusion about those observations. Deductive reasoning moves in the opposite direction; it starts with a generalization and then points to its logical implications with regard to a specific case.

In the context of informative speaking, you can use rational arguments (1) to reconstruct something that happened in the past but can no longer be observed, (2) to interpret the meaning of present observations, or (3) to predict what will happen in the future. In effect, through the use of relevant evidence and logical arguments, you can *infer* conclusions about unobservable issues of fact.

Inferred conclusions based on argument raise major question for which there are no easy answers. For example, how much and what kind of evidence is required to prove an inferred conclusion in the form of a proposition of fact? Widely held standards for answering these questions do not exist. Bear in mind that inferences based on inductive reasoning are not absolute truths. They are *decisions.* The most you can expect is that decisions based on good evidence and reasoning are true at *some level of probability.* In the end, what we call truth is what we *decide to believe.*

Persuasive speaking implies that a speaker sees some basis for disagreement with a listener. In the context of persuasive speaking then, argument is employed in an attempt to resolve an area of disagreement. Disagreements can turn on issues of fact, value, or policy. Accordingly, if a disagreement pertains to a question of fact, arguments should be based on observable evidence; if a disagreement pertains to a question of value, arguments should pertain to speaker and listener likes and dislikes with a probable emphasis on areas of agreement; if a disagreement pertains to a question of policy, arguments should focus on the rationality of a specific proposal in the light of a listener's knowledge and values.

The nature of argument as a logical process is an especially important topic within the domain of speech communication. Accordingly, it provides the entire focus of Chapter Six.

Evidence

Evidence includes a wide variety of verbal and nonverbal materials that are used in support of a proposition of fact, value, or policy. Examples of evidence include statements from individuals who made firsthand observations of events in question; statements from authoritative sources; summaries of data in the form of visual graphs or charts; actual objects in the form of documents or artifacts; or even visual characteristics of physical injury or behavioral trauma.

In the context of informative speaking, evidence can be employed in support of an individual's interpretation of a question of fact, value, or policy. In an attempt to gain a listener's *understanding* of a particular issue, an informative speaker may employ evidence in order to characterize his or her topic in a particular way.

In the context of persuasive speaking, evidence is used in conjunction with claims about what the listener should believe with regard to some

issue, how the listener should evaluate a particular issue, or what action the listener should take.

The impact of the evidence upon the listener depends upon (1) the source of the evidence, (2) the nature of the evidence, and (3) the listener's propensity to accept it. For example, the source of evidence must be reliable. When the evidence consists of testimony about personal observations, the individual who provides the testimony must be demonstrably trustworthy and competent. Evidence should be self-consistent and uncontradictory. Finally, it must be understandable and acceptable to the listener. Table 5–3 summarizes some important tests for determining the practical value of material that anyone can employ as evidence.

Receiver-centered Informative and Persuasive Speaking

In Part I, we advance a receiver-centered perspective of human communication. This perspective stresses the importance of adapting messages to the unique character of a particular listener or audience.

In the context of informative speaking, you must make effective contact with your subject matter and must be able to encode messages that are consistent with that subject matter. But a receiver-centered perspective stresses that an informative speaker must also make contact with the unique characteristics of a particular audience—what the audience already knows about a specific topic as well as their interests in further knowledge.

In the context of persuasive speaking, you must do more than simply advocate a particular belief, value, or preferred course of action. You

TABLE 5–3

Tests for the Evaluation of Evidence*

1. Does *enough* evidence exist to support the conclusion?

2. Is the evidence *clear* to the audience? Are most receivers likely to understand it quickly and easily, especially in terms of what conclusions the evidence is intended to support?

3. Is the evidence *consistent?* Is it *externally* consistent with other information that exists? (Does other evidence tend to corroborate or refute the evidence in question?) Is it *internally* consistent? (For example, does the first part of an eyewitness' account jibe with later parts of his same story?)

4. Is the evidence *verifiable?* Can a speaker go back to original sources to check on the accuracy of statistics, examples, or testimony? Can someone other than the speaker, like a political opponent or a member of the audience, gain access to the same information?

5. Is the source of the evidence *competent?* Has printed material from which examples or statistics are taken come from someone qualified? Is testimony given by someone who observed and was mentally and physically able to report that observation accurately, or whose background equips him or her to provide competent opinions?

6. Is the source of the evidence *reliable?* Is someone who testified trustworthy, truthful, and unbiased? Do printed materials have a good reputation for fairness and thoroughness?

7. Is the evidence *relevant?* Does it support the conclusions that the speaker claims it supports? Does it lead logically and directly to the conclusion?

8. Is the evidence *statistically sound?* Are statistical criteria followed rigorously—such as accuracy, appropriate classification, valid sampling procedures, statistically significant results, reporting in context, and fair visual representations?

9. Is the evidence *recent* or current? This judgment is obviously relative; it depends on the topic. A business executive, attempting to persuade colleagues to adopt a particular investment program, needs up-to-the-minute statistics. In contrast, an advocate for prison reform might need not only reasonably recent evidence about current conditions, but may also use historical materials about past failures in the system.

10. Is the evidence *adaptive* to the information and interest levels of the receivers? Sometimes a speaker with the same topic and purpose must use significantly different supporting materials when speaking to different audiences, like the anti-smoking advocate who used primarily statistical evidence with a group of older smokers, and used extended illustrations with a teen-age group.

*From Freeley, A. (1971). *Argumentation and debate* (3rd ed.). Belmont, Calif: Wadsworth.

must also consider your listeners' current knowledge about the topic, their unique beliefs and values, and their readiness to engage in particular forms of action. It is through this type of listener analysis that a persuasive speaker can pursue his or her goals in terms of what is achievable with a particular listener or audience. In brief, from a receiver-centered perspective, all informative and persuasive speaking involves a *content* issue, a *message* issue, and a speaker-listener *relationship* issue.

Part of the relationship issue includes listener feedback. Feedback can relate to the quality of a speech's content, language or speaking skills, or a speaker's relationship with a listener. Feedback, of course, also varies in quality. It is always necessary for the speaker to determine its value and the extent to which it should influence his or her future activities.

Speech communication can be viewed as (1) a special form of *social exchange* that occurs between a speaker and listener and (2) a form of exchange that leads to important consequences for both. When the speaker provides information, he or she contributes to the ways in which a listener sees a particular condition and concurrently is likely to respond. For example, when we learn that a particular action is *safe,* we are more likely to pursue it; when we learn that a condition is *dangerous,* we are more likely to avoid it. When communication takes the form of *persuasive appeals,* the speaker can also influence what listeners believe about something, how they value it, the kinds of policies they will support, and the actions they will take. Through feedback, listeners can have similar effects upon the speaker. See Figure 5–1 for a moel of the inherent

FIGURE 5–1

A Receiver-centered Model of Speech Communication

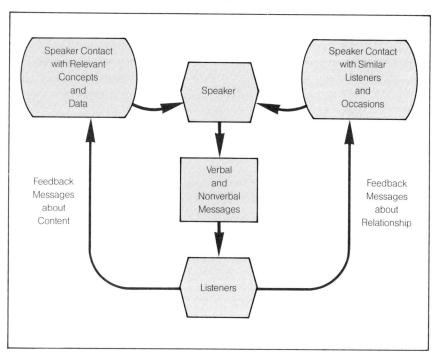

relatedness of content, language and speaker skills, and speaker-listener relationships.

Human communication activities are central to the very nature and quality of our existence. Most of what we know and value about ourselves, about others, and about the world around us is a product of human interaction. To recognize these facts is also to appreciate the central role of human communication as well as the free and open society that makes meaningful communication possible.

Summary

Basic types of speaking are identified as informative, persuasive, ceremonial, or entertaining. However, the business end of most communication activities involves the basic processes of information exchange and interpersonal influence through persuasion. Through information, we provide listener understanding and preparation for effective action. Through persuasion, we try to gain listener belief, evaluation, or motivation for a specific course of action.

The basic processes of informative and persuasive speaking are discussed in terms of topics, issues, propositions, arguments, and evidence. Particular attention is focused on the three types of propositions: fact, value, and policy. Briefly, a proposition of fact is a statement about an observable event; a proposition of value is a statement about personal preferences; and, a proposition of policy is a call for action.

A receiver-oriented model of speech communication is described and informative and persuasive speaking is discussed in terms of this model. All informative and persuasive speaking involves a content issue, a message issue, and a speaker-listener relationship issue.

Questions

1. Why can we say that all language is persuasive? What are some of the persuasive messages typically communicated in an informative speech?

2. How is information an important aspect of persuasive speaking?

3. How can a single topic serve as a basis for either informative or persuasive speaking?

4. Are propositions of value less important because they are not confirmable through methods of observation?

5. How can logical reasoning be employed in an informative speech?

Suggested Readings

BAXTER, L. A. (1984). An investigation of compliance-gaining as politeness. *Human Communication Research, 10,* 427.

BEM, D. J. (1970). *Beliefs, attitudes, and human affairs.* Monterey, Calif.: Brooks/Cole.

LISKA, J. (1978). Situational and topical variations in credibility criteria. *Communication Monographs, 45,* 85.

MILLER, G. R. (1969). Some factors influencing judgments of the logical validity of arguments: A research view. *Quarterly Journal of Speech, LV,* 276.

POLANYI, M. (1958). *Personal knowledge.* Chicago: University of Chicago Press.

Chapter Six

The Nature of Argument

Preview

Most of us like to think of ourselves as rational individuals. We place a high value on the sending and receiving of messages that seem reasonable. Argumentation is a form of communication that is reasonable. In this chapter, we examine some basic concepts in argumentation—logic and reasoning, issues and evidence—and how these elements fit together in the production of rational communication about what we believe to be true, what we believe to be good, and what we believe we should do to improve our circumstances.

The study of argumentation is important because rational arguments, intended to inform and persuade, play an important role in many different contexts—courts, legislative bodies, and public forums. It is important to recognize that rational arguments play an equally important role in less formal settings, too. They are basic to science, the classroom, and any other context where rational decision making is in order—dyads, small groups, or formal public speaking settings.

Objectives

To develop some basic concepts in argumentation

To improve understanding of the nature of logic and reasoning and of their role in communication

To help develop practical skills in arguing a reasonable point of view

To sharpen critical skills in interpreting argumentative communication

SIX   This chapter addresses the nature of argumentation and its role in instrumental communication designed to inform and persuade.

We as humans are rational animals, empowered with an ability to reason and to appreciate that ability. We do not always use this ability or show proper appreciation for its use, but we are nonetheless inspired to do both in some of the more consequential affairs of life.

Argumentation

An argument is a line of reasoning—a set of logically related statements designed to induce belief in the truth of a specific proposition. To argue does not mean "to fight." Unfortunately, the term is often used in that

way. To argue is to engage in instrumental communication that appeals primarily to the rational faculties of the receiver.

No single assertion, proposition, conclusion, or statement constitutes an argument. Remember that an argument is a line of reasoning involving more than one statement. If we merely say, "There is life on Mars," we have not made an argument. We have an argument when we offer at least one more statement showing our reason for believing the truth of the other statement, such as, "We believe this because Mars changes color on parts of its surface as the Martian seasons change." We're not saying this is a particularly good argument, but it does consist of two distinct statements, one lending logical support to the other.

An argument is said to be *valid* if its conclusion follows logically from its premises. When we communicate a set of statements that together seem reasonable, we have made a line of reasoning. The reasonableness of a set of statements depends on two factors—the truth of the individual statements and the logical connections among them. When an argument fails to convince, it fails either because the truth of one or more statements had not been established or because the logical relationships among the statements are not valid.

Logical Reasoning

There are two basic types of logical reasoning: deductive and inductive. Deductive reasoning is based on the rules of formal logic. In a deductive line of reasoning, the conclusion follows logically from its premises by merely restating information that is already implied in those premises. For example, consider a simple deductive line of reasoning consisting of two premises and a conclusion, called a syllogism:

Major premise: All metals conduct heat.
Minor premise: Tin is a metal.
Conclusion:
Therefore: Tin conducts heat.

Notice that the conclusion of this syllogism doesn't really say anything new. What it says is already implied by the premises; it merely clarifies information that is already present.

When we reason deductively, we are simply arranging a series of statements so that the listener can understand how the information contained in the premises leads necessarily to the conclusion. If the premises are true, and if the rules of deductive logic are followed, then the conclusion will be true. Most of us know the rules of deductive logic intuitively and are able to detect faulty reasoning, especially when fairly familiar concepts are involved.

The problem in getting a listener to accept a valid conclusion seldom involves his or her ability to understand the rules of formal logic. Rather, the problem usually has to do with gaining his or her acceptance of the truth of the premises, which is usually a problem in *inductive* reasoning.

In inductive reasoning, the conclusion derived from a set of premises always contains new information that is not already contained in the premises. The plausibility of an inductive conclusion depends on the number and quality of specific premises on which the general conclusion is based. We are reasoning inductively when we generalize on the basis of specific observations

Premises based on observations:	Tin conducts heat.
	Lead conducts heat.
	Copper conducts heat.
	Iron conducts heat.
	Silver conducts heat.
Therefore:	All metals conduct heat.

Notice that the conclusion, a generalization, is by no means a necessary logical consequence of its premises. It would be if every possible metal were included in the premises. Because some are missing, however, the conclusion says more than its premises do. In inductive reasoning, we can never be absolutely certain that the conclusion follows logically from the premises. The best we can expect is a fairly high level of confidence that the conclusion is a valid logical inference.

Evaluating the Validity of a Line of Reasoning

We said earlier that a line of reasoning is valid if its conclusion follows logically from its premises. It is relatively easy to ascertain the validity of deductive reasoning, because the conclusion should restate something implied by its premises. Inductive validity, on the other hand, is not so

readily determined, because the conclusion of an inductive line of reasoning is a generalization inferred from an incomplete set of premises.

Deductive Reasoning

It is possible to judge the validity of deductive reasoning apart from the truth of the individual statements. Considered by itself, validity in deduction has nothing to do with the truth of the premises or conclusion. Table 6–1 illustrates the way logical validity and truth operate independently in deductive reasoning. The quadrants of a 2-by-2 table are called cells. Cell A contains a valid syllogism with true premises and true conclusion. In cell B, both premises and conclusion are true, but the reasoning is invalid because the conclusion is not a logical consequence of the premises. As written, the syllogism fails to identify the logical relationships among the terms and does not measure up as a line of reasoning, even though all three statements are true.

Cell C is a syllogism with three untrue statements, but the reasoning is valid because the conclusion follows logically from its premises. In cell D, both premises are true, but the conclusion is false. The syllogism itself is invalid, and in spite of the true premises, there's no guarantee of a true conclusion unless the reasoning is valid.

TABLE 6–1

Logical Validity and Truth

	Validity of Arguments	
	Valid	Invalid
Truth of Conclusions — True	**A** All men are mammals. Leonard Bernstein is a man. Therefore, Leonard Bernstein is a mammal.	**B** Some students are athletes Some athletes wear glasses. Therefore, some students wear glasses.
Truth of Conclusions — Untrue	**C** All beagles have feathers. Charlie Brown is a beagle. Therefore, Charlie Brown has feathers.	**D** Many tennis players are men. Chris Evert Lloyd is a tennis player. Therefore, Chris Evert Lloyd is a man.

FIGURE 6-1

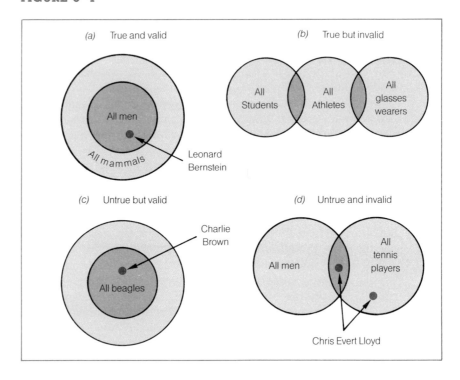

When confronted with a problem in determining the validity of a deductive argument, it may help to draw a *Venn diagram*—a set of overlapping circles, each of which represents all the members of a particular categorical set of objects. Figure 6–1 shows Venn diagrams, indicating the relationships implied by the premises of the syllogisms in Table 6–1.

Inductive Reasoning

Unfortunately, no one has ever been able to discover an adequate set of rules for determining with certainty when an inductive conclusion follows from its premises. There are not handy devices, such as the Venn diagram, to help us judge the validity of induction, so we use informal, somewhat intuitive rules as a test.

In general, however, the logic of induction is the logic of *probability*. When we infer something on the basis of past experience and state our inference in terms of probability, we are reasoning inductively. The validity of an inductive argument is intimately related to what we believe to be the truth of our conclusion—the strength of our belief in its accuracy. Suppose you find that it rains every time you invite friends over for a barbecue. You are planning a barbecue for next weekend, and you say, "Chances are it will rain next weekend because I'm giving a barbecue." This is a probability statement. If you tune in to a radio weather forecast and hear, "There will be a 10 percent chance of rain over the weekend," you are hearing another probability estimate. The weather service's estimate is presumably more valid than yours because it is based on more careful and systematic observations, but both are inductive conclusions.

In practical argumentation, most of the difficulties a speaker encounters have to do with disagreements over probability estimates. Some probabilities can be stated precisely and objectively as numbers. For example, the probability of drawing the ace of spades at random from a deck of cards is 1:52. The probability of drawing any ace is 4:52 or 1:13. The probability of drawing any spade is 13:52 or 1:4. Reasonable people will (probably) not dispute these odds.

Subjective estimates of probability are a different matter. If you ask ten different people what the chances are that China will attack the United States with nuclear missiles within fifteen years, you'll find a wide range of estimates. Most issues we argue about—in law, politics, religion, science, morality, or whatever—involve important estimates of subjective probabilities. None of us can escape the obligation of making such estimates and of basing our actions on them. For example, if you are driving a car and see a child by the roadside, you must make a subjective probability estimate of the likelihood that the child will dart into your path. If you estimate wrong and hit the child, you may be held accountable.

When an individual is called to account for some action in a court of law, the concept of the "reasonably prudent person" is invoked to decide whether or not the action was defensible or justifiable. It is assumed that there are community standards for estimating subjective probabilities, and that a defendant should be held legally accountable for failure to understand and act on those standards. How many times have you heard statements like the following offered in defense after a catastrophe:

"I didn't know the gun was loaded."

"I never expected the kid to dart out in front of my car."

"I was only kidding about hijacking. Can't you take a joke?"

"I never expected that when I told them to get the information 'by any means necessary' they would actually break into the office."

"I had the right-of-way after all."

Each of these statements illustrates someone's failure to make a reasonable subjective probability estimate of the consequences of some act.

Arguments on issues of public policy require many different kinds of probability estimates. Should marijuana be legalized? What are the chances that this would lead to increased abuse of more dangerous drugs? Should the United States unilaterally limit the development of strategic arms? What are the chances that this would lead to aggression by the communist superpowers? Should we permit abortion on demand? What are the chances that this would result in the abuse of abortion as a means of routine birth control? Because we have no way to assign objective probability estimates to these potential outcomes, we must base our decisions on some sort of consensus about subjective probabilities. Thus, you can see that the validity of an inductive line of reasoning depends upon our confidence about the possible truth of its conclusion.

Let's consider an example. The artificial sweeteners called cyclamates were banned in 1969 by the Food and Drug Administration (FDA) because researchers found that high dosages of cyclamates can produce cancers in rats. Some opponents of the ban argue that dosages used to induce cancer in each rat were the equivalent of between one hundred and five hundred bottles of soda pop per day and that, therefore, the probability of human cancer owing to cyclamates must be assumed to be minutely small or nonexistent. The FDA and certain consumer health advocates argue that the evidence shows a risk, however small, and that the ban should stand. Ask yourself these questions: Even if we knew the exact probability of contracting cancer from cyclamates in normal doses, what would you consider to be an acceptable level of risk? Because we have no such objective probability, what is your subjective estimate of the risk based on the evidence we have? To decide the validity of the FDA's argument, you must make intelligent guesses on both questions.

The persuasive force of an argument involving probability estimates depends on the quality and quantity of evidence on which the estimates are based. In a later section, we discuss the nature of evidence and its role in estimating probabilities.

Deductive and Inductive Arguments

Rational argumentation would be child's play if we were equipped with an exhaustive list of major and minor premises that are true. All we would have to do is apply the rules of formal logic to tease out valid and true conclusions. We have no such list, however, so we must base our deductive reasoning on premises inferred inductively. In other words, it isn't possible to rely exclusively on deductive reasoning because the premises used in deduction are themselves *conclusions* based on inductive reasoning.

When reasoning deductively, be sure that your listener *accepts the premises as true,* and that your logic *conforms to accepted formal rules.* This should result in agreement on your conclusion. What may seem reasonable to you may not appear so to someone else, however. No message is inherently true and reasonable. Judgments of truth and reasonableness are made by interpreters as they assign meaning. Personal standards of truth and reasonableness vary, and productive argument requires that you and your listener come to a shared understanding of each other's standards of judgment.

When arguing inductively, you have two major tasks to accomplish. First, you must convince receivers that your probability estimates are accurate. Don't bother with numerical estimates unless you have an objective basis for calculating them. Use verbal qualifiers, such as, "It is *highly likely* that . . ." rather than, "The probability is 0.84. . ." when objective probabilities are not demonstrable. Second, you must convince listeners that your estimates forecast gain or loss for them or someone they care about. Suppose you know that even one bottle of soda pop sweetened with cyclamates produces a 10 percent increase in the chance of malignancy. By itself, this information may not convince your listeners

to avoid cyclamates. Only if they consider this figure to represent an unacceptable risk will they avoid it. Or, suppose that you could convince a listener that a 10 percent increase in defense spending could reduce the risk of war by 20 percent. Only if your listener finds this cost-benefit ratio acceptable will he or she join you in advocating the increase.

This is why it is important, when reasoning inductively, to know what a listener already believes about the relevant probabilities. There's not much point in trying to convince people of something they already believe. Spend your energy speaking to the probability estimates on which you disagree.

In practice, most arguments take the forms of *categorical, causal,* or *analogical* reasoning. Almost all categorical reasoning is deductive. Its purpose is to identify the membership of events or objects in various categories. All the syllogisms discussed earlier include instances of categorical reasoning. Causal reasoning is inductive and consists of describing and explaining events and phenomena in terms of cause-effect relationships. Some serious philosophical and methodological problems are involved in causal reasoning, but building a case without it is almost impossible.

An *analogy* is a figurative illustration in which the properties of a familiar object or event are used to describe or explain the properties of a less familiar object or event. Comparing the flow of electricity through a wire to the flow of water through a pipe is analogical. This kind of reasoning is rhetorically powerful, but also highly susceptible to abuse because analogies can be misleading. Analogical reasoning is purely inductive.

An analogy is a reasonable argumentative device if and only if two conditions are met: (1) the analog, familiar object, corresponds on all important features with the object of comparison, and (2) the analog introduces no irrelevant but potentially misleading features for which there are no meaningful correspondences in the object of comparison.

Try these two tests on the following analogies:

A woman without a man is like a fish without a bicycle.

Breakfast without orange juice is like a day without sunshine.

Letting students participate in university government is like letting the inmates run the asylum.

Capital punishment is tantamount to institutionalized murder.

Laws making possession of marijuana a crime are as foolish as the Eighteenth Amendment to the U.S. Constitution (prohibition).

Of these three types of arguments, the categorical variety is probably the most rational (and also the most trivial), and analogical arguments the least. The more rational forms are not necessarily the most persuasive, however, because the persuasiveness of an argument does not depend on logic alone.

To illustrate these three types of arguments, let's turn to a topic that produces vigorous argumentation in contemporary society—abortion. We list some arguments frequently advanced on this topic and offer them as examples only, not because we necessarily agree with any of them.

Categorical Argument   Abortion is murder, because murder is defined in the law as the willful and premeditated taking of a human life; and a human embryo is certainly both living and human.

Causal Argument   The availability of abortion on demand fosters irresponsible behavior in the form of failure to take adequate precautions to avoid unwanted pregnancies.

Analogical Argument   A human embryo is not a person just as a kernel of corn is not a plant. An embryo, like a seed, is a set of plans for a person. To abort an embryo is no different in principle than to prevent any given sperm cell and ovum from getting together in the first place.

Whatever your views may be on the reasonableness of these arguments, it may be helpful for you at this point to analyze the reasoning in them. Before you read on, take a few minutes to examine each argument and try to create rebuttal arguments for each.

An argument is not the same thing as a fully developed informative or persuasive speech or essay. It takes several arguments to make a complete presentation. An argument is a logically coherent subunit of a speech—like a single girder or span in a bridge—leading to the speaker's ultimate conclusion. A speaker who expects to lead listeners to his or her conclusion must be sure that the bridge is complete. A missing argument may weaken the bridge or make the crossing impossible.

The Structure of Argument

When you have occasion to create an argumentative presentation, you must address each of the following objectives:

1. Clearly and concisely identify the crucial issues to be considered.
2. Show how each issue is related to the major issue to be resolved.
3. Establish a claim about every issue.
4. Support each claim with convincing evidence—evidence that is relevant, substantive, self-consistent, credible, and sufficient to the requirements of your listeners. *Document your sources!*
5. Demonstrate the logical connections between each piece of evidence and the claim it supports.
6. Organize your message so that the arguments presented build on one another to form a logically coherent whole.

If your presentation reflects careful attention to each of these objectives, you will be effective. Even if you do not convince your audience of the truth of your position, you will probably win its respect for that position and for yourself.

Toulmin (1958) has developed a structural model of argumentation that is useful in preparing and analyzing rational discourse. The model is applicable to both inductive and deductive lines of reasoning. Its components, which are different statements or phrases that perform special functions in an argument, are as follows:

Drawing by Stan Hunt; © 1984 The New Yorker Magazine, Inc.

"The talks are in a delicate stage."

Data   Data are statements about evidence and serve as premises. *Data* and *evidence* are synonymous terms. In an argument, data are statements that are generally acceptable to the listener without additional proof and are offered to provide support for a conclusion or claim that does require proof.

Claim   A claim is simply a conclusion requiring proof—a statement that takes a position on the ultimate issue.

Warrant   A warrant is a connecting premise, such as the minor premise in a syllogism, showing the logical connection between a data statement and its corresponding claim.

Backing   Backing consists of statements supporting the warrant, when the warrant itself requires additional explanation or proof.

Rebuttal or Reservation   A rebuttal is a statement about the warrant, showing how the data and the warrant could conceivably lead to an alternative claim to the one being advanced. Usually, the rebuttal is a statement anticipating conditions under which, given the data and the warrant, the claim would still not necessarily follow.

Qualifier   A qualifier is a word or phrase in the argument, indicating the degree of certainty of the speaker's belief in the claim. The qualifier discloses the persuader's probability estimate that the claim is true.

Let's analyze some arguments with the Toulmin model. You can see from the illustrations in Figure 6–2 how the Toulmin model can be used to diagram the logical flow of an argument from premises to conclusions. The model is not a formula for structuring a fully developed argumentative speech, but it should help you to organize your thinking about a topic and to develop lines of reasoning from available evidence. It can assist you in discovering issues needing consideration and can help you anticipate potential rebuttals to your claims.

The most important component in the Toulmin model is the warrant. The warrant provides the logical connection between data (premises) and conclusions. Arguments that fail to gain acceptance usually lack a sufficient warrant, leaving listeners wondering how the speaker got from point A to point C and if they've missed a crucial point B.

The Rational Persuasive Speech

A complete persuasive speech may consist of many arguments. Each argument must stand as a logically coherent subunit of the speech. No arguments should be included unless they are relevant to the ultimate issue, which means that they should contribute meaningful proof toward its resolution. No argument that is required to prove the ultimate claim to the satisfaction of the target listeners should be omitted.

The following arguments might be used in a speech advocating a proposition of policy, the proposition being "that additional standards be imposed for admission to practice of trial law, above and beyond the successful completion of state bar examinations."

FIGURE 6–2

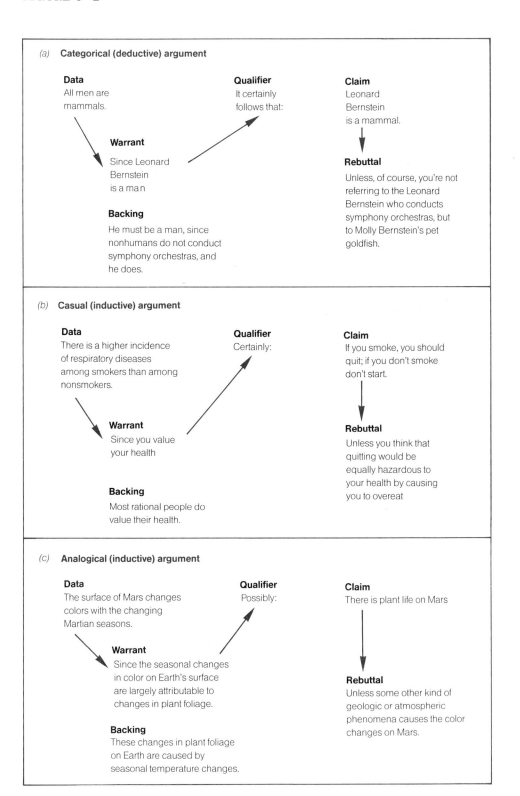

ARGUMENT

Contention or Claim:	Every citizen of the United States who enters into civil litigation or is brought to trial on criminal charges is entitled to representation by competent counsel.
Evidence:	The Sixth Amendment to the Constitution guarantees a criminal defendant the right to assistance of counsel.
Evidence:	The Fourteenth Amendment guarantees the citizen "due process of law."
Evidence:	Citation of several Supreme Court decisions based on the Sixth and Fourteenth Amendments that apply to concrete situations.

The issue addressed here is, "What are the rights of U.S. citizens respecting representation by an attorney in courts of law?" The claim advanced may need more or less support in the form of elaboration of the evidence, depending upon the audience. For example, a group of judges and lawyers may already be familiar enough with the Constitution and with recent applicable Supreme Court cases to warrant a cursory review of the evidence, but a lay audience may need more detailed and fully documented information about its rights.

ARGUMENT

Contention or Claim:	In recent years, there have been numerous cases in which trial lawyers have performed inadequately in representing their clients in the trial courts.
Evidence:	Public comments by such authoritative sources as F. Lee Bailey and Chief Justice Warren Burger.
Evidence:	Increased incidence of appellate reversals of trial court verdicts based on grounds of incompetent or inadequate representation by counsel.

The issue addressed by this argument is absolutely essential to the purpose of the speech—"Is there a need for change?" Several subordinate issues may need to be addressed to advance an adequate answer to this question, including the specific question posed here—"Has the performance of trial court lawyers met the standards implied by the U.S. Constitution?"

Once again, depending on what the audience knows about the claim and the evidence used to support it, the evidence may need further elaboration. For most persons, F. Lee Bailey and Warren Burger are familiar names and are recognized as credible authorities on jurisprudence, but for some, mere reference to their views on the subject may not be persuasive. Similarly, some listeners may require additional support for the evidence cited on the increased incidence of appellate reversals, perhaps in the form of actual cases and in the citation of sources through which listeners can find court opinions.

ARGUMENT

Contention or Claim:	Law school training alone does not equip an individual with the skills necessary for competent trial practice.
Evidence:	Survey of law school curricula showing that law students receive minimal training in trial advocacy; law students spend most of their time reading and listening to lectures, and very little time arguing cases in moot court settings.
Evidence:	Great Britain has long recognized the different skills demanded of the trial lawyer, and provides different training for barristers (trial lawyers) and solicitors (office lawyers).

Here again, the argument speaks to the issue of the need for change. The specific question is whether or not our law schools provide adequate trial law instruction. Note that even if our evidence gains the listener's acceptance of the claim, we still haven't proved that there's anything wrong with our law schools. That's another issue entirely, and one that we may or may not choose to address, depending on our best estimate of the solution to the problem posed.

We still haven't proposed a solution to the problem, although we've implied that one way to deal with the problem is to augment law school instruction in trial advocacy. But there might be a better way to solve the problem, for example, by requiring trial lawyers to complete an internship program similar to that required of medical doctors. It might not even be necessary to advocate a plan for solution to the problem. Remember that the policy proposition advocated refers only to "additional standards. . .for admission to trial law practice," and says nothing about how these standards might be implemented. This exemplifies the importance of clearly specifying the purpose of the speech, preferably in a single proposition of fact, value, or policy that points directly to specific issues needing attention.

A persuasive speech on this proposition would need to include arguments on additional issues. It might be useful for you to do two things after you've finished the last few pages of this chapter: (1) make a complete list of the issues you believe are relevant to this proposition, and (2) create arguments on these issues, perhaps using the Toulmin (1958) model to diagram your reasoning.

As with any kind of speech, the persuasive speech must be organized in such a way as to help the listener understand it. A logical progression of statements helps a listener remember, and a speech that is remembered is more likely to be accepted than one that is forgotten.

Above all, remember that the meaning of a message is assigned by the listener. In persuasion, this means that the reasonableness of a persuasive speech depends on the critical criteria of those hearing the speech and is not something inherent in the message itself. A poorly designed and delivered message may be effective with uncritical listeners, but a critical listener may reject even a very sound conclusion if it is based on sloppy reasoning.

When you wish to communicate rationally, there is one important principle to keep in mind. Rational communication is not just a matter of finding the right answer or reaching the correct conclusion. What matters is how you get there.

Summary

Argumentation is instrumental communication that appeals to reason. An argument is a line of reasoning—a set of logically related belief statements. Lines of reasoning take two basic forms, inductive and deductive. Deductive reasoning yields conclusions that merely restate information implied by a set of premises, whereas inductive reasoning produces conclusions containing new information.

A line of reasoning may be evaluated against two criteria: logical validity and truth. Reasoning is valid when a conclusion follows logically from its premises. Thus, validity is a test of entire arguments. Truth is a test of the individual statements in the argument. Truth and validity can be evaluated independently of one another in deductive reasoning.

Most arguments are of three basic types—categorical, causal, and analogical. Categorical arguments are concerned with membership of objects in categories, causal arguments with cause-and-effect relationships, and analogical arguments with similarities between objects or events.

Toulmin's (1958) model of argument is a useful tool for designing and analyzing the structure of arguments. Applicable to both inductive and deductive arguments, it permits systematic analysis, showing how various statements made in arguments fit together to make a coherent whole.

Questions

1. What is the difference between inductive and deductive reasoning?

2. Can you think of any evidence that would enable you to assign probability estimates about the occurrence of the following events:
   Worldwide zero population growth by the year 2000
   A nuclear war by 1995
   Manned exploration of Mars before 1995

A cure for most forms of cancer by 1999
The likelihood of a snowfall in Denver during June, 1989
That Lee Harvey Oswald acted alone in the assassination of John
F. Kennedy

3. Discuss the nature of categorical, causal, and analogical arguments.

4. Name the components of the Toulmin model and explain their functions.

Suggested Readings

BEARDSLEY, M. C. (1966). *Thinking straight* (3rd ed.). Englewood Cliffs, N.J.: Prentice-Hall.

BETTINGHAUS, E. P. (1966). *Message preparation: The Nature of proof.* Indianapolis: Bobbs-Merrill.

FEARNSIDE, W. W., AND W. B. HOLTHER. (1959). *Fallacy: The counterfeit of argument.* Englewood Cliffs, N.J.: Prentice-Hall.

FREELEY, A. J. (1981). *Argumentation and debate* (5th ed.). Belmont, Calif.: Wadsworth.

HUFF, D., AND I. GEIS. (1954). *How to lie with statistics.* New York: W. W. Norton.

KAHANE, H. (1971). *Logic and contemporary rhetoric.* Belmont, Calif.: Wadsworth.

SHERWOOD, J. C. (1964). *Discourse of reason.* New York: Harper and Row.

III Practical Public Speaking

Public speaking derives much of its uniqueness from its one-to-many format, whereas dyadic and small group activities gain much of their character from the one-to-one format. A major advantage of public speaking is that it provides a means by which we can reach a sizable audience in a relatively short period of time. By way of contrast, the major advantage of dyads and small groups is that they encourage considerable human interaction and immediate feedback among participants.

In Parts II and III of this text, we separate public speaking from diadic and interpersonal activities for convenience and clarity, and because speech communication classes are often divided in similar ways to permit a focus on specific activities. Clearly, however, all communication activities overlap in important ways and often require similar types of knowledge and skills.

Public speaking enjoys the longest of all academic histories. The first textbook on public speaking was probably that of Kegemini and

Ptahhotep of Egypt about 2600 B.C. Public speaking was one of the three academic areas included in the first formal curriculum of the Middle Ages. The *Trivium* of the Middle Ages included (1) rhetoric, the theory of speech composition and delivery; (2) grammar; and (3) logic. Later the *Trivium* was expanded to include the *Quadrivium*: (1) arithmetic; (2) astronomy, (3) geometry, and (4) music. Public speaking continues to serve as one of our most important means of human communication. We employ public speaking to transmit information, to persuade, to highlight ceremonial events, and to entertain.

The four chapters in this section of the text focus on the development of practical public speeches. Chapter Seven deals with basic issues in getting started; Chapter Eight focuses on speech composition; Chapter Nine addresses visual aids; and Chapter Ten confronts speech delivery.

Chapter Seven

Speech Development: Getting Started

Preview

There are a variety of issues that are fundamental to the task of developing and delivering public speeches. This chapter addresses a selective list of these issues and offers a number of suggestions and recommendations. Through a consideration of these basic topics, you should be able to approach the development of public speeches with a greater sense of understanding and confidence. Immediately following this introductory material, we focus on speech composition *(Chapter Eight),* visual aids *(Chapter Nine), and* speech delivery *(Chapter Ten).*

Objectives

To examine motives for giving speeches

To offer suggestions for negotiating a speech

To explore the sources of speech materials

To provide suggestions for choosing a speech topic

To provide suggestions for developing appropriate language style

To provide suggestions for selecting an appropriate presentation form

SEVEN   Individuals who have little experience in speech preparation often find it difficult to choose a topic or get beyond the first sentence of a speech outline. Many approach speeches as though they were entering a wholly new world in which all their previous knowledge, experiences, and common sense are irrelevant. These attitudes not only are unrealistic, but also can be a major obstacle to progress in developing speeches. The novice does not approach the public speaking task wholly unprepared, nor need he or she be intimidated by it. In approaching the task of speech preparation, it is important to recognize that the public speech is a familiar event in which past experiences and common sense remain as useful guides to the speaker. Then, we need to look closer at the unique demands placed on a public speaker as well as at the techniques and skills needed to effectively satisfy those demands. With only minimum amounts of training and experience, most individuals quickly achieve significant levels of effectiveness in the development and delivery of public speeches.

Motivation for Giving Public Speeches

Individuals and organizations achieve their goals through the creation, distribution, and consumption of information. They also seek understanding and support for their activities through the use of persuasive messages. These vital communication activities occur in a variety of interpersonal contexts and, inevitably, include the presentation of relatively formal public speeches.

   The specific motives for active participation as a speaker or listener are as various as the interests of people. These motives can reside primarily with the speaker or with the listener.

Speaker-initiated Speeches

An individual may be able to achieve progress toward personal, professional, or social goals through public speaking, and therefore may seek opportunities for speaking engagements. A business executive may wish to inform his or her employees of new developments within the business organization. The president of a professional organization may wish to appear before the community to explain why its members are on strike, or a member of a government agency may wish to meet with community representatives to explore the feasibility of constructing an atomic generator near that community. In any case, an individual who wishes to negotiate a public speech should consider some of the following issues:

1. What are the speaker's specific goals?
2. Which speech communication format is most conducive to achieving those goals?
3. What speech materials are needed to achieve the goals?
4. Which individuals should receive the speaker's messages or participate in the communication exchange?

Public speaking is expensive. It demands a considerable amount of the speaker's time and energy. It also can require the purchase or rental of audiovisual equipment, the rental of appropriate facilities, and travel and living expenses. The effective speaker will want the greatest return on this investment. Accordingly, a speaker should be clear about goals, and should be selective in the choice of messages and audiences that should hear those messages.

Requested Speeches

An organization frequently can contribute to its purposes by contacting speakers. Typically, an organization will initiate negotiations with an individual who possesses needed information or skills. The members of an organization may desire special information from an expert in a given field; they may wish to learn more about a candidate for political office; or they may want an interesting speaker who can provide an entertaining after-dinner speech.

Although it is flattering to receive speaking invitations, the speaker should evaluate the implications of accepting a speaking engagement. He or she is entitled to accept only engagements that are likely to compliment his or her own personal, professional, and social values. Clearly, the speaker should understand the motives, interests, and expectations of the requesting group. Because speech preparation and delivery are demanding in terms of speaker time and energy, it also is reasonable for him or her to consider the potential payoffs in accepting a given invitation.

A speaker might accept an invitation to deliver a speech for a number of reasons. He or she may be in sympathy with the goals of the requesting organization, may view the invitation as an opportunity to help fulfill community responsibilities, or may perceive the opportunity to gain exposure for his or her ideas. In some cases, he or she may be attracted by a speaker's honorarium. On the other hand, the speaker may conclude that the payoff is minimal or, worse yet, that an appearance could compromise his or her own standards or contribute to unnecessary conflict and hostility.

Negotiating the Public Speech

A decision to give a public speech usually results from negotiations between a speaker and some social agent. The speaker can be any individual who is available and willing to prepare and deliver a speech. The social agent can be a club president, a business executive, a church leader, or any other person representing a group that constitutes a potential audience. Prespeech negotiations may be initiated by either the speaker or the organizational representative. Occasionally speeches are negotiated by a third party, such as the League of Women Voters.

There are many basic similarities in the process of developing speeches for different audiences. At the same time, each public speech poses its own unique set of circumstances. In negotiating to give a speech, you need to consider the reasons for presenting a particular topic as well as its suitability for a particular audience. You also need to consider the unique setting in which the speech is to be delivered, and the ways in which effective and productive speaker-audience interactions can be generated and managed.

Checklist for Negotiating a Speech

The following list identifies some important issues that should be considered in negotiating a speech:

1. What is the purpose of the speech?
2. What is the nature of the audience?
3. Where and when is the speech to be given?
4. How much time will be allowed for the speech?
5. Will the speech be followed by two-way speaker-audience communication?
6. Is the speaker donating his or her services or is an honorarium provided?
7. Does the speaker introduce himself or herself or is he or she introduced by someone else?
8. If the speaker is introduced by another person, does that person have adequate information about the speaker and the speech?

In all speech settings—including the classroom—you are more likely to meet your own expectations as well as the expectations of others to the extent that you develop mutual understandings as to the nature of your commitments and specific responsibilities.

Sources of Speech Materials

The basic ingredients of a speech are messages. Ideally, they are well-selected messages that carry similar meanings for both speaker and

listeners. As noted in earlier chapters, speaker messages are both verbal and nonverbal. They include language statements in the form of words and sentences as well as nonverbal messages in the form of gestures, charts, pictures, and various physical relationships between speaker and audience. In some cases, a speaker's messages are the products of his or her own unique experience and insights. But to be well informed on a particular topic, it is usually necessary for the speaker to go beyond his or her own level of information and seek additional ideas and data from others.

The Speaker as a Source

The speaker is a depository of experiences, ideas, information, attitudes, and unique ways of viewing the world. These resources should be used to the extent that they contribute to the purposes of a speech. For example, if your purpose is to achieve self-expression on a given issue, you might achieve this goal by relying entirely on your own resources. If, however, your purpose is to inform the audience of the amount of heat energy that is lost through each square foot of window pane, your own knowledge may be wholly inadequate; therefore, you may need to discover and review the most recent data on this topic and utilize this information as the basis of the speech.

Others as a Source

When a speaker concludes that personal resources are not the best available for accomplishing the purposes of the speech, he or she turns to others. In doing so, the speaker must consider the expertise and reliability of these sources. Usually, the speaker will rely on people who, through training or experience, have demonstrated special knowledge concerning the speaker's topic.

Individuals who possess reliable, current, and specialized information are usually referred to as "experts" or "authorities." As we continue in our evolution toward a more complex society, people find it increasingly difficult to keep abreast of the most recent developments that bear on any given speech topic. Accordingly, the speaker must frequently turn to the experts and rely on the information that they can provide. Because it may be difficult to evaluate the accuracy of the information available from a single source, some measure of safety is assured if the speaker takes care in the selection of sources and checks the information of one against others.

The speaker can have many good reasons for incorporating outside source materials in his or her own speech: (1) quoted material may provide information or facts needed in the speech; (2) authoritative material may lend support to the messages of the speech; (3) literary statements from prose or poetry may give appropriate expression to the speaker's ideas or help to present them in a novel or interesting way. It is not only acceptable for speakers to employ quoted materials; in many cases it may be imperative! However, you should recognize the ethical and legal obligation to identify the sources of quoted material used in a speech. The ethical question is rather straightforward: the person who created the original statements deserves the credit for those statements. The speaker who presents another's material as his or her own is engaged in an unfair and unnecessary deception.

The legal question is sometimes clear and sometimes not. If a speaker were to "borrow" someone's original poem and present it as his or her own, it is likely that the poem's author could bring a legal suit, provide evidence of authorship, and win damages from the speaker. At the least, the author could cause the speaker a degree of discomfort and embarrassment. At the same time, some information has been well diffused throughout the community and is viewed as part of our public domain. Such information can be employed without credit to its creator.

Whether the question is one of ethics or law, the speaker can satisfy both considerations by providing (1) the name of the person who generated the statements, (2) the approximate date on which the statements were made, and (3) the medium through which the statements were presented. For example, "In a 1977 article by Dr. David Gibbon, published in the *Saturday Review*, the following information is revealed." Or, "During a recent interview conducted by a *Time* magazine staff writer, former Senator Mike Mansfield was reported to have made the following statement." Or, "A line from Shakespeare's King Lear makes the point quite clearly. . . ."

By using these kinds of statements to introduce quoted materials, you can accomplish several goals. Most ethical and legal obligations are satisfied; the audience is given the opportunity to know and thereby evaluate sources; and a useful transitional statement is created that indicates the point at which original material stops and quoted material begins.

The novice speaker will wonder how much quoted material is appropriate. That's similar to the question, "How long should a dog's tail be?"

Just as the appropriate length of a dog's tail should depend on the dog, the amount of quoted material should depend on your purpose and the appropriateness of available materials for accomplishing the purpose.

In general, it is reasonable for you to rely upon personal resources in choosing your purpose and in selecting, organizing, and developing ideas. Nevertheless, we advise you to incorporate direct quotations where they will provide additional credibility for your ideas or will enhance your style and rhetorical effect.

Choosing a Topic

In choosing a speech topic, you will want to consider your own motives for giving a speech as well as the needs or interests of the audience. Some factors that deserve consideration are as follows:

Speaker Knowledge

In looking for an appropriate speech topic, a major consideration should be your level of knowledge. Developing a speech requires considerable effort—even when a speaker is well informed on the subject. Additionally, you should consider the availability of related materials. If a speaker starts with considerable knowledge about the topic and is also aware of related publications or interview possibilities, the information problem is quickly solved and he or she can get on with the task of speech development.

Speaker Interests

A second major consideration should be your own interests. Developing and delivering speeches requires considerable time and energy, but the

whole task is much easier when you are *intrinsically* motivated to pursue your topic (it isn't work when you enjoy what you are doing).

Audience Knowledge or Belief

A central issue is audience knowledge. Quite simply, it is doubtful if any useful purpose is served by telling an audience what it already knows. Similarly, little is achieved through persuasion if the audience already shares your point of view. In any case, providing the audience with something new is seldom a problem. Few of us are experts at more than one or two things, and through some concerted research efforts, we can soon discover useful information that the audience is likely to find new and interesting.

Audience Interest

Although you should select a topic that is likely to hold interest for a particular audience, some inexperienced speakers make things unnecessarily difficult by trying to find the "perfectly fascinating" topic. Whether experienced or not, we consider it a mistake to search for the "fantastic." A more reasonable goal is to select a topic that is in some way *related* to audience interests, then simply get on with the job of developing the best speech materials in the time available.

Limiting the Topic

Part of the problem of choosing a topic is determining how that topic will be treated. As a practical matter, you should be able to deal with the topic within allotted time limits. Yet, you will want to develop the topic to the extent that you feel is appropriate.

As a general rule, we suggest that *you should control the topic*—as opposed to the topic having undue control over you. Speaker control over a topic is achieved when the speaker *selects the specific aspects of the topic to be covered in a particular speech.* Do not try to solve the world's problems in a single speech. Further, consider the capacity of the audience to deal effectively with presented materials. A reasonable goal is to *limit* the topic so that something of value is fully achievable within available time constraints.

Appropriate Language Style

In general, we encourage you, in your efforts to communicate to listeners, to develop a relatively simple, clear, and direct style of language. Most audiences—even highly sophisticated ones—are likely to appreciate a language style that is easily grasped and understood. A language style that is simple in appearance, however, usually requires considerable training and effort. In the absence of this training and effort, it is easy to deviate from standards of good grammar and to generate awkward sentences and organizational patterns that are difficult to follow.

Although *intelligibility* through *simplicity* is the basic goal of most language usage, it is also the case that overall effectiveness and stylistic appeal are related to one's language facility. Additionally, standards of appropriate usage vary with the *formality* of the occasion, the *complexity* of the subject matter, and the nature of the *audience*.

Formality of Occasion

A wide spectrum of public speaking activities can be characterized as "informal" and "conversational" in style. Nevertheless, if you move into positions of increased responsibility or leadership, you are likely to address a variety of audiences including formal ones. Accordingly, if you develop a reasonably elaborate vocabulary and a repertory of effective language skills, you have the advantage of being able to adapt to a variety of occasions—formal or informal.

Complexity of Subject Matter

A popular misconception is that any topic can be dealt with in fairly simple terms and that "difficult" terms are to be avoided. In general, however, *commonsense concepts and popular terminology* are only applicable to *commonplace events and popular activities*. As you address more specialized topics, technical vocabularies are required in order to adequately deal with the subtleties, complexities, or other unique features of those topics.

In any case, it is all too easy to lose sight of how quickly you can develop specialized knowledge and terminology. The problem then develops when you unload all of these terms on an unprepared audience. Clearly, while the use of particularly appropriate terms should not be avoided, you must be sensitive to the needs of the audience and, when necessary, should define key terms when they are introduced.

Nature of the Audience

Consistent with the receiver-oriented perspective on speech communication, we encourage you, as a speaker, to adapt your language to the needs of a specific audience. Ideally, however, you can adapt in *two directions,* that is, to more popular audiences as well as to the more specialized and discerning ones. Accordingly, we encourage you to take full advantage of opportunities to develop a richer vocabulary and additional language skills. Both English and speech classes can contribute significantly to your overall language facility—and language facility is a loyal ally in virtually all communication settings.

Presentational Form

Fundamental to all public speaking tasks is the issue of *how* to *develop* and *rehearse* the materials for a specific presentation. A decision on this issue should be made early on because it will guide and influence all aspects of speech development. Alternatives available are:

1. *The memorized speech:* You can draft messages word for word, can rehearse and memorize them, then can deliver them entirely from memory.
2. *The manuscript speech:* You can draft messages word for word, and can develop them into a neatly typed *manuscript* that you can read to an audience.
3. *The extemporaneous speech:* You can draft basic messages and can arrange them into a neatly organized *outline.* After sufficient rehearsal, you can deliver the speech from the outline.
4. *The impromptu speech:* You can draw upon prior knowledge and experience and, with only a moment's notice, simultaneously formulate and deliver the speech.

Your choice of presentational form should be based on the nature of the occasion, the audience, and the task. Additionally, a particular form should be adapted to your needs. All speakers differ somewhat in the ways a presentational form affects their delivery and overall effectiveness.

The Memorized Speech

In general, the memorized speech is only appropriate on rare occasions when someone is giving a *very brief* presentation—as might be the case with a speech of "introduction," "acceptance," or "thanks." Even on these occasions, however, a few notes can ensure that important names as well as other materials will be available when needed.

In most cases, the memorized form of presentation is problematical, and sometimes downright dangerous. It can be time-consuming to memorize materials—even brief ones. Additionally, there is the ever-present danger of forgetting. Finally, giving a speech from memory usually has a negative impact on a person's delivery. Memorized speeches are more likely to sound "mechanical" and "predictable," that is, "memorized."

The Manuscript Speech

There are a few occasions when it can be highly advantageous to present messages from a prepared text. For example, you might wish to rely on prepared comments when speaking on a specific technical or legal issue, when stating your position on a controversial issue, or when addressing a potentially hostile audience. The need for accuracy and precision in messages is often a function of the consequences they can produce. Specifically, the more critical the likely consequences, the greater the motivation to speak from a carefully prepared manuscript. There are also occasions when you might find it useful to quote another person's statement, or a piece of prose or poetry—and want to get it right!

Except for purposes such as these, however, the manuscript format is usually a poor choice. Like speaking from memory, manuscript speaking usually results in a less natural and spontaneous delivery. Also, to the extent that you must keep eyes glued on the manuscript, you are likely to have poor eye contact with the members of the audience.

The Extemporaneous Speech

The extemporaneous style of presentation is adaptable to a wide range of occasions, and overall, it is the most frequently used.

Through sufficient development, revision, and rehearsal, the extemporaneous format can produce a relatively precise, organized, and articulate message. Yet, because not every word or sentence is precisely planned, there is room for an element of spontaneity and naturalness in delivery. Further, with appropriate editing and rehearsal, you need only glance occasionally at notes and can be free to maintain a considerable amount of eye contact with members of the audience.

The extensiveness of an outline and notes will vary with the complexity of the topic, the formality of the occasion, as well as with an overall level of experience in similar speech settings. In any case, a reasonable goal for most occasions is to develop the minimum outline that is actually needed. Most people find that they can do a maximally effective job with a minimum of notes if they understand their material, carefully prepare and edit their outline, then engage in sufficient rehearsal.

The Impromptu Speech

Eventually, we all encounter occasions when we are suddenly asked to share information or voice an opinion. Additionally, with only a moment's notice, we may discover an opportunity to make a point or to achieve a goal through presenting a few comments.

In most cases, your interests, experience, and training provide the basic content needed for these impromptu speeches. At the same time, training and experience in a variety of speech settings can contribute significantly to your ability to quickly formulate a speech and present it in an articulate and interesting manner. In general, as you gain skill in the development and delivery of extemporaneous speeches, you will find that the same skills are highly useful in impromptu settings.

Summary

A speaker can be motivated to give a speech in order to achieve his or her own purposes, or to help others to achieve theirs. In either case, it is important to negotiate an agreement covering the details of a specific presentation.

The materials for a speech may come from a speaker's own experiences, or they may be available from "authorities" who have special training and experience. As speech topics become more specialized, the speaker will increasingly need to rely on outside sources for at least part of the materials needed in the development of a speech. In most cases, an individual will choose a topic that is closely related to his or her current knowledge and interests; importantly, a speaker will always check for the availability of needed materials.

You are encouraged to develop a relatively simple, clear, and direct style of language. Basic courses in English and speech can contribute substantially to the achievement of this goal. Four presentational forms were discussed: the memorized speech, the manuscript speech, the extemporaneous speech, and the impromptu speech. We recommend the extemporaneous format for most speech occasions.

Questions

1. What makes a person qualified to speak with authority on a particular topic?

2. Identify ten topics that most college students can address with considerable expertise.

3. Under what circumstances should a speaker provide documentation for statements used in a speech?

4. What are the most important factors in the development of an effective style of language usage?

5. Why does the extemporaneous format usually result in good eye contact and a more natural speech style?

Suggested Readings

BROOKS, W. D., AND R. W. (1985). *Speech communication* (5th ed.). Dubuque, Iowa: Wm. C. Brown.

DEVITO, J. A. (1985). *Human communication: Basic course* (3rd ed.). New York: Harper & Row.

ROSS, R. S. (1984). *Essentials of speech communication* (6th ed.). Englewood Cliffs, N.J.: Prentice-Hall.

Chapter Eight

Speech Development: Composition

Preview

Under the best of circumstances, speech composition is a complex task. This task becomes easier however to the extent that you learn basic composition strategies and techniques, and then apply them to specific speech assignments. This chapter describes a six-stage process of speech development and illustrates a variety of specific techniques that can be quickly acquired and adapted to the development of more effective speeches.

Objectives

To discuss the important role of a speaker's purpose

To illustrate how to divide material into major topical areas

To discuss basic patterns of speech organization

To discuss the nature and use of supporting materials

To suggest techniques for introductions and conclusions

To discuss editing and techniques for improving clarity and style

To suggest ways of organizing notes for extemporaneous speaking

EIGHT   This chapter suggests a general sequence of steps for creating and developing a well-organized and effective speech. You are encouraged to consider this general plan as long as you follow one hard and fast rule: *when you seem to have a good idea, write it down!* Ideas don't come along in a nice neat sequence. Even as you work on one section of a speech, ideas that pertain to other sections will come to mind. Accordingly, record ideas as they occur; eventually, you can work them into your speech if they serve a useful purpose.

It is helpful to *record* your ideas, issues, pieces of evidence, or whatever on separate 3-by-5-inch or 5-by-8-inch index cards. Each card becomes a building block that can be arranged and rearranged among the others until the most desirable speech pattern is achieved. Eventually, the ordered set of index cards becomes a roughly composed speech, which can be condensed into fewer cards for the presentation of a shorter speech, or expanded for the presentation of a longer one.

With these general thoughts in mind, we now turn to a simple six-stage sequence of speech development:

1. Develop a clear statement of your central purpose.
2. Identify major topics or arguments that relate to your purpose.
3. Select an overall plan for organizing topics or main ideas.
4. Develop each main idea with supporting materials that clarify or substantiate those ideas.
5. Add an introduction and conclusion.
6. Edit for clarity and style.

Prepare a Statement of Purpose

The Mock Turtle advised Alice that "no wise fish would go anywhere without a *porpoise*. . . . Why, if a fish came to me, and told me he was going on a journey, I should say 'with what porpoise?' " It might also be said that no wise speaker would go anywhere without a *purpose*. If you

came to one of us and said that you were going to give a speech, our first question would probably be, "What is your purpose?"

The importance of being able to state the specific purpose of a speech might appear obvious. Nevertheless, many novice speakers devote a good deal of energy to a speech before really understanding what they are trying to achieve. Before working on the speech, you should be able to write a simple and direct statement identifying your major purpose. Frequently, you will need to rewrite this statement a number of times before it accurately states what you wish to achieve.

A common mistake is to develop a statement that is too long, too vague, and too general. Here are examples of such statements.

The purpose of my speech is to *talk about* energy conservation.

The purpose of my speech is to help *develop more understanding* of energy conservation.

The purpose of my speech is to *develop more appreciation* of the energy-conservation problem.

These statements do little more than identify the general topic of the speech—that is, energy conservation. The fact is, several thousand different speeches could be written on the subject of energy conservation, each requiring a different direction and the selection and development of different types of materials. You can greatly simplify your task by narrowing the range of possible subjects with a more specific statement of purpose. For example:

The purpose of this speech is to identify and describe the best ways to achieve efficient use of kitchen appliances.

The purpose of this speech is to describe specific ways to better insulate your home.

The purpose of this speech is to describe alternative lifestyles that would result in less energy consumption.

By clarifying the purpose of a particular speech, a speaker helps focus on the particular direction he or she wishes to select and the particular kinds of materials need to achieve the purpose. A speech should not be viewed as so many minutes filled with words. A given speech should have a specific purpose, and only those materials that contribute to that purpose should be reviewed for possible inclusion.

A clear statement of purpose helps the speaker clarify the intended direction, identify appropriate speech material, and avoid expensive false starts. Having served the speaker in these ways, however, the statement of purpose is not usually a part of the presentation. The purpose of a well-developed speech will be apparent to the audience; the speaker should not need to hang a sign on the speech to identify its direction.

Identify Major Topics or Arguments

Once a speaker has clarified the essential direction of an informative speech, it is easy to develop a list of relevant subject areas and determine which topics make a substantial contribution to that purpose and which do not. Consider the following statement of purpose:

The purpose of this speech is to describe specific ways to better insulate a home.

Topic areas related to this purpose include:

1. Insulating the ceiling
2. Insulating the floors
3. Insulating the windows
4. Insulating the doors

If further examination indicates that these major topics contribute to the stated purpose, the speaker can turn his or her attention to the development of each topic area. To this end, the speaker first develops a list of subtopics that appear necessary for each major topic area. For example:

Insulating the ceiling

1. Types of ceiling insulation
2. Cost-effectiveness of each type of insulation
3. Recommended amounts of insulation
4. Installation

In an informative speech, the final selection of major topics and essential subtopics constitutes a basic outline for the speech. In some cases, the outline will follow a neat pattern of development; in others, the topics may need some reshuffling before they fall into a convenient pattern.

In the case of a persuasive speech, it is frequently effective to develop your materials around a list of specific *arguments* (that is, around reasons why a person should adopt a particular belief or evaluation, or should take a particular action). A first step is to identify possible arguments and then to narrow the list to those that are likely to be the most effective.

For example, you might advocate that a highway should be built in a particular area:

1. *Because* that location would provide the shortest route
2. *Because* that location would provide the most scenic route
3. *Because* that location is least likely to disturb the natural habitat of wildlife

In a persuasive speech then, basic arguments often provide the essential structure of a speech. Once the basic arguments are identified and clearly stated, they are open to further development. For example, they can be clarified through explanations or illustration, or supported with the appropriate evidence.

Select an Overall Pattern of Organization

You as a speaker are more likely to present your ideas in an orderly and coherent fashion if you can devise an overall design or pattern that provides a clean structure for the materials. Several overall designs can be useful in the preparation of informative or persuasive speeches. These include (1) the time pattern, (2) the topical pattern, (3) the problem-solution pattern, and (4) the logical pattern.

The Time Pattern

In many cases, the events we describe in a speech can be ordered in a time sequence. This pattern of organization is particularly appropriate for (1) giving step-by-step instructions on how to perform a specific task or (2) describing a sequence of events that has led to a particular state of affairs. For example, we have followed this pattern in describing some of the important steps involved in writing a speech: first, writing a statement of purpose; second, identifying major topic areas needed to achieve the stated purpose; and third, developing a list of subtopics needed to explain, illustrate, and further develop the major topic areas.

Many of our speeches provide step-by-step instructions, and many others deal with events that occur in a time sequence. The time pattern, therefore, is useful for a wide range of public speeches. Fortunately, it also is one of the easiest ways of organizing speech materials.

The Topical Pattern

A speaker's comments often can be developed under a few major topic areas. Suppose, for example, that you are summarizing recent developments in our energy crisis. You might organize the materials around the following topics: (1) political problems, (2) economic problems, and (3) social problems. By organizing speech materials under major topic areas, a speaker is less likely to jump back and forth between ideas that pertain to the different topics.

Sequence is a factor in the topical pattern as well as in the time pattern noted previously. The speaker discussing developments in the energy crisis, for example, should consider whether members of the audience may need information on political problems before it can fully appreciate information on economic and social problems. Experience and common sense will usually lead to an appropriate sequence for the ordering of speech topics.

The Problem-Solution Pattern

On the surface, the basic approach of the problem-solution pattern is quite simple. In the first part of the speech, present a problem, and in the second part present a solution to that problem. Nevertheless, a well-developed problem-solution pattern can be relatively complex and sophisticated.

In many cases, the problem part of the speech is actually an informative speech. In order for the speaker to *identify* and *delineate* the problem and to show the *magnitude* of the problem, he or she must provide the necessary information. The pattern used in this phase could follow any of the informative patterns. For example, you could trace the chronological development of the problem (time pattern), or could discuss the various topics that shed light on the problem (topical pattern).

Occasionally, a thorough analysis of the problem will point to an almost inevitable solution. For example, if a speaker can show that the problem is the amount of heat loss in the home, and if he or she can further show that the problem can be easily and economically solved by placing insulation in the attic, the simple facts of the situation can point to the obvious solution. More frequently, however, a problem can be solved in a variety of ways. The variety of possible solutions combined with variations in audience attitudes, tastes, and values means that some measure of advocacy, or persuasion, is needed to gain support for a given solution. In effect, the solution phase frequently consists of a persuasive speech structured around a pattern of logical argument. Taken together, the arguments develop logically toward the speaker's preferred solution.

There are several essential ingredients in most problem-solution speeches:

1. The problem phase
   a) The problem phase should include a clear *description* of the *problem*; that is, the central concern of the speaker should be obvious to the audience.
   b) The speaker should provide information that documents the *importance* and *magnitude* of the problem.
   c) When possible, the problem phase should show *how the problem relates* to members of the audience.
2. The solution phase
   a) The speaker should provide a clear description of his or her solution including such major points as:

      (1) The *nature of the solution.*

      (2) The *estimated cost* of the solution in time and/or money.

      (3) How the solution can be *initiated and/or administrated.*

    b) The speaker should be able to demonstrate the *relative advantages* of the solution—that is, how the solution is both *practical* and *beneficial.*

The relative time spent on the problem or solution will vary with each speech. In general, when the problem is familiar to most members of the audience, the speaker can simply summarize it and use the greater portion of time to develop the needed solution. If, on the other hand, the audience is not aware of a problem or convinced of its importance, the speaker might devote most of the time to the problem and merely suggest the direction of possible solutions. In fact, simply gaining audience awareness of an important problem may be a major contribution, particularly if it is coupled with a clear, if brief, closing presentation on an appropriate solution.

The Logical Pattern

The logical pattern employs a line of reasoning that includes two or more logically related statements. For example:

Statement 1   Evidence shows that men and women have similar abilities to perform many of the essential tasks that are common to our armed services.

Statement 2   Therefore, both men and women should have the opportunity to be admitted to our service academies and to receive academy training.

The organizing concept in many speeches is a line of reasoning. A speaker can bring order to the speech by developing materials around a sequence of *arguments* (contentions) that develop into a line of reasoning. A popular logical pattern consists of a series of *arguments,* each supported by items of *evidence.* Each argument advances the contention that something is true or that some condition exists, and items of evidence are employed to support each argument.

Various logical patterns are available, but their effective use usually requires some study of their structure and development. In Chapter Six, the structure of argument is analyzed in considerable detail. A review of that material may prove especially useful if you plan to organize material around a line of argument.

Develop Supporting Materials

Hammers and saws are useful tools. A hammer is useful if you want to pound something, and a saw is useful if you want to cut something; neither has much value, however, unless used for the proper purpose. There are several tools at the disposal of the speaker seeking to *clarify* or *substantiate* major points in a speech. An understanding of the alternative supportive techniques and the purposes they can serve will enhance the speaker's ability to prepare effective speeches. Specific techniques considered here are: (1) explanation, (2) example, (3) specific instance, (4) analogy, and (5) statistics.

Explanation

Explanation simply consists of verbal narrative or description, and it accounts for most of our simple and direct communication. The purpose of explanation is to transmit or exchange information. We employ words and sentences to tell someone about something, to show how something works, to give directions, and to define the way in which we are using a word or concept. For example, consider the use of explanation in the following statement:

The rubber seal on a refrigerator door will tend to deteriorate over time. Eventually the seal does not do its job, and cold air escapes. To check to see if your refrigerator is properly sealed, do the following: Place a dollar bill at a point where the door closes against the refrigerator and close the door. Then with gentle jerks, try to pull the paper dollar from the door. If your refrigerator is properly sealed, you will meet with some resistance; a slight "tug" will be necessary to

remove the dollar. Repeat this process at various points around the door. if you find spots where the dollar bill slips easily from the closed door, you should arrange to have the seal replaced.

Simple explanation, without further development, is frequently an adequate means of transmitting relatively simple messages about familiar objects. When the topic is less familiar or the subject more complex, explanations might require further clarification through visual demonstrations or other illustrative devices. For example, in explaining a method of spraying additional insulation into the attic, you could use visual diagrams to help clarify critical steps in the spraying operation, or could provide an actual demonstration.

The Example

The example is probably one of the most useful tools of speech construction. Although most of us are familiar with examples, many of us have not considered the essential nature of an example or developed a composition style that uses well-chosen examples appropriately.

An *example* may be viewed as a *specific sample* of a more general condition. The essential value of an example is that it gives precision to our messages. We frequently speak in general terms regarding an issue or topic, and the general nature of our messages results in vagueness and misunderstanding. A well-chosen example can *specify* and thereby *clarify* the meaning of a general statement. Consider the following generalization and how it is clarified through the details of an appropriate example:

Generalization: *Many homeowners are terrible energy wasters.* Mr. Jones, for example, has no storm sashes on his windows, and he heats all rooms in his house even though three are rarely used. He has large cracks around exterior doors; the insulation in his attic and under the floors is minimal; and the temperature of his hot-water tank is set at such a high level that it is continuously heating the water.

Although we are all familiar with examples and use them regularly in our everyday conversations, the more experienced speaker does not use examples in a hit-or-miss fashion. Rather, he or she will review the speech with an eye for generalizations that are in need of further clarification and specificity.

Specific Instances

Whereas an example serves as a representative sample, *specific instances* simply *identify a series of cases* or conditions by name or brief reference. For example, an individual presenting a speech on energy conservation might provide a series of specific instances to identify essential ways in which the audience can conserve energy in the home.

The homeowner can turn the thermostat to 68 degrees.

The homeowner can install storm sashes on all windows.

The homeowner can check all doors to see that they are properly sealed.

The homeowner can add insulation to ceilings and floors.

The homeowner can check the water heater to make sure it is not heating the water to an unnecessarily high temperature.

If the homeowner is familiar with the specific instances mentioned, simply listing them may be an adequate reminder that leads to action. All homeowners know how to turn down the thermostat; however, many do not know how to install storm sashes or ceiling insulation. Depending on the speaker's purpose, then, he or she may need to follow certain references with an explanation or demonstration that more fully develops the specific instance.

The Analogy

Like an example, the *analogy* is a useful device for *clarifying* a message. It is particularly useful for introducing *relatively new* and *unfamiliar* ideas. Through the comparative process of the analogy, we can show the relationship of something new and strange to something old and familiar, and in showing this relationship, we can help the audience discover the nature of the new and strange.

If you are trying to distinguish between "abstract" and "concrete" language styles; you might start with a general statement such as, "Abstract language provides perspective, whereas concrete language provides details." You could then *clarify* that narrative statement through use of the following analogy:

Picture a helicopter sitting on the ground with a camera attached to its bottom and pointing straight down. Now, imagine the pilot taking a picture of the earth. Most likely the picture would reveal small rocks, a weed or two, and a few blades of grass. Now imagine the pilot flying to five hundred feet and taking a second picture. That picture will no longer reveal the small objects, but it will include a larger picture of the airport. Now imagine the pilot taking a picture at ten thousand feet. This picture is likely to provide a general perspective of things. That is, it is likely to reveal large objects like clouds, landmasses, and large bodies of water; it also will provide a general perspective of the geographic relationships among these objects.

It is safe to say that language operates much like the camera on the bottom of the helicopter. That is, concrete language gives us the specific details like small rocks, weeds, and blades of grass. Abstract language gives us perspective; it provides the bigger picture of things; it shows the clouds, the landmasses, and the lakes; and it shows the way these things are related to each other. Depending on one's purpose, a speaker will want to use both concrete and abstract language. He or she will use concrete language when specific details are needed, and will use abstract language when an overall perspective is needed.

The above analogy was used as a device for clarifying the nature of concrete and abstract language. Clarification was achieved by comparing concrete language with low-level pictures and abstract language with high-level pictures.

Analogies fall into two main categories: *figurative* and *literal. Figurative analogies* point to a *similar quality* in two different situations. In the preceding analogy, for example, the common quality in high-altitude pictures and abstract language is the level of abstraction. *Literal analogies* point to a *quantitative relationship* between two different situations. To illustrate this quantitative relationship consider the following:

Many individuals consider the small crack around the front door of their house to be a minor source of heat loss. Yet a recent study revealed that the open space provided by that small crack is often the equivalent of a hole in the wall ten inches in diameter!

This analogy is literal in the sense that it points to a measurable equivalent for the amount of space provided by the crack around the front door— namely, the amount of space provided by a ten-inch hole in the wall.

Figurative and literal analogies are two of the most useful tools in speech construction. They can provide *clarity* and *vividness,* and their process of comparison can contribute a novel *stylistic effect.* At the same time, you should be aware of the limitations of these tools. For example, the figurative analogy can only point to general qualitative similarities; if misused, it can grossly exaggerate the similarity of two different situations. The literal analogy frequently requires the quantitative assessment of a qualified mathematician or engineer. In any case, the ability of a speaker to formulate ideas in communicative language is directly related to the ability to employ useful language tools, such as the figurative and literal analogies.

Statistics

Statistics provide a convenient language for summarizing quantitative relationships. The appropriate statistic will typically allow the speaker to assign a simple numerical value to an overall characteristic of a body of data. For example, statistics can provide measures of central tendency (average scores) or measures of dispersion (spread of scores).

When the speaker wishes to communicate summaries of quantitative data, the appropriate statistic can be the most useful of all available tools; in some cases, it is the only available tool. As with other forms of support, however, the speaker's ability to employ statistics successfully will depend on a knowledge of statistics, including their advantages and limitations. Because of the frequent use of statistics in speeches and because of the contribution they can bring to a speech, we advise you to gain a reasonable familiarity with this tool.

In general, you should employ statistics in cases where they will provide clear and accurate summaries of important data. At the same time, you should avoid unnecessary statistics that simply cloud the issues at hand and serve to confuse the audience. In the Carter-Ford debates, for example, criticism was directed at both contenders because of what appeared to be an unnecessary and confusing use of complex statistics.

Add the Introduction and Conclusion

A speaker's primary efforts will be directed toward a clear statement of his or her purpose, and the development and organization of main ideas and supporting materials. After achieving these central tasks, the speaker will turn to the preparation of an introduction and a conclusion appropriate for the particular speech, the occasion, and the audience. At the very least, the speaker should develop a few written statements that can serve as introductory and concluding remarks.

Although a well-developed speech should be the central concern, getting off to a poor start can diminish the overall effectiveness of a good speech. In addition, the speaker who does not have a clear stopping point might end the speech abruptly and awkwardly. Worse yet, for lack of a convenient stopping point, a speaker may wander into new territories that prolong the speech and deviate from the central purpose. Many well-planned ten-minute speeches are excellent for ten minutes but become poor at the end of fifteen and unbearable at the end of twenty.

The Introduction

In general, the introduction is designed to achieve one or more of the following purposes:

1. It can serve to recognize the significance of the occasion and the presence of distinguished guests.
2. It can provide the speaker a chance to express appreciation for the opportunity to appear before that particular group.
3. It can make reference to preceding events and connect them to the current speech, thereby providing a transition between those events.
4. It can be used to gain attention; however, a speaker usually has the audience's attention for the first minute, and there usually is little need for attention-getting devices in the introduction.
5. In almost all cases, it should include statements that prepare the audience for the forthcoming speech. For example, the speaker might use a rhetorical question such as: "Do you know the three most important ways of saving energy in your home?" Or the speaker might use a simple declarative statement that focuses audience attention on the central issue of the speech: "If you are an average homeowner, your monthly utility bill is twice as high as it needs to be!"

Frequently, the introduction is a kind of audience briefing in which the speaker provides a survey of the territory he or she intends to cover. In this case, the speaker may simply indicate the nature of the speech and the major topics to be considered.

The lay speaker often seems to feel that a speech should start with a joke, probably in the belief that a good joke will establish a friendly and more relaxed relationship between himself or herself and the audience. But what happens if the joke "bombs?" If you feel that a joke can contribute to your presentation, there is an excellent strategy for preventing its backfire. Always select a joke that *ties directly* to the ideas in your speech. If a joke ties directly to a point that you are about to develop, it will seldom backfire. If the audience responds, so much the better; if it doesn't, the joke still serves a useful purpose by introducing your next point.

In some cases, it may be desirable to make last-minute changes in the introduction to a speech. At public gatherings, a number of events occur just before a speaker's presentation. A prior speaker may have stressed a major point; the person introducing the speaker may have included a comment that deserves a response; or a sudden noise may have startled the audience. An imaginative speaker might use one of these events as a springboard to his or her own speech. The effect can be a creative and original transition from prior events to the speaker's presentation. Nevertheless, a speaker should not assume that he or she will be blessed with a last-minute stroke of genius. A preconsidered and planned introduction should be available and utilized except when last-minute changes suggest a novel approach.

The Conclusion

The conclusion of a speech is usually influenced by the purpose of the speech. If the purpose is to inform, the speaker is likely to provide a summary of the main ideas. If the purpose is to persuade, the speaker might summarize the main arguments in support of his or her point of view. Typically, the concluding remarks serve to restate or emphasize ideas already developed in the main body of a speech.

The speaker occasionally can achieve a more stylized or dramatic effect by employing a piece of prose or poetry that captures the essential meaning of the messages. Or the speaker might conclude with an enthusiastic call for action on the main proposal of the speech. In any case, if the speaker is able to achieve the major purpose, he or she is likely to do so in the body of the speech. Usually, the conclusion can do little more than provide a sense of completion and closure and can summarize or emphasize points the speaker has already developed.

Edit and Revise for Clarity and Style

Finally, then, after the basic speech is developed, the speaker will usually spend some time reviewing the product. The energy devoted to this task will depend on the available time and the importance of the speech event. During this final review, the speaker will typically ask such questions as:

1. Do all materials contribute to my central purpose?
2. Are all materials sufficiently clear and organized for my intended audience?
3. In the case of informative speeches, are all topics sufficiently developed through appropriate explanation or illustration?

4. In the case of persuasive speeches, are all arguments sound and adequately supported?
5. Are planned introductions and conclusions appropriate for the purposes of this speech?

There are a number of specific composition techniques that can add substantially to the overall clarity and effectiveness of a public speech. Four of the most effective are (1) parallel constructions, (2) internal summaries, (3) internal introductions, and (4) restatement. These techniques are often incorporated in the original composition, but can be added or improved upon during the final stages of editing and revision.

Parallel Constructions

One of the most effective ways of constructing a neat and coherent speech is through the development of parallel sentences. The technique of parallel construction can be employed in a variety of ways throughout a speech. In an informative speech, for example, major *topics* can be introduced through the use of parallel sentences:

"To achieve a well-insulated house you will want to do four things:

First, you will want to insulate the ceiling.

Second, you will want to insulate the floors.

Third, you will want to insulate the windows.

Fourth, you will want to insulate the doors."

In persuasive speeches, it is possible to organize materials around the *reasons* why a particular course of action should be taken. And, each of the specific reasons can be clearly stated in parallel sentences, for example:

"There are four major reasons why a college student should make every attempt to complete a baccaulaureate degree:

1. *Because a degree usually provides* better job opportunities
2. *Because a degree usually results* in higher lifetime earnings
3. *Because a degree represents* the achievement of a major personal goal
4. *Because a degree usually results* in a more attractive self-concept"

Interesting stylistic effects can also be achieved through the use of parallel sentences in introductions and conclusions. The usual effect is to show the relation between introductory and concluding statements and to give a sense of closure. Other stylistic effects can also be achieved through the use of parallel sentences at key points throughout the entire speech.

Internal Summary

The summary technique is an obvious means for concluding a speech. There are other uses of the summary, however, that are frequently overlooked. For example, the internal summary can be an extremely useful technique for amplifying crucial points throughout a speech and for recapping essential points. In general, internal summaries are more useful as the speech becomes longer. In speeches that approach five minutes or more, members of the audience can experience difficulty in sorting out the speaker's major ideas. By including a brief summary of major points after each key division of the speech, you can increase the audience's focus on central ideas.

Internal Introductions

Just as the introduction to an entire speech can prepare an audience for the type of materials it is about to hear, *internal introductions* can prepare the audience for the materials to be presented in separate sections. Through the use of *internal summaries* and *internal introductions,* a speaker can also achieve effective *transitions* between the major sections of a speech.

Restatement

The listener's task is somewhat different from the reader's. A reader can read and reread a given section of an article before moving on to the next section. The listener does not have this advantage. You therefore must clarify messages through adequate explanation and appropriate stylistic techniques. The *restatement* of central ideas at key points throughout the speech is a simple and effective technique for achieving this goal. Consider the dramatic effect of repeating the key statement, "I have a dream," in Martin Luther King's famous speech.

Finally, in all aspects of speech preparation, speaker originality can provide a refreshing departure from the more standard and predictable patterns of speech development. At the same time, originality includes a greater element of risk. You must also consider your motives and must determine whether you prefer the safety and predictability of an established path or the exciting possibilities, as well as the risks, that go with cutting a new path.

Speaker Notes

Up to this point, we have discussed the basic elements that contribute to a coherent, organized, and well-developed set of ideas and supporting materials. We have also suggested that these ideas and supporting materials can be recorded on separate index cards, then arranged and rearranged until you are able to achieve the desired sequence. If you follow this procedure, you may find that index cards provide an adequate, if not preferred, basis for presentation of the speech to an audience.

The organization of speech materials onto index cards offers a number of advantages:

1. Index cards make a neat and convenient package. They can be carried in a coat pocket or a purse.
2. Index cards are unobtrusive. They are less of a visual distraction than large sheets of paper. When handled, they do not make "crumpling" or "rattling" sounds that can be picked up by a microphone.
3. By writing on only *one side* of the index cards, you can move smoothly through the cards without "flipping" them from front to back.
4. Sooner or later neatly prepared materials are dropped on the floor, blown by the wind, or they slide from the speaker's stand. By *numbering* each card in a consistent and visible way, you can easily and quickly reorganize the set of cards and can proceed with a minimum of disruption.
5. You may present the same speech to a variety of audiences that provide different time limits. By organizing separate speech units on separate cards, it is possible to delete certain cards for a shorter speech or add cards for a longer one. To achieve a shorter speech, you may use fewer illustrations or examples or may even eliminate a particular section of the speech. If added time is available, you may wish to include more materials that serve to elaborate main ideas or "localize" the speech by relating ideas to the local community.

A variety of suggestions for organizing your note cards are summarized in Figure 8–1.

FIGURE 8-1

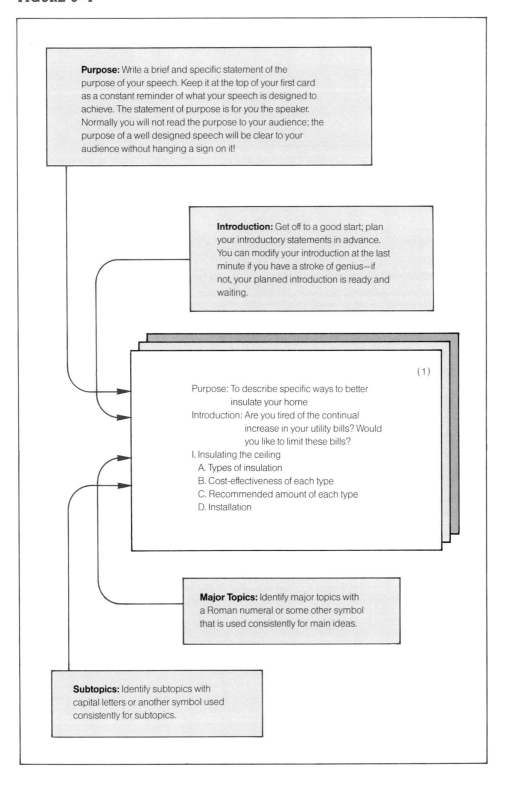

FIGURE 8–1 (continued)

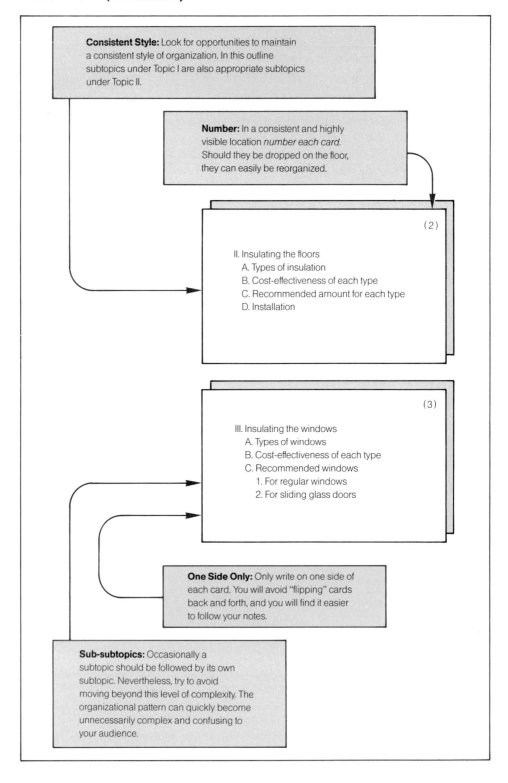

Consistent Style: Look for opportunities to maintain a consistent style of organization. In this outline subtopics under Topic I are also appropriate subtopics under Topic II.

Number: In a consistent and highly visible location *number each card*. Should they be dropped on the floor, they can easily be reorganized.

(2)

II. Insulating the floors
   A. Types of insulation
   B. Cost-effectiveness of each type
   C. Recommended amount for each type
   D. Installation

(3)

III. Insulating the windows
   A. Types of windows
   B. Cost-effectiveness of each type
   C. Recommended windows
     1. For regular windows
     2. For sliding glass doors

One Side Only: Only write on one side of each card. You will avoid "flipping" cards back and forth, and you will find it easier to follow your notes.

Sub-subtopics: Occasionally a subtopic should be followed by its own subtopic. Nevertheless, try to avoid moving beyond this level of complexity. The organizational pattern can quickly become unnecessarily complex and confusing to your audience.

FIGURE 8–1 (continued)

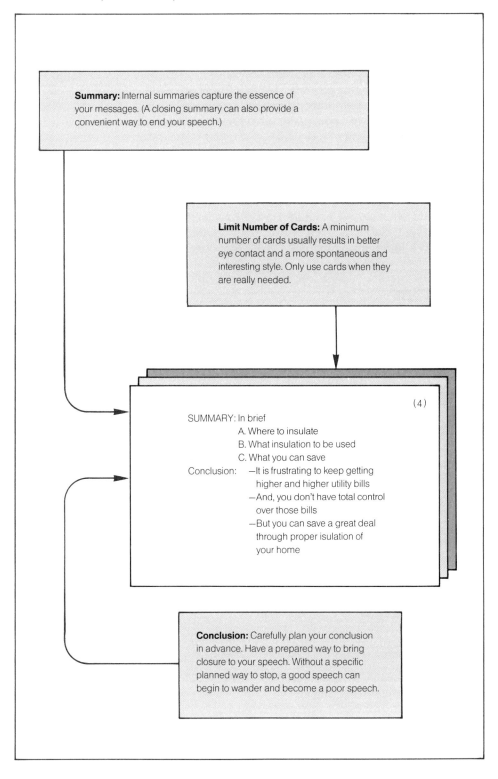

Summary

Our best ideas do not occur in a nice neat sequence. Accordingly, when good ideas come along it is helpful to get them recorded. In general, however, we encourage you to develop your materials in six stages: (1) develop a clear statement of purpose, (2) identify topics or arguments that relate to this purpose, (3) determine an overall plan of organization, (4) develop appropriate supporting materials for main points in the speech, (5) develop an appropriate introduction and conclusion, and (6) edit for clarity and style.

We discussed several patterns of speech organization. These are (1) the time pattern, (2) the topical pattern, (3) the problem-solution pattern, and (4) the logical pattern. Also, techniques were described for the development of supporting material: (1) explanation, (2) example, (3) specific instance, (4) analogy, and (5) statistics.

We included a number of stylistic techniques: (1) parallel construction, (2) internal introductions, (3) internal conclusions, and (4) restatement.

Questions

1. Are some organizational patterns especially suited to an informative speech? Explain.

2. Are some organizational patterns especially suited to a persuasive speech? Explain.

3. Are the various forms of support interchangeable or does each form serve a unique function?

4. Suggest occasions when it would be appropriate to employ: a rhetorical question, parallel sentences, internal introductions, and internal summaries.

Suggested Readings

ANDREWS, J. R. (1973). *A choice of worlds: The practice and criticism of public discourse.* New York: Harper & Row.

BARTLETT, J. (1980). *Familiar quotations* (15th ed.). Boston, Mass.: Little, Brown.

HODGES, J. C., and M. E. WHITTEN. (1984). *Harbrace college handbook* (9th Ed.). San Diego, Calif.: Harcourt Brace Jovanovich.

MOREHEAD, A. H. (Ed.). (1982). *Roget's college thesaurus: In dictionary form.* New York: Signet.

Chapter Nine

Speech Development: Visual Aids

Preview

With tongue in cheek, someone once said, "Confucious talks too much, he should show more pictures." A verbal presentation, of course, does not always require further development in the form of visual aids. Nevertheless, on some occasions visual aids are useful; they may serve to clarify and therefore compliment a verbal message. On other occasions, visual aids may be central to the speaker's purpose; they can provide the focus of an entire presentation.

Objectives

To discuss different types of visual aids

To illustrate some basic visual aid formats

To provide suggestions on the preparation and use of visual aids

To discuss the demonstration as a special form of visual aid

NINE   Public speeches include a visual dimension. The audience sees the speaker, his or her posture, dress, and movement. But the visual aspects of a speech can be more fully utilized when the speaker develops and employs specific devices to help clarify or enhance some of the more important messages. If poorly selected or displayed, however, visual aids may also distract or confuse. You should not assume that, once conceived, the visual aspects of a speech will take care of themselves; careful planning is necessary.

Types of Visual Aids

The visual materials that can be adapted to a speech setting are so numerous as to be limited only by imagination and creativity. Nevertheless, some general *types* of visual aids can be identified and described so as to give you a clearer sense of the broad range of possibilities.

The Human Body

When a speaker personally demonstrates a particular behavior (like swinging a tennis racquet, doing yoga exercises, or operating a machine), his or her body becomes a visual aid that provides information above and beyond normal animation. In addition to personal demonstration, the speaker may select another individual to help, as with a speech on self-defense maneuvers, lifesaving or first-aid techniques, or clothes modeling. The main advantages of the body as a visual aid are animation, adaptability, and realism. We can move around to appropriate positions and postures, change behavior to meet unexpected situations, and actually show how a particular activity is performed.

One problem with the use of our own bodies for demonstration is the difficulty in maintaining an effective speech delivery. We once saw a speaker demonstrate modern dance steps. She became so winded that her speech was uttered in strained, awkward gasps. Another problem is greater difficulty in using notes during the physical demonstration. If another person participates, he or she may behave with awkwardness or embarrassment and may become distracting.

Physical Objects

Audiences appreciate seeing appropriate physical objects. If the object being discussed is physically present, we have the advantages of exactness and realism. Sports equipment, products of arts and crafts, and various mechanical devices are common visual aids in this category.

Objects are sometimes too big or too small to be practical for a particular speech environment (New Trends in Single-Engine Aircraft, Techniques of Diamond Cutting). With some objects, we are unable to show the inner workings (The Catalytic Converter in U.S. Automobiles). Some objects are unavailable for display (Primitive Artifacts), and others may have to be shown out of proper perspective or context because the larger objects of which they are a part cannot be exhibited (Radar Devices in U.S. Missiles). Nevertheless, you will discover that objects, when appropriate, can attract attention and can enhance a complicated verbal explanation.

Models

Models are replicas of the real thing. Their size can be varied to be practical (Aerodynamic Features of the SST, The DNA Molecule), and cutaway views in some models permit us to concentrate on the important aspects. For example, medical instruction often utilizes plastic models of body parts that can be further disassembled to show inner workings. Models also can prevent embarrassment, as with the life-size dummy used for demonstrating mouth-to-mouth resuscitation.

Unfortunately, appropriate models are often expensive and difficult to obtain. They are less than realistic, and precise model dimensions and features are difficult to achieve. But for some types of instructional messages designed to train people for specific tasks, either real objects or their replicas are crucial.

Electronic Media

Included in the electronic media category are projections of slides, filmstrips, movies, and transparency materials. The category also includes videotaped replays on television monitors. Such visual aids can supply movement, variety, color, and rapid changes of image. They can also provide large amounts of information in a brief time. Most instructional programs developed in the last few years utilize electronic media to some extent.

Though the advantages are significant, visual aids that depend on electronic media can pose significant problems for the one-time-only informative speech. Equipment and facilities are usually costly. Setup of devices requires technical expertise and adds significantly to speech preparation time. Many more things can go wrong during the speech with electronic media than with other types of visual aids—power failures and faulty equipment, for example, can cause havoc. Most important, the

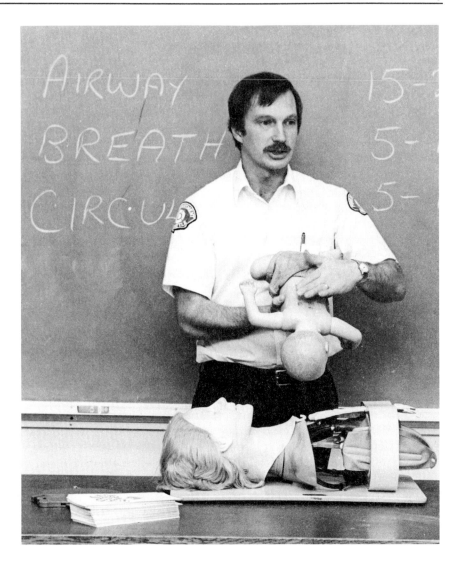

personal audiovisual appeal of the speaker is minimized, especially when lights are dimmed, sound is loud, and most of the audience attention is directed to the visual media rather than to the speaker's commentary. Use of electronic aids requires practice, but these aids are clearly becoming more popular than any other form of visual support, and most public speakers will have to learn to use them.

Pictures and Diagrams

Almost any audience likes to look at pictures, photographs, paintings, and drawings; they can enhance the interest and clarity of a presentation. They are usually easy to obtain, and we can develop them especially for a particular speech. Obviously, topics involving particular places, people, or artistic themes must rely heavily on pictorial content (Western American

Artists, My Vacation in Scandinavia, Famous Actors I Have Known).
Diagrams or drawings of actual objects can depict three-dimensional
views and concentrate on important features.

Certain kinds of pictures, like large color photographs or original paintings, are sometimes too expensive or inaccessible for a one-time-only
presentation. Some speakers make drawings and diagrams too complicated with irrelevant information or too small to be seen by a large
audience. Other speakers may be unable to prepare these visual aids
themselves because of the artistry or time necessary for effective results.

Graphs and Charts

Charts and graphs illustrate statistical and conceptual relationships. The
bar, line, and pie graphs can summarize bulky statistical information in
relatively simple form, and the statistical chart can show interrelationships
(for example, the amount of rainfall according to year and location).
Organization charts demonstrate the links between various subgroups.
A flow chart can identify a sequence of events as they occur in a series.
(See Figures 9–1 through 9–4)

The problem with a graph or chart is that the viewer must spend time
getting oriented to what it is designed to show and to how it should be
read. For example, if you were discussing economic trends over the past
few years, you would first have to explain carefully the terms, symbols,
and lines on the graph. From reading some textbooks, we know how
long a process that can be. Furthermore, because the speaker usually
utilizes only a portion of the data, the excess information in the chart or
graph may become distracting.

Maps

Because they show dimensions, shapes, contrasts, and geographic relationships very well, maps are often indispensable. Speeches on the
weather, international politics, travel, transportation, military activities,
historical topics, and various business and government issues usually
demand the effective display of maps.

Appropriate maps often are hard to obtain without considerable expense. Printed maps are usually too small and almost always show
unnecessary details that either confuse or distract, as with a common
automobile road map. Hand-drawn maps are rarely precise or neat,
though they can be constructed to the appropriate size and without
irrelevant data.

Chalkboards

By far the most popular visual aid, the chalkboard is readily accessible
in almost any public speaking environment, often in the form of a mov-
able panel. The speaker can adapt a writing or drawing for the size of

FIGURE 9–1

Bar Graph

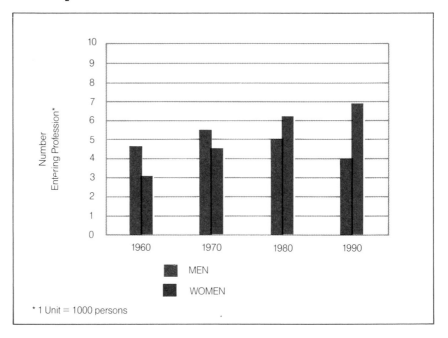

FIGURE 9–2

Line Graph

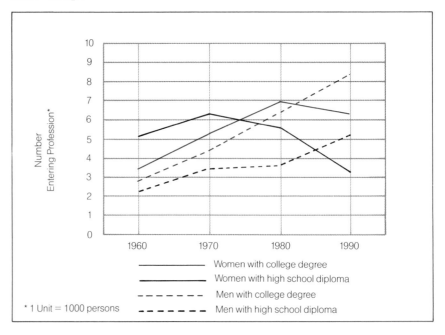

FIGURE 9–3

Pie Graph

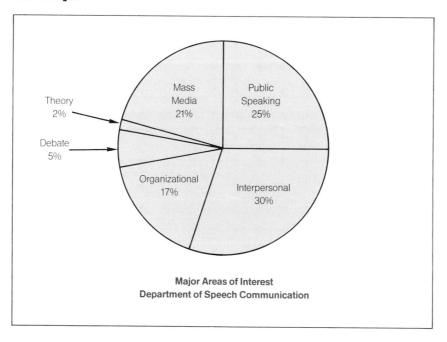

Major Areas of Interest
Department of Speech Communication

FIGURE 9–4

Flow Chart

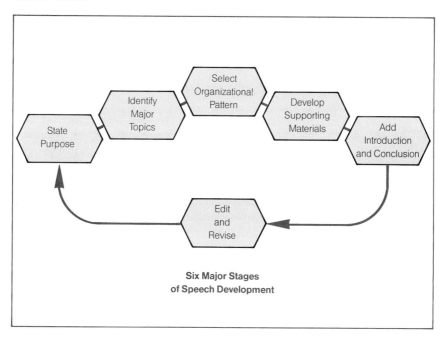

Six Major Stages
of Speech Development

the audience, and ease of erasure permits spontaneous modifications.

This aid sounds ideal, doesn't it? We take quite the opposite, and probably controversial, point of view that *except for everyday classroom situations, the chalkboard as a visual aid should be avoided.* We believe that speakers commonly use the chalkboard as a substitute for better visual alternatives because they lack energy and creativity. They lose audience contact while they are writing or drawing. The materials are rarely neat, precise, or artistic. Previous erasures show as messy smudges, and the new writing is sometimes not dark enough to be seen clearly. Glare from lights or a window may restrict the view of part of the audience.

The availability of a chalkboard also tempts unplanned use on the spur of the moment. Suppose you sense some confusion in the audience. Instead of simply elaborating verbally, you say, "Well, uh, perhaps I can show you what I mean here on the board." You search for chalk, draw an image that is inaccurate and too small, hunt up an eraser, try again, and perhaps eventually write or sketch something that may or may not clarify your point. The audience watches you struggle and may lose interest. The haphazard attempt to use a quick visual medium has actually detracted from the speech. Again, we urge that the chalkboard be used sparingly; there are better ways. A possible improvement over the chalkboard for spontaneous sketching or writing is a large tablet on an easel, with colored felt-tip markers. This aid is portable and less messy. And, if a speaker prefers to prepare information beforehand, the tablet is also superior to the messy and erasable chalkboard.

Visual Aids Preparation

The effective use of visual aids requires careful planning and preparation of the materials, always with an eye to the purpose and main ideas of the speech and to the audience for whom it is intended. The following suggestions will help you achieve maximum effectiveness of the visual dimension of your speech.

Advance Planning and Preparation

Prepare visual aids well in advance of the speaking situation. Last-minute attempts to find appropriate pictures, draw charts, or arrange for demonstration equipment is not only a hectic process but also reflects negatively on the speech. The audience can usually sense the lack of careful preparation. If the visual aid involves other people, it is crucial to discuss their roles with them beforehand so that they will know *precisely* what is expected of them. Spontaneous volunteers rarely do an optimal job in a demonstration and may even sabotage (usually unintentionally) your objectives.

Relevance

Make the visual aid and all its components relevant to the speech topic. Too often, informative speakers toss in extra materials as an afterthought simply because the aid is available, looks good, and "might as well be shown." We once heard a slide-illustrated lecture about a trip through Aztec ruins in Mexico. The speaker could not resist spending about five minutes showing slides of his wife and children on a side trip through Disneyland!

Sometimes speakers use visual aids simply to impress an audience with their advance preparation, even though the materials are not needed; perhaps they want to prove to their auditors (or to a speech instructor) how hard they've worked on the project. You should screen visual materials carefully. Are these devices really necessary? "What do I hope to achieve that cannot be gained without them? Will I insult my audience's intelligence by using an aid for so simple an idea?"

Simplicity and Clarity

Make certain the visual aids are simple and clear. If you must make a lengthy explanation about what the visual materials are supposed to illustrate, the materials become less "aid" and more new speech topic. Visual aids must be large enough to be seen, and dark or contrasting colors can help. A series of simple charts, graphs, or pictures may be more comprehensible than one large complicated one.

Rendering Style

If the visual aids involve writing or drawing, be neat and artistic. Speakers in business or professional settings often have artists or printers prepare their visual aids because they know that sloppiness causes a *transfer* of negative attitudes about the visual aids to the speaker's own speech objectives and ideas. Frequently in this text, we have argued that the verbal and nonverbal processes are intertwined and inseparate. Thus the speaker with verbal fluency can be betrayed by the nonverbal impact of a pencil-drawn chart on a torn piece of notebook paper, a graph on smudged posterboard, messy writing on a blackboard, and even an object or model in disrepair.

Practice

Practice using the visual aids beforehand. This step in speech preparation is frequently overlooked. A speaker practices the verbal message orally and occasionally *thinks,* "At this point I will pick up the object and show how it is used." But he doesn't actually *do* the demonstration ahead of time; he just imagines himself doing it. As a result, many speakers have been surprised by unexpected problems. Perhaps the color slides were not in order, or a device would not work properly, or an important detail had been omitted from a diagram, or the aids were bulky to hold, clumsy to manipulate, and difficult to set up. Practicing will not guarantee that unexpected problems will be avoided, but it can significantly reduce their likelihood and improve speaker confidence. We especially encourage you to rehearse *in the presence of a listener,* asking that person to interrupt whenever he or she cannot see or understand.

The Presentation

No matter how well prepared, visual aids that are ineptly presented can be at best useless and at worst a distraction. The following suggestions will help optimize your use of visual aids during a presentation.

Audience Viewing

Make certain that visual aids, during use, remain in clear and constant view of the entire audience. Do not let hands, body, podium, or other visual aids obstruct the vision of particular audience groups. Everyone should be able to see without effort or strain. If some cannot, they will either lose interest or become resentful that the speaker does not appear concerned with their well-being. Except for a few well-planned lecture or conference rooms, most speaking environments are *not* ideally suited for visual presentations. Hence, the speaker may have to spend some time moving around with the visual aid so everyone has an opportunity

to benefit from it. Some speakers nervously play with demonstrated objects, bouncing them around as the audience struggles to focus on them. As a rule, touch the visual aids only when absolutely necessary for displaying them.

Eye Contact

Maintain *eye contact* with the audience. Visual aids may become security blankets. We find it more comforting to look at them because, unlike the audience, these *things* we have prepared do not glare back at us, do not threaten us. Hence, you may look at the visual aids throughout the entire speech. As with touching the materials, you should look at them only when absolutely necessary—when you must see where to point or when you must manipulate them in some way. The listeners may decide whether they want to look at you or at the materials. Because eye contact has much potency for maintaining audience attention, the speaker cannot abandon this crucial tool.

Timing

Use or display visual aids at the *proper psychological point* in the speech. The use of visual materials usually has only two possible outcomes: (1) improved audience understanding and interest, or (2) distraction of the audience from the message. If visual aids are in view before or after a speaker actually applies them, the audience will notice. The speaker cannot simply say, "Don't pay any attention to that; I'll get to it in a minute." The audience *does* notice and is thus prepared psychologically to think about it. We recall the speaker who was discussing poisonous snakes. He had a cage with a live rattler moving around inside. The cage appeared to be open at the top so the snake could crawl out. As the audience squirmed nervously, the speaker tried to present five minutes of background information about snakes in general before he described the live one in the cage. He remained naively unaware that the audience didn't hear a word he said!

Though sometimes it is impossible to hide the visual aids (like an intricate blackboard drawing that must be done beforehand, a large object like a motorcycle or a large animal), you should make every attempt to assure that materials are *visual* only when you want them to be.

Handouts

In general, the most effective handout consists of printed materials that are distributed at the *end* of a speech. On some occasions, for example, a speaker may refer to a long list of worthy investment possibilities, or perhaps a rather complex set of instructions for achieving some task. Because materials such as these can be difficult to remember, having them in print for future audience reference can be highly useful. Nevertheless, it is almost always a mistake to hand them out *during* a speech. This practice is usually noisy, time-consuming, and tends to break the rhythm of a well-developed speech. Further, it is inevitable that many audience members will read this material during the remainder of a speech; in effect, by passing out materials during a speech, you create competition for the audience's attention. Finally, of course, you should not pass out materials at the end of a speech if they are likely to interfere with an additional speech that is to follow.

In the context of a persuasive speech in which action in the form of writing a congressional representative is called for, a speaker might pass samples of appropriate letters, or even appropriately addressed envelopes. Again, however, you should consider the most convenient moment for these activities.

"Passouts" also can include such items as pictures on various kinds of objects or artifacts. By handing out these types of materials however, it inevitably means that at any particular moment, three or four people are not listening; they are looking at the handout or are involved in passing or receiving it. Meanwhile, a person in another part of the room notices the handout's progress and thinks, "I'll bet the speaker is finished before I get to see it." Some people see the handout at the wrong time, after the speaker has already moved on to another point. Where possible, it is much better to find ways to let everyone see these types of visual aids at the same time, perhaps by using larger materials or by asking people to come up after the speech has ended to see tiny objects or pictures. Presentation of a single picture or object to the entire audience directs attention to material at the times and in the preferred manner.

The Demonstration

Perhaps the most challenging use of visual media is the *demonstration*. A demonstration is not simply the *display* of visual aids but includes their *use* in showing the audience a process or procedure. Table 9-1 identifies some of the differences between visual "exhibits" and the demonstration.

As an instructional device, demonstrations are crucial on topics such as arts and crafts, athletics, and equipment operation. In demonstrating a process, however, many things can go wrong. What if you must thread a needle? Carefully slice a vegetable with a razor-sharp knife? Bring water to boil quickly? Comb the hair of a frisky dog? We have seen many well-prepared speakers fail because of unexpected events in the "doing" phase. One student demonstrated karate. Because of nervousness, he could not concentrate fully and broke his hand instead of the brick! A woman explaining wine tasting accidentally sent a fifth of cabernet sauvignon crashing to the floor. An ardent golfer swung his three wood and demolished a light fixture. A guitarist broke a metal string and spent several minutes replacing it before she could continue. Most speech instructors can describe numerous horror stories of the demonstration-gone-awry.

In preparing speeches that involve demonstrations, you should remember an important axiom: whatever *can* go wrong *will*. You must be able to predict potential trouble spots. Ask these questions beforehand:

TABLE 9-1

Demonstrations and Visual Exhibits

Visual Exhibits	Demonstrations
A chart showing proper tennis court positions and strategy	Using a tennis racquet to show proper serving techniques
Color photographs of imaginative food servings	Preparing and mixing ingredients for a new recipe
Slides or films that illustrate techniques of firearm maintenance and safety	Dismantling and cleaning a firearm
Charts and graphs that show the effects of exercise on cardiovascular functioning	Doing pushups, running in place, and then taking blood pressure, pulse, and respiratory readings
Showing human models with new hairstyles	Styling a person's hair

What events have to happen as planned for my speech to succeed? If one of these events does not go smoothly, what are my options? What visual materials can become defective? After considering potential trouble spots, try to eliminate them ahead of time. For example, if you anticipate that nervousness will lead to trembling hands, you may want to do some of the intricate manipulation ahead of time (threading a needle, pin-striping with paints, assembling tiny machine parts, and the like).

Be especially conscious of *time*. Rarely does a demonstration run shorter than expected; it almost always takes longer. Run through the speech ahead of time, precisely as it will be done during the actual presentation. If it is too lengthy, ask again the crucial question: Which portions of the demonstration are really necessary and which are not? Any demonstration should have carefully limited objectives. Speakers who encounter problems are frequently those who tried to do too much in a short time.

At all times avoid the demonstration that is potentially *unsafe* or may be especially problematical. it is doubtful that the nature of a presentation will justify the use of potentially dangerous weapons (including the unloaded gun), unmanageable animals, or possession of illegal drugs. Questionable items such as these are best presented in the form of pictures or photographs.

Finally, avoid extended *silent demonstration*. Though there are exceptions to this rule, most audiences expect continuous commentary from the speaker. Experienced demonstrational speakers actually plan for filling periods of physical activity with anecdotes or additional information. They know that some people become uncomfortable during these silent phases, and continuity in speaking eases the problem. If the speaker has practiced using the visual aids, he or she knows when these moments of silence

are likely to occur and can plan accordingly. Anyone who has ever watched helplessly as a speaker quietly struggled with a troublesome visual aid knows how useful supplementary verbal materials can be for this type of situation. Although speakers need not apologize for circumstances beyond their control, they should frankly explain the problem and trust the audience to be reasonable. Audiences are usually not malicious or sadistic people who enjoy seeing a speaker flounder in unexpected problems. Most of us feel real empathy for the speaker in difficulty. Some people will even try to help with the demonstration.

Summary

Many speeches include a discussion of complex events or relationships that are difficult for the speaker to describe and the audience to grasp. In cases such as these, the best solution is often found in the development of an appropriate visual aid; that is, one that captures the essential aspects of the information. In general however, visual aids should only be used when they clearly contribute to the speaker's purpose.

You have many options for visual aids: the human body, objects, models, electronic media, pictures and diagrams, graphs and charts, and the chalkboard. These aids must be used carefully, however. Clear, neat, and artistic results are crucial. You should practice using the aids. Special concern should be directed at maintaining an unobstructed audience view, maintaining eye contact, and using visuals at the proper point in the speech. In general, handouts should be avoided unless distributed at the end of a speech; if the materials could interfere with other planned activities, they should be distributed only at the conclusion of an entire program.

In contrast to *visual displays, demonstrations* involve activities that show how something is done, or how some object works. Demonstrations have strong audience appeal but are more prone to unexpected problems; accordingly, the demonstration speech requires special care in preparation and rehearsal.

Questions

1. Identify occasions when a visual display could be crucial to a well-developed speech.

2. Identify occasions when a demonstration could be crucial to a well-developed speech.

3. In general, under what circumstances can visual aids be entirely avoided?

4. Identify major features of a well-designed well-constructed visual aid.

5. Describe guidelines for the incorporation of visuals into a speech.

Suggested Readings

HILL, H. (1957). Bringing figures to life. *Communication Quarterly 5,* 11.

KEMP, J. E., and D. K. DAYTON. (1985). *Planning and producing instructional media,* (5th ed.). New York: Harper & Row.

Chapter Ten

Speech Development: Delivery

Preview

Public speaking is an artistic enterprise, not only in the preparation of a speech but also in its actual presentation. Listeners may not be preoccupied with a speaker's delivery, but they are often affected in important ways by how a speaker looks and sounds. As a society, we tend to appreciate people who are fluent and attractive in a one-to-many communication setting. Public advertising, news broadcasting, and political speaking are examples of communication events in which we expect articulate, fluent delivery.

In relatively serious informative and persuasive settings, the importance of delivery should not supersede the importance of what one has to say. But delivery is important; it always makes a difference. If two speakers essentially have the same message, the one with better oral and visual style will usually be more successful in gaining the desired audience response. Delivery is also important to the speaker who wants to be thought of as an effective communicator. In this chapter, we offer suggestions to help you develop your delivery skills, noting that without those significant skills messages may go unheard and unappreciated.

Objectives

To address problems of communication apprehension

To suggest standards for appropriate delivery style

To discuss audible and visible aspects of delivery

To discuss situational variables related to delivery

TEN   We have discussed some of the factors involved in the development of a well-organized and effective speech. Although speech preparation is crucial to good public communication, for many it is by no means the most difficult or intimidating element of speech making. A much more threatening prospect is the actual delivery of a public speech.

Nagging questions continually arise. "What if I forget what I want to say? Will the right words come to me where I need them? Will the audience like me? How should I dress? What should I do with my hands? What if I say the wrong thing? Can everybody hear me? What if people get bored, fall asleep, or walk out while I'm talking?"

Our concern for *delivery*—the actual presentation of the message—is not unjustified. We know it will affect the speech outcome. No matter how good the speech content, the speaker's oral and visible effectiveness is crucial to audience understanding and approval. Because we recognize that many things can go wrong during a speech presentation, we want to be assured that we have made the best choices among the many strategies available. In this chapter, we explore most of the typical problems associated with speech delivery. We also suggest specific strategies for dealing with them. With appropriate knowledge, adequate preparation, and ample rehearsal, most individuals are quick to develop an effective style of delivery.

Communication Apprehension

Perhaps no problem is more overwhelming for the beginning speaker than communication apprehension—the tension, anxiety, and sometimes panic that you can experience when faced with relatively new or demanding speech tasks. A common reason why some students avoid a basic speech communication class is not necessarily that they feel communication to be unimportant, but rather that they are thinking ahead to the inevitable public speaking projects in which they will have to stand alone before the class and present their ideas for the scrutiny of critical listeners. Because the problem of communication apprehension is so common and so compelling, we begin our discussion of speech delivery by addressing this problem "right up front."

We can make several generalizations about communication apprehension; these generalizations point to its nature and effects and help to provide a realistic perspective on the topic. Specific suggestions with regard to the management and control of speaker apprehension also will help to alleviate some of the concerns you may have about speech delivery.

First, communication apprehension is common to nearly any situation in which a person's behavior is open to immediate scrutiny by others. Athletes, actors, ministers, politicians, musicians, singers, teachers, dancers, attorneys, broadcasters, and many others regularly report anxiety before and during their audience-centered activities, even after years of experience. When the beginning speaker assumes that he or she faces special or unique problems of nervousness, he or she is grossly inaccurate and impedes progress. Communication apprehension is an exceedingly common response; it is not restricted to an isolated few.

Second, most communication apprehension symptoms are not visible to the audience. Accordingly, they do not diminish the audience's evaluation of the speaker. Our experience is that speakers *overestimate* the degree to which their presentation is affected by communication apprehension and the extent to which audiences perceive these symptoms.

Third, reasonable levels of communication apprehension serve as an ally that *contributes* to effective speaking. A public communication event should not be a totally relaxed, casual experience. A speech should be a challenge for which you prepare psychologically. Just as an athletic coach worries when the team appears to be too blasé about the approaching game, so you should be concerned if you do not feel at least a twinge of apprehension. If worry and nervousness do not play a part in speech delivery, the actual presentation will probably be bland and the speaker will be unenthusiastic.

Forth, some of the more uncomfortable apprehension symptoms will quickly dissipate as you get into your performance. One reason that accomplished speakers are not overly concerned with communication apprehension is because experience tells them that those symptoms will not adversely affect their performance.

One of the most important benefits derived from speech training is that almost all speech students discover that they can perform well—in spite of certain symptoms of apprehension. Most discover that a certain level of apprehension is *necessary* for an alert and enthusiastic performance.

Speaker Control Over Communication Apprehension

In order to keep apprehension symptoms within tolerable limits, you can experiment with a variety of strategies and techniques. Consider the following ten suggestions that we have found especially helpful.

1. Pursue opportunities for *instruction* and *training* in various speech activities. As a communication event becomes familiar and manageable, communication apprehension tends to subside. Twenty-five years ago, space flight was a frightening prospect. We were facing the unknown. Yet for several years, astronauts traveled into

space with little observable apprehension. When Neil Armstrong landed the first U.S. spacecraft on the moon, for example, his heartbeat was within the normal range for everyday activities. Two factors in his or any other astronaut's coolness must have been a detailed understanding of space science—orbital mechanics, propulsion theory, communication and navigation equipment, and so on—and confidence in their ability to perform. Similarly in public speaking, you can learn much about the variables of a one-to-many communication situation. This knowledge means that you are not confronting the unknown, but you have an accurate comprehension of a reasonably familiar environment. One means of developing this awareness is a basic speech course, which can render speech apprehension much less intimidating.

2. Develop a *plan for self-improvement.* To some extent communication apprehension is a form of learned behavior. Accordingly, under new learning circumstances, you can "unlearn" excessive apprehension behaviors and can develop a higher level of self-composure. Developing and implementing a realistic plan for self-improvement can accelerate the learning of more effective delivery behaviors. A widely accepted strategy is to start with achievable goals that are likely to result in success. Then approach more ambitious goals in small steps that are also likely to provide success. If you experience unusually severe symptoms of communication anxiety, start with courses in small-group communication, where less emphasis is placed on individual presentations before an audience.

3. *Preparation* tends to reduce communication apprehension. When you *know* that you have a well-researched and well-developed message designed to meet the needs of a particular audience and occasion, your apprehension will tend to subside. Conversely, when you know that you are not well prepared or have not adequately rehearsed, you will usually find that your level of speech anxiety is much higher and can interfere with your delivery. A poorly prepared and poorly rehearsed speaker is likely to encounter unanticipated problems, and these problems have a way of making the speaker even more uncomfortable. This negative cycle can feed on itself and can generate additional problems.

4. *Rehearsal* tends to reduce communication apprehension. Rehearsal of speech materials can reveal needed revisions in notes, and can help to establish the appropriate verbal repertory so that it is available when needed. The amount of rehearsal required can vary considerably among speakers. With experience, however, you can quickly discover the amount needed for a particular type of speech event. In any case, the experienced speaker soon learns that there simply is no substitute for adequate preparation and rehearsal. Through instruction and experience, you gain confidence and learn important skills and techniques. You also learn that adequate levels of preparation and rehearsal are always necessary to ensure an effective performance. Fortunately, when any of us puts forth the needed effort—those efforts are almost always reflected in our performance.

5. Well-organized *speaker notes* help to reduce communication apprehension. When notes are organized and easy to use, you can approach the speech occasion with less anxiety. While rehearsing, it is also helpful to include cues for appropriate delivery in your notes. This is especially true in the case of manuscript speaking because it is easy to fall into a monotone or a monopattern. In developing your notes, focus special effort on *introductory remarks*. Getting off to a good start can produce positive audience feedback and can quickly boost confidence. Also, be sure to have a clear stopping point with appropriate *concluding remarks*.

6. Appropriate *visual aids* can share the burden of speaking and thereby can reduce communication apprehension. Visual aids also provide

a legitimate reason for moving about during a presentation and burning off excess energy.

7. *Dress* appropriate but comfortably. Your confidence can be enhanced when you know that you are appropriately attired. At the same time, you should dress comfortably; clothes that bind or interfere with movement or breathing can be distracting and can induce anxiety.

8. Develop an appropriate but comfortable *speaking posture.* We are usually attractive and comfortable when we stand on both feet in an upright and balanced position. Do not lean on the podium!

9. Experiment with various *relaxation exercises.* Chewing gum for fifteen to thirty minutes prior to speaking can relax most of the muscles used in speech production; however, never chew gum while delivering a speech! Some individuals also indicate that deep breathing and even meditation exercises are helpful. Others report that walking and stretching exercises reduce muscle tension and anxiety.

10. When presenting a speech, try to focus on your *prepared messages* and the task at hand. Although it may be helpful to discuss your anxieties with friends prior to a speech, such comments should be avoided during the actual presentation. In most cases, your comments only serve to emphasize any delivery problems that you may have.

Appropriate Delivery Style

Standards of appropriate delivery are a social phenomenon—the product of our culture. Most individuals unconsciously adopt many of the practices of their family, teachers, peers, and other people with whom they have considerable contact. Increasingly, television also plays a major role in standardizing what our culture defines as "acceptable" or "desirable" standards of speech delivery style. In any case, it is easy for all of us to fall into delivery habits that prevent us from achieving our maximum potential as a communicator. Accordingly, we can all benefit from constructive feedback that alerts us to possible problems and points in the direction of more desirable standards.

A speaker's style can take one of two major directions—the *formal* style and the more *informal* or *conversational* style. Many famous public speakers have used a stately, oratorical style with carefully planned inflection, dramatic pauses, increased volume, overly precise enunciation, and other vocal traits that give the speech a formal ceremonial tone. We can all remember speakers who, when they got behind the podium and began to speak, seemed almost to become different people because their oral style changed so radically. When you get up to speak, you may find yourself changing your delivery style to fit audience expectations as you see them.

But the point of any speech should presumably be the content, the *message* you want the audience to receive. Your goal should not be to impress an audience with a beautifully modulated voice; rather, it should be to maximize the chances that the audience will attend to and understand your message. For most public communication, therefore, we

suggest the second option—a more natural, conversational style. With this style, you use language and vocal inflection much as in normal, face-to-face conversation. The emphasis given to words and phrases, the speed and loudness of the delivery, the word choices—indeed, all audible characteristics of the presentation—are then similar to your oral style in everyday interaction.

Of course, some changes from a purely conversational delivery may be necessary. You may have to talk more loudly or articulate more carefully because of poor acoustics. More specialized language usage may be required to assure message accuracy as, for example, with a technical engineering report. In addition, key points sometimes need special vocal emphasis, which might not be characteristic of a natural delivery. In general, however, we recommend that you strive for a conversational, spontaneous style when you speak in public.

The conversational strategy fits especially well with the extemporaneous style of delivery. Anyone appears more relaxed and warmer in this mode; most people are more relaxed simply because they exert less effort in presenting the message. Still, habits and stereotypes may make it difficult to escape from a more formal style. You may want to remind yourself not to lapse into an unnatural delivery by inserting reminders in the outline notes to "relax!" or to "be conversational."

For most people, a conversational style is easy to develop and causes few problems. As in normal conversation, you can expect some imperfections in fluency—an audible pause like "uh," a minor pronunciation error, a grammatical slip, or a slurred phrase. Fortunately, while you may notice these minor errors, the people in the audience rarely do. As in more casual interaction, listeners filter out these flaws and focus on content. In general, you can conclude that any aspect of delivery that compliments a speaker's messages is good; any aspect of delivery that distracts from the speaker's messages is bad.

Variables Related to Effective Delivery

The major variables that determine the effectiveness of a speech delivery can be discussed in terms of (1) audible and visible speaker variables, and (2) situational variables. Audible speaker variables pertain to how the speaker sounds, whereas visible variables pertain to how the speaker looks. Situational variables concern the ways in which a speaker adapts the presentation to the unique aspects of a particular audience and setting.

Audible Speaker Variables and Effective Delivery

There are several questions that need to be considered with regard to audible style: How loudly should you speak? How rapidly? How precisely should sounds be enunciated? How varied should the inflection be? How planned or calculated? Are there oral mannerisms or problems that should be avoided?

For most speakers, the conversational style naturally integrates the audible dimensions of the delivery. However, all of us are capable of drifting into distracting mannerisms that draw attention away from our essential messages. In cases such as these, constructive feedback can point to problems that usually can be corrected with some conscious effort. Fortunately, our speech-producing mechanisms are extremely flexible and adaptable to preferred or normative standards.

In general, the audible style recommended for most speech occasions might be described as "articulate" and "poised" but somewhat "conversational," "natural," or even "spontaneous" in appearance. These terms can be misleading, of course, because for some, a considerable amount of training may be necessary before they are able to appear conversational, natural, or spontaneous.

Essentially, there are four categories of audible communication behaviors that can contribute to a more natural and conversational style of delivery: *voice, articulation, rhythm,* and *language usage.* In the following paragraphs, we recommend some desirable standards of performance as well as practical suggestions for achieving these standards.

Voice　The human voice consists of three primary variables: (1) pitch, or the vibrations that determine high to low frequency sounds; (2) volume, the force or loudness of the sound; and (3) quality, or overall characteristics of the vibration and resonance of sound waves.

The high to low sound frequencies that we refer to as pitch result from the thickness of the vocal folds, the size of resonating cavities, and other anatomical characteristics. In most cases therefore, a woman's voice tends to have a higher pitch than most men's. Nevertheless, with heightened tension, our voice mechanisms tend to contract and produce a much higher—and sometimes very distracting—pitch. Typically, however, this problem is easily resolved through awareness and conscious effort to relax the muscles employed in speech production.

On occasion, an individual tries to stress a particular word or phrase by employing a higher pitch. A more effective approach, however, is to stress important messages by increasing *volume* while maintaining a more natural and pleasant pitch.

Volume or loudness is one of the most familiar and recognizable voice variables. And here, quite simply, the problems usually consist of talking so softly that you cannot be easily heard, or talking too loudly or with insufficient volume variety. Almost *all* individuals are equipped to speak with sufficient volume. Accordingly, speaking too softly is usually a question of habit. It also appears that some novice speakers speak softly in an attempt to "play it safe." Nevertheless, inadequate volume is frustrating to listeners and can cause them to "turn off" a speaker. By contrast, continuous high-volume speech can be extremely abrasive and offensive.

Clearly, you should try to find an acceptable volume for the nature of the setting. Additionally, however, volume should vary with the interpretation that you are trying to achieve for a particular message—with more important messages receiving the appropriate emphasis through increased volume.

Vocal quality is much more difficult to identify and define than pitch or volume. We often use vague adjectives like gravelly, strident, hoarse, piercing, mellow, or harsh to describe vocal quality. *Hypernasality,* a more precise term, refers to the occasional problem in which too many of the resonating sound waves pass through the nasal cavities instead of through the oral passage. In the English language, only the *m, n,* and *ng* sounds are formed with air passing through the nose. When other sounds, especially vowels, are uttered with most of the air going through the nasal passage, a speaker is hypernasal, and the vocal quality is unpleasant. In contrast, *hyponasality* (also called *denasality*) results when the air that should be resonating in the nasal passage passes through and resonates in the mouth instead. We experience this problem when we have a severe cold, as do a few people who have permanent sinus or bone structure problems that can only be corrected by surgery. You can experience denasality simply by holding your nose and saying, "Spending money is nice." The *m, n,* and *ng* sounds become more like *b, d,* and *k,* and the sentence becomes, "Spedink buddy is dice."

A hoarse, gravelly, or raspy voice may be caused by swollen vocal folds or mucus on the vibrating mechanism. We notice how distracting speakers can be when they sound as if they need to clear their throat. Audiences may squirm helplessly, totally unaware of the message and preoccupied with the unpleasant vocal quality. Still another problem is *breathiness* in which too much air escapes through the vocal folds, giving the voice a whispery quality. Although the Hollywood starlet may consider breathiness sexy, for the public speaker—especially for one using a loudspeaker or recording equipment—this vocal flaw is highly detrimental.

Many voice problems can be corrected. But because they may be the result of physiological and psychological problems, the speech pathologist—not the public speaking instructor—is probably the best source for advice and therapy. You should become aware of your vocal characteristics. One way to achieve this is to listen to a tape recording of your delivery. At first it may be an unpleasant experience. "That doesn't sound like me" or "I sound terrible" are common responses. Actually, the way we hear our own voice is determined not only by sound waves through the air but also by bone conduction, the sound vibration through the skull. The tape recorder "hears" our voice the way other people do, through air conduction only. Thus, the playback is a fairly accurate indicator of the way other people hear us. Listening to the tape and getting feedback from others can be useful in either confirming effective vocal traits or in identifying particular problems that may be distracting to the audience.

Articulation   Articulation problems essentially concern the improper formation of speech sounds by the articulatory mechanism, consisting of the teeth, tongue, lips, and hard and soft palates. Sometimes the problem is substitution of sounds. The cartoon character Elmer Fudd's error was to substitute *w* for *r*—"I'll twap that awnwy wabbit!" Another example is Tweety Bird's classic line, "I tawt I taw a puddy tat!" Some substitution is due to different cultural backgrounds. People of German background may substitute *v* for *w* ("I vant it"). A native-born Japanese may insert *r* for *l* ("flied lice" for "fried rice"). People on the East Coast may substitute *er* for the final *uh*, as in "Ameriker" or "Afriker." And, of course, we are aware of substitutions in a southern accent, as in "oil" pronounced like "all." But audiences are not necessarily distracted by articulation errors that stem from cultural differences. The problem instead is in improper articulation that is not tied to regional language or culture, errors that stand out from the rest of a speaker's generally correct speech.

A common substitution is the lisp, using *th* for *s*. American culture has regrettably come to associate a male lisp with effeminacy and a female lisp with childishness. It is almost always distracting.

Another articulation problem is distortion. Some speakers simply do not enunciate carefully enough, and sounds become slurred and partially omitted. Others are hampered by organic problems, as in the case of a person with a cleft palate. Still others have dental devices, like bridges or orthodontic retainers, that impede clear articulation. Whatever the cause, distorted or mumbled speech may call attention to itself, thus distracting the audience away from the speaker's message.

Rhythm   One rhythm problem is a delivery that is *too rapid*. Though some people speak at an acceptable rate in normal conversation, the speed of delivery may increase in the public situation. The cause may simply be anxiety, a desire to make the unpleasant speech situation as brief as possible. Another cause is the tendency to try to cover more information than can be presented in a limited time. We have all heard the rapid-fire disc jockey reading a commercial. Presumably the sponsors want to say as much as they possibly can in a thirty- to sixty-second time slot. We have heard professors who, anticipating the bell, rush through the last portions of a lecture. There is evidence that increasing the number of words per minute cuts down the time available to comprehend each verbal symbol and, beyond a certain speed, leads to a decrease in understanding (Foulke, 1968; Sticht and Glasnapp, 1972).

The obvious corollary of a rapid delivery is one that is *too slow*—that is, the regular intervals between words and phrases are too long. Even at the normal English delivery speed of about 100 to 125 words per minute, the audience can think much more quickly, somewhere between 400 and 500 words per minute (thought speed). This means that listeners can anticipate what might come next and can even think about other unrelated ideas. When the speaker's delivery sinks below normal rates, the audience may become nervous and impatient, anticipating words that are too slow in coming. Or the audience may discover that it can attend to other things and still listen enough to understand the message. The most important flaw of too slow a rhythm is that it closely resembles a monotone style because the longer pauses between each sound make the pattern of naturally varied inflection more difficult to hear.

A third rhythm problem is the *unnatural pause*. Speakers who rely on a manuscript or quote from printed material too often pause at the ends of printed lines, after all punctuation marks, or after a predictable grouping of five or six words. An example of unnatural pauses is the novice actor trying to read Shakespeare. Although the great playwright utilized a poetic form called *iambic pentameter* (ten-syllable lines with a two-syllable rhythm pattern), he did not intend the lines to be read in predictable one-line patterns like those of a children's poem. If the novice actor pauses at the end of each line rather than at the end of a complete thought unit, the meaning may be lost. Another example might be an inexperienced broadcaster who has not yet learned to read conversationally; his awkward rhythm patterns are distracting. In summation, the pause is a meaningful rhythm characteristic that we use every day without thinking. But when poorly timed or omitted, it can retard an otherwise effective delivery.

A final rhythm problem that is especially serious is *stuttering*. Though stuttering is a complicated disorder and difficult to define, for our purposes, we can simply think of it as an obvious and distracting interruption in the flow of speech, one that is likely to recur. It can include repetitions of single sounds or "blocking" on particular syllables or words (inability to utter the sound at all). Severe stuttering may be accompanied by facial distortions or other unnatural body movement. Most stutterers are well aware of their speech problem, and may tend to avoid public communication situations. Those who do speak publicly have learned to manage their stuttering. Although severe stuttering is rare, *we all have some occasion to repeat or hesitate on speech sounds.* When these situations arise, we should not be preoccupied with the problem. Because it occurs in normal conversation, there is no reason to try to eliminate it from public speaking. As you gain experience, you will learn to disregard occasional stutters and focus instead on the message.

Language Usage   Language is a symbol system used for communication. *Language disorder* is a broad term that refers to a person's limited ability to use the symbol system in oral communication. Common language problems faced by public communicators are errors in *pronunciation* and *grammar*. A speaker may distract or confuse an audience if his or her natural speaking style includes improper use of language from the audience's point of view. The key factor is audience perspective. Some usage is not improper though listeners may think it is. For example, for many years speakers who used the so-called black English were considered "substandard" in their use of language. They pronounced words differently, appeared to err in grammar and syntax, and used a vocabulary that was unfamiliar or confusing to nonblack audiences. Black English is a legitimate and systematic variation from general American dialect, yet even today, some black speakers have difficulty gaining acceptance from audiences due to their language usage.

Many language problems are linked not to culture but to individual characteristics. A person's educational background may have limited his or her language development. The home, school, and community environments of children sometimes preclude varied and accurate language learning. Problems may be caused by emotional or neurological deficits during childhood. Sensory deprivation, like hearing loss, also causes language deficiencies. Anyone who has observed language training for deaf children knows what an enormously handicapping problem deafness can be.

Fortunately, most public speakers are not bothered by serious language handicaps, but people who make errors in normal conversation are likely to transfer those flaws to the public arena. For example, a speaker may show a limited *vocabulary* by using the same descriptive terms continually throughout the speech. We recall a student speaker who was describing her trip to Europe with the aid of color slides. For nearly every slide, she noted that the experience it depicted was "really interesting" or "a lot of fun." After more than thirty slides, this vocabulary flow became tedious for the audience. Younger speakers today use "like" and "ya know" repetitiously and usually as substitutes for more varied descriptive language.

Pronounciation errors are deviations from a culturally accepted or dictionary prescription of word sounds. Standards of pronunciation are based on conversational utterances of educated or literate speakers. Standards vary with region, of course, and are subject to gradual change. Most of us have a general awareness and expectation of "good" pronunciation. Glaring errors distract us from a speaker's generally fluent delivery, especially when they are committed by experienced communicators like newscasters, politicians, clergy, or teachers.

In general, pronunciation errors include the use of the *wrong sound* (*February*, "feb RU ary," not "feb YOU ary"); the *omission* of a *sound* (*police*, "po LEECE," not "PLEECE"); the *insertion* of an *extra sound* (*drowned*, "DROWND," not "drown-DED"); the *misplacement* of an *accent* (*cement*, "suh MENT," not "SEE ment"). Whenever a public communicator reads or quotes from a manuscript, he or she should try to anticipate pronunciation errors and even write the difficult words phonetically so that they will not cause a glaring distraction.

Grammar can be broadly defined as the choice, forms, and placement of words in a sentence. Fortunately, most speakers exhibit reasonably correct grammar in normal speech. But occasionally speech habits or colloquialisms divert audience attention from the message. The double negative is common, as in, "I won't never do it." "This here" and "them there" are substandard. So are improper verb forms ("I've been woken up" or "I drunk it all down"). Hundreds of examples of such grammatical errors can be found in any basic composition text. In general, when we consider a sentence like, "My daddy he done it real good," rather than, "My daddy did it well," we can understand why some ungrammatical speakers have difficulty communicating with an audience. People sometimes equate poor grammar with low intelligence, bad ideas, or other negative qualities. The irrepressible Dizzy Dean never suffered because of poor grammar. "He slud into second base but got throwed out anyways." Some speakers purposely use an uneducated language style as a ploy to win favor of an audience they believe to be uncultured. But for most of us, a failure to detect and remedy common grammatical errors will usually be a serious handicap in many different communication situations.

Visible Speaker Variables and Effective Delivery

People in an audience notice two things about the speaker's visible presentation. They notice the speaker's appearance—physical features and clothing. They also observe the speaker's behavior. Both elements combine to affect the speaker's impact on the audience.

A primary requirement of clothing is that it be comfortable. Some high-heeled shoes, tight-fitting pants or dresses, and heavy, hot fabrics may be distracting and physically uncomfortable. Dress and grooming habits can also affect a speaker *psychologically*. A new hairstyle, new glasses, or avant-garde clothing might be a source of apprehension if the speaker fears audience disapproval.

Even more important than comfort is message effectiveness. Obviously, if listeners become distracted by your physical characteristics, attention to and comprehension of your message may be lost. What is appropriate physical appearance? It can be argued that suitable dress and grooming criteria can only be determined by each individual. Some people use a self-reference criterion, applying purely personal needs and tastes to what is acceptable appearance with little regard for audience expectations. A speaker who adopts the "do your own thing" standard has every right to do so, but he or she should not be surprised at negative responses from some audiences.

We suggest that a more meaningful point of view is *accommodation:* a move away from a speaker-centered orientation ("I'll do what makes me happy") toward a more audience-centered basis for communication behavior. If the message you wish to communicate is truly important, if receiver understanding and acceptance are sincerely sought, you should be willing to adjust to audience standards of acceptable physical appearance. Accommodation means neither deception nor abandonment of personal convictions. Rather, it is simply the willingness to make minor adjustments in normal preferences so as to increase the chances of communicative effectiveness. By considering the relative formality of the speaking occasion and dressing appropriately or by avoiding clothing or accessories that are distracting, you can enhance speech effectiveness with attention to appearance.

Eye Contact   The importance of eye contact can be demonstrated with a simple experiment. In a casual conversation with a friend, try closing

your eyes while that person is talking. Your friend will probably stop abruptly and ask you what's wrong. You then reply, with eyes still closed, "Nothing is wrong. I'm hearing you. Go right ahead with what you were saying." Your friend will probably be unwilling to continue the conversation until you respond to his or her message with "normal" eye contact. This little test suggests the effect of eye contact on our motivation to communicate. Like students who become frustrated with a teacher who buries his or her head in notes, we in the audience want the public speaker to acknowledge our presence and importance with direct eye contact.

A by-product of good eye contact is an increased ability to hold attention. If you look directly at a person in the audience, your eye contact has a "grabbing" effect. Most teachers know that the easiest way to get a daydreaming student to listen to the lecture is to look directly at him or her. Conversely, looking away from a person is a kind of psychological "release" that permits the listener to attend to other things. Although eye contact cannot guarantee complete audience attention, especially if the message is inherently uninteresting, it is an important factor in audience receptivity.

A common mistake is to glance only at audience members who are located in central areas near you. Many members of the audience will experience a sense of exclusion if you do this. In attempting to achieve and maintain good eye contact, we suggest the following: Make occasional visual contact with the people at the outer perimeters of the room, including those at your extreme left and your extreme right. With conscious effort and practice, good eye contact can soon become a regular part of your delivery style.

Not surprisingly, the *amount* of audience eye contact is usually correlated with the extensiveness of a speaker's notes and need to rely on those notes. In general, the more elaborate the notes, and the speaker's dependency upon them, the more the speaker's eye contact must be directed at those notes and away from the audience. Accordingly, time spent in editing notes into a better organized and briefer style usually pays significant dividends in the form of improved eye contact.

Gestures   A second factor in the speaker's movement is gesture or *body action*. Though facial expression can be included in this category, for the moment we will consider hand and arm movements, body stances or postures (including postural changes), and "footwork" or shifting of positions in front of the audience. Obviously, the different kinds of gestures and combinations of movement are practically infinite; we have an enormous range of options. Almost any movement, positioning, or posturing carries symbolic content or meaning. Hence, animation serves as a potentially flexible and varied tool for enhancing audience comprehension and increasing message impact. A speaker obviously cannot ignore the action dimension of his or her presentation.

For several reasons, a formal gesture strategy is usually inappropriate. First, as with other nonverbal factors, a planned movement or gesture may appear unnatural and thus may distract or confuse the audience. A planned gesture may be mistimed, appearing out of proper sequence with the idea being expressed. It may be overdone or seem stiff or awkward. Like facial expression, the planned gesture also may lack congruence with the spoken idea. Natural gestures accompanying normal conversation, in contrast, are nearly always properly timed and appropriate to the ideas being expressed. You may recall a heated argument, a conversation at a party, a child describing a new toy, or a salesperson closing a deal—all illustrate that body action need not be planned to be meaningful. We all gesture fluently every day and usually without conscious thought.

Body action may require serious attention, however, if particular mannerisms become distracting. A common problem is random pacing. Some speakers wander back and forth at regular intervals, often as a subconscious release of tension. Another problem is repetitious hand and arm gestures. A typical movement is the "apple-picker gesture" in which a speaker moves his or her hand out and back, out and back (like a person picking apples) almost as if he or she were reaching out to grab the words that come next in the speech. Another overused gesture is a perpetual chopping motion with one hand. A postural distraction is the constant shifting of weight from one foot to the other, with possible shuffling of whichever foot is not supporting body weight. And, of course, facial mannerisms, like a nervous tic, can also bother the listeners.

Inappropriate movement not only hampers message effectiveness, it also neutralizes the potentially potent tool provided by the visual dimension of a presentation. The inventory of potentially distracting gestures is large. The important thing is to get adequate feedback from students or instructors so that you will recognize your unique mannerisms in a simulated situation rather than in an actual one.

Facial Expression   Another visual factor is facial expression. The facial muscles are capable of enormous variation in movement and positioning. As we know from actors and pantomimists, facial communication can be highly meaningful (certainly the focal point of body posture), and can also be developed through practice. In other words, facial expression can be a *conscious* strategy for the communication of feelings and ideas.

The problem with *planned* facial expression is that it too often appears contrived and insincere. The painted smiles in automobile showrooms, beauty contests, and political campaigns are good examples. But the opposite extreme—passive, expressionless facial features—is equally unacceptable. When you are discussing happy themes, you should look happy. Grave or unhappy messages should be accompanied by more serious looks of concern and even sadness.

How can you make facial expression congruent with the mood of your message without appearing artificial? If you use the conversational speaking style, facial expression is likely to develop naturally. If you select topics of personal concern and are enthusiastic or committed, natural expression will be more likely than if you select a topic of only casual interest. Viewing your speech on videotape is a good way of becoming aware of your nonverbal facial behavior in a public situation. You may discover, "I'm really coming across too seriously; I'm too grim. Next time I'll try to smile more." Or, "I really do look bored. No wonder the audience seemed restless. I'll try to show more enthusiasm." In general, however, we caution against becoming too concerned with facial strategy. The normal expressions that you exhibit in everyday conversation will develop, in most cases, as you grow increasingly familiar with the public speaking situation.

Situational Variables and Effective Delivery

In fundamental ways, the effectiveness of a speaker's delivery is a function of message preparation and rehearsal. However, you may encounter situational variables that challenge your ability to deliver a speech as planned. Accordingly, an experienced speaker tries to correctly anticipate and prepare for a variety of situational events that can form an impact on the presentation.

As a general rule, you should always acquire advanced information about the unique features of a particular setting or audience. Through advanced information, you can resolve a variety of potential problems. Contact people who may be familiar with the setting for your forthcoming speech. Will some prior arrangements be made? Will there be a loudspeaker system? A blackboard? Demonstration area? How many people are expected? Are distractions or interruptions likely? Will specified people be available to help with last-minute problems? By getting answers to these and other questions, you will also eliminate the element of surprise because you will know what to expect.

Managing the Physical Setting   In addition to getting advanced information about potential problems, you should always arrive at least twenty to thirty minutes ahead of time to survey the scene. A movie or slide projector, a videotape machine, or an overhead projector should be plugged in and tested so that any or all aids will be ready to use with a simple flick of a switch. Similarly, the microphone should be tested, with another person standing at various places in the room to assure proper volume. You should move to various positions around the podium to determine the microphone's sensitivity and how much freedom of movement will be possible without distorting sound reproduction. You can thus avoid awkward introductory comments like, "Is this thing on?" or the shout from the back of the room, "We can't hear you!"

Is a lectern needed? Is one available? Notice its height. Will it restrict audience vision of body movement or visual aids? Would a small portable lectern be more appropriate? If the speech involves physical demonstration of visual materials, where can notes be placed?

Analyze the audience seating arrangement. In most cases, seating will be fixed, and you must adapt to it. If so, survey the room, and notice places where some people may have trouble hearing or seeing. In a few cases, it may be possible to rope off certain sections or let people know where the best seats are. In some environments, the speaker can actually rearrange the seating—in classrooms, conference rooms, luncheon or banquet areas, churches, and public halls. Audiences tend to be more responsive if they are sitting closer together and nearer the speaker than if they are spread out over a large room. Avoid setting up chairs too far to either side of the podium; this arrangement will make eye contact with some people more difficult.

Survey the total environment for potential distractions. Will some of the light be uncomfortable for you or the audience? Is room temperature comfortable and can it be raised or lowered? Will open windows or doors admit distracting sights and sounds? Are the chairs the type that will become especially uncomfortable if the speech is lengthy? (Most folding chairs usually are.)

Beyond anticipating and preparing for unique settings and situational occurrences, you should develop an approach to standard issues, such as the management of audience participation and of situational interruptions.

Managing Audience Participation   Most occasions for public speaking call for an active speaker and less active listeners. The speaker explains or advocates; the audience listens. On many occasions, however, the use of well-planned audience participation techniques can enhance the speaker's effort. Audience participation helps listeners to be more actively involved and can contribute to audience interest.

You can achieve a modest amount of audience involvement by simply asking for a show of hands on certain issues, or by asking volunteers to respond to specific questions. You can also select individuals to participate in purposeful demonstrations.

In some cases, more active audience participation is achieved simply by using a public speech as a preliminary step to be followed by planned audience activities. For example, you might describe the major features of a problem and then arrange the audience into small groups to consider possible solutions. A specific individual in each group can be asked to summarize the results of the group's deliberations and to present them to the entire audience.

A speaker does face some risks in using participative devices. Certain audiences have gotten use to a passive role and feel comfortable with not having to respond. They may resent the speaker's requests. Other audiences are unable to respond because they cannot think creatively about the speaker's ideas. (Most teachers find that, because of the mood of their students on a particular day, they simply cannot generate any voluntary reactions from the class.) Most importantly, the participative framework can be difficult to control. If your audience takes off on a subject, you may not have time to do some of the other things you had planned. Hence, you must either be tactful in getting back on the topic or have the ability to adapt the ideas generated through audience participation to the planned content. Whatever the possible drawbacks, however, audience involvement is a creative and increasingly popular approach.

Sometimes speakers address exceptionally large audiences, with listeners numbering in the hundreds or thousands. Such communication events include large college lecture classes, banquets, and special programs. The large audience presents several unique problems. A speaker can rarely interact with listeners, and audience participation is awkward. Subgroups within the audience may respond differently throughout the speech. People close to the speaker may see and hear easily and may respond enthusiastically, whereas those farther away may become impatient and surly. Audience members are much less likely to share common backgrounds and interests to the extent that members of smaller groups do. The greater the number of people, the greater the chance that the level of information will be too complicated or too simple, depending on the listener. A platform, podium, and public address system may keep the speaker locked to a tiny presentational area.

Although the classroom speaker can encourage questions when anything is unclear, such techniques can become disruptive in an auditorium with two thousand people. Because informal feedback is difficult, the speech may need more careful structuring and elaboration. Clear presentation the first time through is the only reasonable solution. If the speaker will accept audience inquiries, he or she might ask an assistant to collect written questions from the audience and select some of them to answer. Finally, if the communicator regularly speaks to a particular audience, he or she might want to get systematic oral and written feedback *after* each speech to determine how to modify the next one.

Managing Situational Interruptions   In many "real-life" settings, speakers are confronted with a variety of interruptions that can challenge their ability to present the materials as planned. Some members of the audience may engage in distracting, private conversations, a small child may be crying, someone may be staring out the window or falling asleep, others may raise their hands for questions or may interrupt with applause, laughter, or comments. Someone may enter the room unexpectedly; someone else may get up and leave. The audience is a dynamic group engaging in continuous activity, and the speaker is not simply "acting" but is *interacting* with audience behaviors.

The obvious implication is that the speaker must make regular spontaneous adaptions to situational interruptions. Unlike the stereotyped professor who enters the classroom, buries his or her head in notes, reads for an hour, and then walks out, most speakers will be continuously reminded of audience presence. The following are common occurrences and suggestions for adapting.

Audience noise or commotion: Noise or commotion frequently occurs when youngsters are present or when the speech situation involves a volatile emotional issue. Sometimes members of the audience who want to hear will try to silence others, but more often the speaker will have to intervene. Dogmatic statements like, "Be quiet while I'm talking!" are usually too antagonistic to be productive, and a more friendly reaction might be, "Perhaps some people cannot hear because of side conversations; we will have time for comments and questions in a few minutes." In addition to being courteous, such comments should preserve the anonymity of the noisemakers. To single them out might encourage even more damaging behaviors. Only when the disturbance persists should the speaker single anyone out for comment. The key is to be as tactful and accommodating as possible for as long as possible. Do not alienate an audience with an unnecessary command or accusation.

Spontaneous audience questions: Questions that arise spontaneously may interrupt the speaker's trend of thought. In any speech, you should decide in advance whether you want to permit questions during the planned presentation. If precise timing is not a factor, questions might be handled as they arise (a common classroom technique). However, you should be wary of irrelevant questions that divert listeners from the speech topic. You should also avoid belaboring a point by accepting too many questions on the same basic idea. A comment like, "Perhaps we've discussed this notion long enough and should get back to some of the things I wanted to mention," will usually have the approval of most of the audience.

If you feel that questions during the speech will be disruptive to the flow of ideas, you may want to agree to answer all audience questions later on. For example, you might say, "I'm going to talk to you for about thirty minutes. Then I shall be happy to spend a few minutes answering whatever questions you might have." If this tactic is used, however, you *must* reserve the question-and-answer time. An audience is not amused when a speaker sheepishly concludes, "Well, I see I have talked longer than I expected, and we won't have time for questions." For speakers attempting to persuade, like salespersons or politicians, this comment can be deadly to the achievement of objectives. You may also defer the question to a later point in the speech. "If you don't mind, I'd like to come back to that important question when I discuss the issue later in the speech." That response is fine as long as you do indeed refer to the question later. Evasive speakers sometimes use the reply as a strategy for ignoring a tough question, but the person who asked the question (and usually others in the audience as well) will remember what it was and may persist later on, leaving the speaker in an awkward position.

A useful technique for fielding questions is to pause at the end of each main point and ask for questions before moving on to the next.

Whatever the strategy, however, you must realize that the public communication environment is increasingly becoming *two way,* and presentational speaking with speaker-audience dialog is a growing trend that more and more audiences are coming to expect.

The heckler: Though feared by many speakers, the heckler is actually quite rare in public communication. Politicians being covered by the news media may encounter antagonists who recognize an opportunity to make a point and to have it picked up on television, but most of our speeches are attended by reasonably well-mannered, considerate people who do not attempt to embarrass or destroy us.

There is the occasional person, however, who obviously wants to interrupt, challenge, or heckle the speaker, and we cannot ignore this individual because his or her antics may increase. Remember, first, that the speaker usually has legitimacy, and the heckler does not. The person at the lectern, often with a microphone, has an enormous psychological advantage. Second, many audience members are frequently as embarrassed by the heckler's comments as is the speaker. The speaker, therefore, can often count on the audience as an ally rather than as an enemy.

Some people may not be aware of the inappropriateness of their behavior. A brief remark from the speaker may be all that is necessary to quiet them. The following statements are potentially useful responses to the heckler:

"Though you are entitled to your opinions, you've been monopolizing the discussion, and I think we should give others a chance to participate."

I'll tell you what. If you will let me finish my speech without interruption, I'll let you have the floor to answer my arguments."

"Sorry, but you are rude and obnoxious and are wasting the audience's time. I think you should be quiet or leave."

The speaker must be firm and attempt to maintain reasonable control! A grateful audience often will actually applaud and may even assist the speaker in managing the heckler.

Briefly, then, factors related to the physical setting, speaker-audience interaction, or situational interruptions can influence the overall effectiveness of speech delivery. By seeking prior information about a particular setting, by carefully selecting an appropriate format for speaker-audience interactions, and by preplanning appropriate responses to possible types of interruptions, any speaker can increase the overall odds that the presentation can be delivered as planned.

Summary

In this chapter, speech delivery is approached from several perspectives. First, we address the problem of communication apprehension; we note that anxiety and other apprehension symptoms are common to virtually all occasions that involve performance before an audience. Specific suggestions for controlling speech apprehension are offered and in this context, the importance of instruction, adequate preparation, and rehearsal are emphasized.

Delivery standards are discussed, and a natural, conversational, and spontaneous-appearing style is suggested for most occasions.

Variables related to effective delivery are discussed in terms of (1) audible speaker variables (including voice, articulation, rhythm, and language), (2) visual speaker variables (including eye contact, gestures, and facial expressions), and (3) situational variables (including the management of equipment, and of audience participation and situational interruptions).

Questions

1. What are some of the implications of an audience-centered approach to speech delivery?

2. Identify some effective delivery strategies for the following public communication situations:

   Religious service   Business conference
   Political campaign   Orientation session
   Classroom presentation   Televised speech

3. What are some common problems in a speaker's visible mannerisms? Identify some potential solutions.

4. Discuss some of the unexpected problems that can arise in any speaker-audience setting. What specific problems have you observed?

5. How can a speaker maximize speaker-audience interaction without losing too much control over the presentation and the purposes of the speech occasion?

Suggested Readings

BEATTY, M. J., R. R. BEHNKE, AND K. MC CALLUM. (1978). Situation determinants of communication apprehension. *Communication Monographs, 45,* 186–191.

GUNDERSON, D. G., AND R. HOPPER. (1976). Relationships between speech delivery and speech effectiveness. *Communication Monographs XLIII,* 158.

MAC LACHLEN, J. (1979). What people really think of fast talkers. *Psychology Today, 12,* 113–117.

MC CROSKEY, J. C. (1977). Oral communication apprehension: A summary of recent theory and research. *Human Communication Research, 4,* 78–96.

MC CROSKEY, J. C. (1982). Oral communication apprehension: A reconceptualization. In M. Burgoon (Ed.), *Communication Yearbook 6* (pp. 136–170). Beverly Hills, Calif.: Sage.

IV Practical Interpersonal Communication

During the past several decades we have seen the development of a number of new and useful courses in the area of interpersonal communication. These courses have evolved out of a growing realization that the majority of meaningful human communication activity occurs in dyadic and small group situations, and that theory and research into human communication in these contexts have reached a level of advancement that warrants application in communication skills training.

It is through our routine, informal, daily communication activities that we share much information, influence our own behavior and that of others, and learn the ways in which we view ourselves and the world around us.

Part IV begins with an introductory exploration of the dyad and dyadic interaction as a unit of analysis useful in understanding not only intimate one-to-one communication, but small group and public

communication dynamics as well. We then focus on a dyad of special importance to virtually everyone—the interview. Emphasis in this section is on the employment interview.

Two following chapters deal with interpersonal communication dynamics in the small group setting. The first is a general introduction to group communication, and the second focuses on decision making, leadership, and effective participation in small groups.

The section concludes with a chapter devoted to listening and responding, emphasizing once again the central role of receivers in the communication process.

The concepts and principles we discuss in this section were selected because we believe they have direct application to understanding the communication process and to the acquisition of communication competence in the interpersonal context.

203

Chapter Eleven

One-To-One Communication: The Dyad

Preview

For hundreds of years, speech education has centered on a speaker-audience (one-to-many) communication model as students learned to prepare and deliver public speeches. The audience was viewed as a mass of humanity with certain general characteristics, and speakers learned to prepare their messages with these general factors in mind.

Today speech education is increasingly concerned with the uniqueness of each individual in the communication event, regardless of the total number of participants in that event. We have begun to focus on the dyad, or one-to-one communication, as the basis for understanding the communication process.

The dyad is not merely a handy unit for theoretical analysis. It is also a fact of our everyday interaction. We spend more time communicating in dyads than within small groups or to larger audiences. Hence, a superior public speaker may be significantly handicapped as a communicator if he or she cannot interact productively in the dyad, which paradoxically may require more complex adjustments to one's behavior than is required in the public setting.

We think it is crucially important for you as speech communication students to develop awareness of and skill in dyadic transactions. Such competence is the basis for all meaningful and productive human relationships, and has high survival value both for the individual and society.

Objectives

To increase awareness of the enormous complexity of dyadic communication

To identify the role of dyadic interaction in developing self-concept

To discuss dyadic interaction as the basis of intimate relationships

To introduce concepts for analysis of dyadic communication

To enhance the development of dyadic communication skills, emphasizing empathy, openness, and flexibility as critical areas

ELEVEN   The basic unit of interpersonal communication is the *dyad,* which we define as communicative interaction between two persons. The dyad is the building block of human social interaction. Dyadic relationships are vitally important in human affairs, playing a major role in child development (parent-child dyads), social skills development (dating, friendships), family culture (the marital dyad), and careers (superior-subordinate relationships).

In addition, the dyad is a unit of analysis that is useful in situations involving more than two persons. In a small group or even in a public speaking situation, the dynamics of communication are often amenable to analysis in dyadic terms. For example, in a classroom setting, a speech student does not speak to an undifferentiated blob called an "audience," but rather to a set of individuals. He or she relates to each individual in a unique way, as subsequent dyadic two-way communication between the speaker and members of the audience inevitably reveals.

Action, Interaction, and Transaction

In his book about interpersonal communication, *Bridges Not Walls,* John Stewart identifies three perspectives on communication: communication as *action,* communication as *interaction,* and communication as *transaction.* Viewed as action, communication is simply the presentation of a message to stimulate a listener or audience. It is something the source does *to* the receiver or *for* the receiver, and requires no feedback or reciprocal action. An example would be the presentation of the evening news on television, or the recorded presentation of the time of day available on the phone. Viewed as interaction, communication is two way in the sense that sender and receiver exchange roles frequently and exert reciprocal influence on one another by alternately sending and receiving messages. An example would be a dialog between two persons on some subject. Viewed as a transaction, communication is a process involving both action and interaction in which the reciprocal influence that occurs is intimately tied up with the very nature of the communicators themselves. This transactional perspective recognizes at least two important characteristics of human communication missing from the action and interaction points of view: (1) in many communication events, the persons themselves are part of the subject matter of the messages exchanged, and (2) the participants are changed—for better or worse—in the process of interpersonal communication.

The transactional perspective is essential to an understanding of the more important dyads in a person's life, those that develop into intimate, ongoing relationships between people, as in marriage, close friendships, kinships, or work relationships requiring a high degree of interdependence and cooperation. The importance of communication in these relationships cannot be overemphasized; it is the glue that holds them together, the fuel that energizes them, and the ultimate return on the investment in them (see Figure 11–1).

In a sense, an intimate dyad is one in which the task of the dyad is the relationship, or at least is to sustain the relationship. How often do we hear people speak of "holding their marriage together," referring in actuality to communication that serves to maintain the marital partnership. Dyads are characterized by goals for the near, intermediate, and

FIGURE 11–1

Communication as Action, Interaction, Transaction

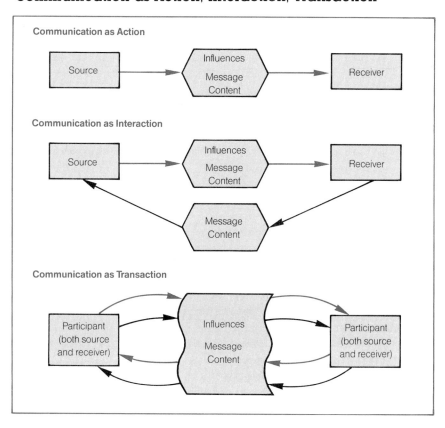

long term. When the long-term goal is to maintain, nourish, and perpetuate the relationship, demands for trust, affection, intimacy, and honesty are more acute.

Origins and Contexts of Dyadic Interaction

A dyad begins, obviously, with someone's conscious awareness of another person. For a variety of reasons, we notice another human being and make some sort of verbal or nonverbal contact. Dyadic communication begins, in other words, when two people perceive each other's presence and behavior and begin to give meaning to those behaviors.

Why the dyad develops and is maintained in particular ways is the subject of entire courses on dyads. The "why" of some relationships might never be fully understood. Think of a personal friendship of your own that has involved affection, intimacy, feelings of attraction (perhaps sexual, perhaps not), and even love. Why did it begin? Because the other person was physically appealing? Fun to be with? Drove a nice car? Had interesting friends? Paid attention to you? Had similar ideas and background? Or is there some kind of inexplicable "chemistry" that drew you together and cannot be analyzed rationally? Such is often the case in strong dyadic relationships, where the reasons for the bond are not fully understood by the partners, and are a total mystery to outside observers. The metaphor "falling in love" remains the most common description of the beginning of one of the more significant dyadic relationships in Western culture. "Falling in love" suggests something more accidental than planned, more attributable to chance or fate than to choice and purpose, and perhaps something scary and dangerous.

Many dyads, of course, begin under controlled and deliberate conditions. We team up to complete career tasks, to share information to persuade, to give and receive needed services, to unite in comradery, to play games for recreation.

Perceiving Self and Other

Apparently a simple social unit, the dyad is actually quite complex. Laing, Phillipson, and Lee (1966) have noted that a dyad involves six "persons" rather than two. Those six, when you and I are the dyad, are:

Who I think I am.

Who I think you are.

What I think you think of me.

Who you think you are.

Who you think I am.

What you think I think of you.

These perceptions of ourselves and of each other will affect our communicative interactions. Suppose that I am your professor in a class, and that I think of myself as competent, fair, and approachable. I assume you see me in the same way. I also assume, based on your good performance in class, that you like school. But what if you actually don't like going to college, and you think I'm rather distant and aloof. We would encounter serious difficulties in developing shared meanings.

Recall that in our discussion of receivers, we stress the importance of our beliefs about ourselves for our communication behavior, and vice versa. We cited the role of self-disclosure in gaining accurate self-knowledge. Most self-disclosure occurs in dyadic relationships, so the degree of agreement between the two real members of a dyad about the other four imaginary members is a function of the amount of self-disclosure that takes place.

The Johari Window

Ingham and Luft (1955) created a model to illustrate interpersonal relationships in terms of awareness. It is called the "Johari window," which sounds like something based on Indian mysticism (see Figure 11–2). It isn't because Johari is just a contraction based on the first names of Luft and Ingham, and it's called a window because the model is a two-by-two table, as depicted below: (We tell you this in case you ever find yourself involved in a game of Trivial Pursuit® in which social sciences is a category.)

The Johari window is useful in analyzing what sort of information is available to partners in a dyad. The quantity and kind of information about the individuals that resides in each of the four areas determines the nature of the relationship—how intimate it is, how it functions for the participants, how much trust exists, and so on.

FIGURE 11–2

The Johari Window

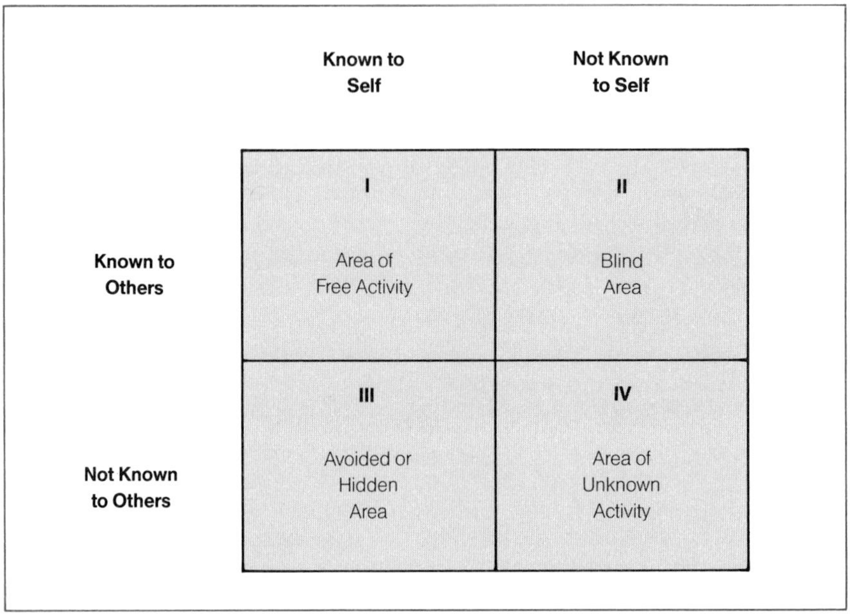

	Known to Self	Not Known to Self
Known to Others	I Area of Free Activity	II Blind Area
Not Known to Others	III Avoided or Hidden Area	IV Area of Unknown Activity

Cell I, the free activity area, contains information about the self that is mutually shared. In a dyad that is just getting acquainted, what little information there is in this cell usually has to do with items that are rich in stereotype value. For example, some of the first things new acquaintances ask each other are about occupation, marital status, length of time in the local area, and leisure pursuits. These topics hasten the acquaintance process by providing stereotypical information more likely than not to be accurate. As the acquaintance develops, more information in cell I is contributed by self-disclosure and direct observation.

Cell II contains information not available to oneself, but available to the other partner. All of us have aspects of ourselves of which we are either unaware or hold false beliefs. The more normal and healthy our communication, the less information exists in this cell. When we seek professional help from a psychotherapist or counselor, we are acknowledging our own ignorance about the information in this area and are inviting the insight of the other. Such insight can be provided by laypersons as well. In healthy, productive interpersonal relationships, information moves from cell II to cell I in the normal course of interaction, increasing accurate self-knowledge. When a person's ordinary interpersonal relationships fail to perform this function, then the person must seek professional help.

Cell III contains information known to oneself, but unknown to the other partner. Even in the closest and most intimate relationships, individuals refrain from disclosing certain information about themselves to their partners. A person's reasons for withholding information may vary, ranging from fear of negative evaluation if the information is socially unacceptable to a simple desire to remain interesting to the other by leaving things yet to be discovered, to a concern about hurting the other's feelings or arousing discomfort.

Cell IV contains information unknown to either partner. The amount of information in this area is large for individuals who do not enjoy a variety of sustained interpersonal relationships in which self-disclosure takes place, and self-knowledge is thereby enhanced. If this area gets too big, the individual is out of touch both with social contacts and with reality.

Obviously as relationships grow, the information about participants moves around. Too, the information in each cell varies from relationship to relationship. For example, the free area in cell I usually contains different information in parent-offspring dyads than in other dyads involving the offspring. In other words, "My wife knows some things about me that my mom doesn't, and it's a damn good thing, too."

As a general rule, it is good when a relationship has a large free area for each participant. This indicates that the relationship is one in which a lot of shared meaning has occurred with respect to the persons themselves, and that they are comfortable with the sharing, which suggests high levels of *acceptance* of both self and other, in the context of the relationship, for both partners.

Acceptance and Rejection

In his book *Why Am I Afraid to Tell You Who I Am?* (1969), John Powell explains that fear of rejection prevents persons from self-disclosure. This

is a recurrent theme in the literature of communication. Fear of rejection, or the need for acceptance, operates in every communication situation.

In the dyadic context, rejection may be particularly fearful because of the importance of the other partner in the dyad. It is one thing to disclose information about ourself and have it rejected by someone unimportant; it is quite another to be rejected by a valued friend, loved one, or associate.

Self-disclosure is thus a risky enterprise, and what is risked is not just the acceptance of the other, but our very concept and evaluation of self, or self-esteem. This fact makes the establishment of intimate dyadic relationships a high-risk—high-return activity.

Dance and Larson (1976) discuss the responses typical of persons subjected to rejecting feedback on aspects of self that they communicate. Citing three typical response patterns they call reevaluation, amplification, and salvaging, these authors describe them as follows:

Reevaluation: Reevaluation refers to changing perceptions of the person who has communicated rejection. To illustrate, suppose a friend of Tom Selleck tells him that he (Selleck) isn't particularly good looking. Selleck is very likely to reevaluate his friend, concluding that he or she is not quite as perceptive as he once thought.

Amplification: Amplification refers to a person's efforts to reinforce another's perceptions of some aspect of self that has been rejected, by some insistent message that says, "I am so" (whatever it is that the other has not accepted)! Larson illustrates amplification with an adolescent who believes himself to be responsible and mature but gets rejecting feedback from his parents on this belief. Amplification might include a premature marriage or, perhaps, joining the Marine Corps as an expression of maturity and independence.

Salvaging: Salvaging refers to letting go of a belief about oneself as a consequence of rejecting feedback, and to advancing some compensating factor in its place. Suppose, for example, that an athlete who has tried hard to qualify for a competition is finally told by the coach, "I'm afraid you're just not Olympic level talent." A salvaging response might be to accept the accuracy of the coach's appraisal but say to oneself, "Maybe not, but I'm persistent and a hard worker, and that's more important anyway in the long run."

Dance and Larson go on to describe the circumstances likely to predict which of the three types of response that will result from rejection. Reevaluation, they believe, is most likely to occur when the rejected person has high self-esteem based on accurate self-knowledge. Such a person knows who he or she is and what attributes he or she possesses, is comfortable with that knowledge, and will reevaluate another person who denies it. Amplification is most likely to occur when the rejecting communication comes from a significant other person, such as a parent or loved one—someone involved in an intimate dyad with the rejected person. Salvaging is likely to occur when the rejection is consistent—coming from many other persons over a period of time, and corroborated by other available evidence.

Sometimes, it is wise and humane to give people rejecting feedback about themselves when their beliefs are unrealistic, but doing so requires utmost sensitivity and skill. Too, it is vital to a person's development to receive accepting feedback on realistic self-descriptions and appraisals. This is especially true for children, but some adults need such feedback as well. The intimate dyads in a person's life are where these needs can be fulfilled.

Exchanging information with one another about our perceptions of self is a crucial aspect of human relationships. Knowing what to disclose, when to disclose, how to respond to disclosure, how to handle acceptance and rejection, and how to respect the privacy of the other individual underlie the communication skills required in dyadic interpersonal communication.

Dyadic Communication Skills

In dyadic communication, skills that facilitate the initiation, nurturance, maintenance, and perpetuation of relationships consist mainly of three kinds: *empathy, openness,* and *flexibility.* We discuss the nature of these attributes and the kind of behavior that communicates them in turn.

Empathy

Empathy refers to a person's ability to assume the role of the other person, not just intellectually, but emotionally as well. It is not the same thing as sympathy, or feeling sorry for someone else. Empathy is more than *feeling for* someone; it is *feeling with* someone, and not just sorrow, but whatever emotion the other person is experiencing—joy, anger, grief, disgust, or whatever. Thus, the empathic person is one who may cry when a friend is hurt, and jump for joy when the friend feels joy, as if whatever caused the feelings in the friend affected the empathic person in exactly the same way.

The behaviors that exhibit empathy between people are therefore fairly simple to describe, but difficult to enact for persons who do not actually *feel with* their partner in the dyad. Emotional empathy is expressed nonverbally by way of crying, laughing, jumping for joy, touching, smiling, and so on. These actions convey empathy much more credibly and sincerely in many cases than verbal communication. When we say, "I know how you feel," we may be sincerely acknowledging an intellectual understanding of how the person feels, but perhaps may not be indicating that we feel the same way ourselves at the moment. When we let out a "whoopee!" to match that of a friend's who announces her acceptance by her first choice among medical schools, we've probably empathized. But empathy, like beauty, is in the eye of the beholder. No matter what we actually feel or how we act on those feelings, our dyadic partners may not view us as empathic unless we behave in a manner consistent with their expectations. If the things we do to display our feelings and express our thoughts do not match those expectations, we are not seen as empathic by the other.

The ability to empathize is the central communication skill, although it is too complex an ability to be considered a single skill. Empathic ability is the essence of a receiver-centered approach to communication, and functions in all communication contexts, not just in the dyad. It is especially crucial in the dyadic situation, however.

Empathy is probably more likely to occur between similar individuals whose past experiences, self-concepts, value-systems, and behavioral repertoires have much in common. Persons with similar backgrounds generally share the same "codes" with respect to the cues that signify empathic communication. The common bonds and shared codes that facilitate empathy are frequently less visible to dyadic partners from different cultural or social backgrounds, making communication difficult. A person not steeped in the culture of the Far East, for example, does not fully understand the significance of "losing face." Similarly, an Iranian youth would have difficulty comprehending the strong feelings of many young Americans about their music.

Openness

This term refers to an individual's willingness and ability to do two things— disclose information about the self as appropriate to the situation, and be receptive to information from his or her partner in communication. Receptivity implies a lack of defensiveness and an ability not to pass judgment in responding to others.

Individuals who do not exhibit appropriate levels and kinds of self-disclosure have difficulty in establishing relationships. When they succeed in establishing relationships, they have trouble maintaining them. Without self-disclosure, there is no information base upon which dyad partners can build intimacy and trust. We've said earlier that self-disclosure is risky, because it makes the discloser vulnerable to *rejection* from the other, which may take the form of denial of the accuracy of the self-disclosure or of a negative evaluation of the self-disclosed content. We've chosen to exemplify this with self-disclosure about sexual preferences, because sexual intimacy is sometimes an objective of one or both partners building a dyadic relationship, and is usually a topic of disclosure even among close friends whose relationship is nonsexual.

Suppose a person with whom you are starting a friendship discloses to you that he or she is a homosexual, and you react with disbelief because this information is not consistent with other information you know about the person. Or, you might accept the information as accurate, but downgrade your evaluation of the other person because you dislike homosexuality.

Receptivity to information from the other is also illustrated by the preceding example. The way a person responds to another's self-disclosure signals acceptance or rejection, and gives powerful clues as to whether or not the respondent is interested in continuing the interaction and pursuing the relationship.

Behaviors that communicate openness include appropriate kinds and levels of self-disclosure at various stages of development of the relationship, and nondefensive, nonjudgmental responses to the disclosures of the other. Often, the content of self-disclosure signifies acceptance, without further comment. For example, consider the following response in the situation described previously:

"I'm a confirmed heterosexual, myself, so we haven't got much in common there. How do you feel about that?"

This response simply states facts about the speaker's self-concept, makes no judgments, suggests no defensiveness, and invites further discussion on the matter. As such, it typifies a high degree of openness in communication. Some contrasting examples follow:

"Oh, that's too bad. Well, good luck on your exams. See ya."

This response includes a judgment, and a hasty leave-taking that indicates nonreceptivity to further communication at this particular time, on this particular topic, with this particular person. The leave-taking may well be permanent.

"No, that can't be true. You're so feminine!"

This response signifies a denial of the content of the disclosure, bolstered by a claim offering support for the denial.

"Oh, yeah? Well no thanks. I'm sorry for you, but I'm disappointed in you, too."

This response suggests a judgment, implies that the discloser's original motive may be seduction, and then makes explicit two negative judgments.

Flexibility

Flexibility is having a diverse repertoire of communication behaviors and being able to enact them as the occasion requires. Although dyadic communication is usually informal and free-flowing, it can be regarded as a series of tasks or goal-oriented activities. Some of these tasks are peculiar to a given dyad at a particular encounter. Others are routine kinds of tasks that need to be performed in every encounter, such as initiating the interaction, sustaining it, and taking leave when the time is right. These tasks may seem rather obvious and mundane, but they do produce awkward situations in dyads where the participants lack an appropriate repertoire of skills.

A common problem in dyadic communication is defensiveness. When an individual is threatened in some way, by implicit or explicit criticism, by conflict over beliefs, or perhaps by inattentiveness, a common response is to become defensive. Defensiveness is often expressed by judgmental communication as a retaliatory tactic. Defensiveness often breeds more defensiveness, resulting in a vicious circle. A person whose approach to communication is limited to a posture of "attack and defend" is inflexible.

Flexibility means being able to suspend judgment even when your feelings are hurt—to find out what the other person is doing and how he or she is feeling rather than simply fighting back or going away. Flexibility means taking stock of your own thoughts and feelings in an encounter, taking responsibility for them, and being deliberate about what you are going to do about them.

Taking responsibility for our own feelings isn't easy for many of us, because we sometimes tend to moralize with ourselves about our feelings, believing that some of them are bad or improper. Feelings of anger are often seen in this light, for example. When this happens, there's some comfort in believing that something or somebody else made us have these bad feelings. A more realistic view is that feelings are neither good nor bad in and of themselves, and have no moral significance until we act on them. For example, something you said or did may make me feel angry. (See what you *made me* feel?) But I can choose how I will respond to those feelings of anger. If I choose to express them, it makes more sense to do so in a way that implies my own responsibility for them, rather than blaming you—"I feel angry"—as opposed to, "You make me angry." If I don't choose to express them, but rather to explore with you the meanings of whatever it was you said or did that angered me, it's possible that my feeling of anger will quickly subside, enabling me to respond more empathically to you.

How do we acquire a broad repertoire of response options, and an inclination to use them? The same way we acquire other complex behaviors—by learning. No one is born with communication skills. Some of us are better endowed genetically to learn them, and some of us benefit from early learning environments that helped us acquire them fairly easily, but no one came by them automatically.

Learning from role models is probably the best, if not the only, way to become aware of new ways of responding to communication. Watch other people deal with sensitive situations, and when you discover a new way of managing a transaction, try it out yourself when an appropriate occasion presents itself. Be patient with yourself and with your partners. Expect some frustration and false starts, just as you would when trying a new move in a sport or a performing art. Persist, and you'll develop a sense of confidence and control in dyadic communication based on the knowledge that you have choices in how you respond.

Our behavior in dyadic interaction affects our attitudes toward human relationships. It is only when we develop and refine our behavior that we fully appreciate the rich potential of interpersonal communication.

Summary

The dyad is the basic unit of interpersonal communication, and the context of life's major human relationships. For this reason, a transactional perspective is necessary to understand the dynamics of dyadic communication.

A major function of dyadic interaction is the development of self-knowledge through self-disclosure. Acceptance by others of an individual's expressed concepts of self is a major concern in the dyadic setting.

The central skills in dyadic interaction are empathy, the ability to take the role of the other; openness, willingness to disclose and to receive disclosure from the other; and flexibility, the ability to practice a diversity of response options in dealing with others.

Questions

1. How many important dyads are you now involved in?

2. Why is dyadic interaction important in terms of an individual's psychological and sociological well-being?

3. Discuss the concepts of action, interaction, and transaction.

4. What is meant by *empathy, openness,* and *flexibility* in the dyadic context?

5. What are some of the behaviors that communicate these attributes?

Suggested Readings

DANCE, FRANK E. X., and C. LARSON. (1976). *The functions of human communication.* New York: Holt, Rinehart and Winston.

POWELL, J. (1969). *Why am I afraid to tell you who I am?* Chicago: Argus Communications.

ROGERS, C. (1961). *On becoming a person.* Boston: Houghton-Mifflin.

SATIR, V. (1976). *Making contact.* Millbrae, Calif.: Celestial Arts.

STEWART, J. (1982). *Bridges not walls* (3rd ed.). New York: Random House.

VILLARD, K. L., and L. J. WHIPPLE. (1976). *Beginnings in relational communication.* New York: Wiley.

WILMOT, WILLIAM. (1980). *Dyadic communication (2nd ed.). New York: Random House.*

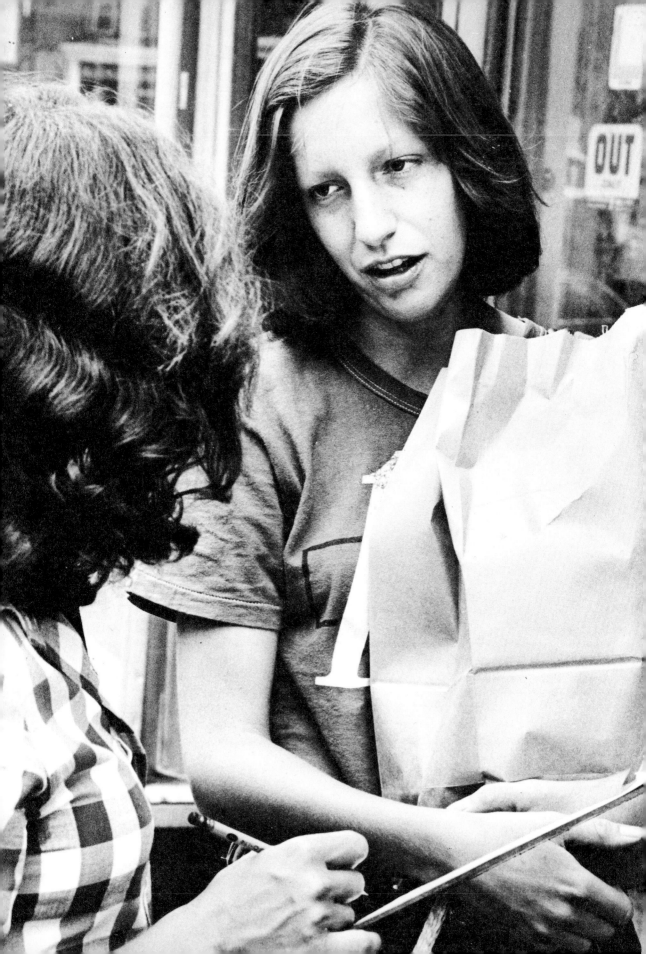

Chapter Twelve

A Special Dyad: The Interview

Preview

The formal dyad commonly known as the interview plays a crucial role in most of our lives. Interview dyads are used to screen applicants for employment and advanced education, to conduct performance appraisals, to obtain information for the news media, to conduct research, to provide counseling and therapy, and to accomplish a host of other important tasks. The quality and quantity of information that can be exchanged through the interview cannot be matched in terms of efficiency by any other format. Interviews and their outcomes are frequently critical, life-changing episodes. More routine interviews may be less potent in terms of consequences, but may serve essential purposes in accomplishing tasks. Your communication training is not complete without an understanding of the interview process and the development of skills necessary for effective participation both as an interviewer and interviewee.

Objectives

To identify various types of interviews and their special requirements

To provide concepts useful in planning and preparation for interview participation, both as interviewer and interviewee

To suggest procedures for follow-up to the interview experience

TWELVE Most everyday dyads develop spontaneously and are fairly casual and unstructured. A special type of dyad, the interview, is usually more formal and structured—both in content and in its setting. Huseman, Lahiff, and Hatfield (1976, 153) give the following definition of an interview: "goal-directed communicative behavior between or among two or more individuals who, through <u>direct</u>, structured interaction in a given environment, exchange information." Though this definition implies that an interview may include more than two people (as, for example, a three-member interview with a grade-school teacher and two parents), most of these communication events are dyadic. In this section, we examine interviews separately because they are common and important events in most of our lives. It is important to remember, however, that the interview is subject to all the variables and problems of dyadic communication discussed in earlier chapters. And the central objective—shared meaning—remains the same.

Types of Interviews

Formal dyads vary significantly in their specific purposes. Listed below are some common types.

The *employment interview,* also termed a *selection* or *hiring* interview, is probably the most common type. Job applicants usually have to go through at least one and sometimes several interviews before they can be hired. The interviewer seeks specific information about the interviewee and also evaluates more subjectively his or her manner and appearance. The applicant in turn attempts to present that information in the best possible light and to learn more about the potential employer and job opening.

The *performance appraisal* interview brings together a supervisor and an organization member to discuss the member's past performance and plans for future performance goals. Like the employment interview, performance appraisal sessions are uneven dyads in terms of relative power; the supervisor clearly is dominant and usually controls the communicative transaction. It can also be a threatening dyad with the supervisor occasionally having to criticize the employee's performance and the latter responding defensively. Some more progressive organizations try to make the performance appraisal session a positive event, with the two participants attempting to focus on *future* performance standards and less on rehashing past problems. In some cases, the interview is a mere formality, a meeting to explain the contents of official written evaluations.

The *news interview* is usually conducted by the press or other public information agencies. Interviewees include anyone with special or news-worthy information. The interview may be essentially unplanned, as in an eyewitness account of a traffic accident; or it may be carefully or-chestrated, as in a television news program like "Meet the Press"; or it may be a staged political press conference. A common problem with the news interview is that limited air time or newspaper space usually forces the interviewer to condense the information gleaned from the interview and use only short and sometimes misleading excerpts in a televised or printed message.

Briefing and debriefing essentially involve giving instructions and get-ting feedback. In a briefing dyad, the person conducting the interview imparts information for a job or assignment; in the subsequent debriefing, that same person asks for information on how the instructions were carried out. The briefing/debriefing interview is a useful supplement to written memos and reports because it permits elaboration and clarifi-cation in a face-to-face dialog.

The *research interview* is designed to collect information through a set of questions structured to support conclusions. Public opinion polls rely heavily on the research interview as do many laboratory studies. Orga-nizations sometimes use this type of dyad to find out about employee attitudes and company problems. A person preparing a research paper or public speech may use this type of interview as he or she would use a library, to obtain authoritative information from experts.

Counseling and correctional interviews are designed to change attitudes or behaviors or to resolve conflicts. Job, marriage, and psychological

counseling sessions are examples. In an organization, interview objectives may range from clarifying information to issuing reprimands to terminating an employee. The real artistry needed to draw out information from reluctant interviewees suggests that interviewers should have special training for their role.

The *grievance interview* involves a complaint by the interviewee about a matter over which the interviewer has some control. For example, the complainant might be an employees' representative who describes poor working conditions to a supervisor. Should that supervisor appear insensitive to the grievance or react defensively about the complaints, this interview may actually increase the antagonism instead of resolving disputes. For legal reasons, many grievance interviews now include taped or written records of what transpired, a strategy that may further stifle open, candid information exchange.

The *exit interview* occurs between a representative of an organization and someone who is voluntarily leaving that organization. Often overlooked, this type of interview can help an organization identify possible problems in its operations because the employee can provide insights about why he or she is leaving—what caused that person to seek work elsewhere. The event can be unproductive, however, if the employee is bitter about leaving and burns some bridges with this last opportunity to unload pent-up hostility against the employer.

The *sales interview* is an attempt to persuade someone to buy a product or service. If possible, the interview should also maintain good public relations for the salesperson and the product. These dyads may involve high-powered sales representatives and corporate executives or simple door-to-door campaigns. Because of the potential personal gain for the initiator of the dyad, the persuader, this type of interview is prone to incomplete or deceptive messages by unscrupulous communicators. Potential buyers may become wary, and the entire interview may be conducted in an atmosphere of suspicion and distrust.

Interview Planning

Because most interviews are less spontaneous than informal dyads, there is usually some time for preparation and planning. In fact, the communication event begins when the interview participants begin to think about the approaching interaction, sometimes long before they see one another and begin to speak.

There are two important questions for both parties. "What is the purpose of the interview?" "What sorts of information must be exchanged?" In a recent job interview, an employer became so engrossed in telling the applicant about the company and locale that he never achieved his main objective—finding out how the interviewee could respond to tough questions. The interview was a pleasant communicative experience, but little relevant information was exchanged.

Once the purpose of the interview is established, all other plans follow from it. The interviewer will often prepare questions that will elicit information in support of the interview objectives. This plan may be a formal questionnaire or interview schedule (some organizations use a standard question form or guide for all hiring interviews), or it may simply be a list of key topics. The interviewee may try to predict some of the questions likely to be asked, the topics on which he or she should be informed. The interviewer should also devise some unobtrusive yet accurate method of recording information.

Sometimes we are not careful enough in selecting the people to participate in interviews. For example, an executive who has no training or experience in interviewing may fall into the role quite by accident and may know little of the company's expectations for new employees. He may select the wrong people to interview and may be inefficient in the actual dyadic transaction. He may get the wrong information and not know how to evaluate it properly. In press interviews, organizations may select a person to answer questions who has a good grasp of the information but cannot communicate it well. Progressive organizations recognize the importance of interviews and develop specific teams to handle employment interviews, job counseling, research, briefings, and press conferences.

Environmental factors, like personal appearance, setting, and time limits, should also be considered ahead of time. Why is this office or conference room appropriate for the event? Why not a coffee shop or lounge? Why thirty minutes? Why not five minutes or an hour? What outside events, like a phone call or a knock on the door, might interrupt progress? How should the participants be dressed? Why? In most dyads, the participants have some control over the environment; in the planned interview, that environmental manipulation may be the key to productive communication.

During the Interview

In most interviews, the *opening phase* is crucial because it sets the tone for the rest of the event. If the dyad involves a distinct power or status differential (as in employment, grievance, appraisal, and counseling interviews), it may be necessary for the interviewer to set the interviewee at ease so that subsequent interaction may be more open and relaxed. A few moments spent in casual "break the ice" conversation may be a time-saving investment compared to the "get right down to business" style that stifles personal contact and the free flow of information. Also important is a clear understanding by both parties about the specific objectives of the interview. What does each expect to accomplish? Ulterior motives, innuendos, and subtle strategies usually breed suspicion and restricted exchange of information. Confused objectives also waste time and leave the dyad partners groping for appropriate messages.

The *middle phase* is the heart of the interview, the time in which both parties attempt to achieve their goals. The productivity of this phase depends on two elements: structure and questioning techniques. *Structure* means the organization plan for approaching various topics. For example, in a structured or directive job interview, the questioner might ask first about the applicant's credentials, then go on to more general discussion of ideas and goals, and finally move to answering questions about the company. Interviews can also be fairly unstructured or non-directive in that the interviewer lets the discussion proceed spontaneously. Counseling and correctional interviews often take this form, though both participants should nevertheless remain aware of process as well as information content, regularly reminding themselves of where they are in terms of achieving their objectives.

Questioning techniques refer to the types of questions selected to elicit particular kinds of information. Brooks (1974) suggests five basic types of questions, which are paraphrased below:

1. *Open questions* ask for an answer of more than a few words and give the respondent some leeway as to the kinds of information to be included.
   "What do you think about this problem?"
   "What would you hope to accomplish in this job?"
   "Why do you feel that way?"

2. *Closed questions* demands a very specific response, usually requiring only a few words, like yes or no or specific data.
   "Do you have a college degree?"
   "Where have you previously worked and for how long?"
   "Are you Republican, Democrat, or independent?"

3. *Mirror questions* simply rephrase a previous answer so as to get more extensive information. It says, in effect, "Tell me more."
   "You say you think you can help this company?"
   "You have some experience, then, in this kind of work?"

4. *Probing questions,* like mirror questions, attempt to elicit more information from the respondent or the reasons behind particular opinions and feelings. Probes are the short "why's" and "how's" or utterances like "uh-huh" or "oh?" that encourage the respondent to keep talking. Silence can also be a probe as the interviewee feels that he or she should keep talking rather than let the conversation stop.

5. *Leading questions* tend to direct the respondent toward a specific answer the interviewer is looking for. It is asked in such a way as to suggest an expected or appropriate response.
   "You aren't advocating government intervention, are you?"
   "Would you say you have significant experience for this job?"
   "What do you think of this stupid policy?"

The style of questioning behavior can affect the interview outcome. Open, mirror, and probing questions will mean a much longer interview, one that is usually less structured, because the respondent has much greater freedom to elaborate and move in new directions. Closed questions are efficient for obtaining specific factual data in a short time (as in some job interviews or public opinion surveys) but can also seriously restrict the amount and depth of information. The limited information from closed questions can be deceptive. Leading questions should be avoided. They are prohibited in the courtroom, rejected by careful researchers, and run counter to the real goals of the interview—to obtain complete, unbiased information.

The *concluding phase* brings the interview to a close. A simple summary is a good technique. In hiring, counseling, or grievance interviews, the interviewer should specifically indicate what will happen next, such as, "We will call you within a week to let you know our decision" or, "I'll take your complaint to the board and get back to you in writing." As in any conversation, many interviews may conclude with some casual, nonsubstantive remarks to reaffirm the interpersonal relationship that has developed during the interview.

Postinterview Considerations

The communication event has not necessarily ended when the dyad breaks up physically, because the participants may still be responding to what took place. It is essential to have some reliable way of organizing, evaluating, and using the interview information. What do we know now that we didn't know before? Opinions? Problems? Factual data? Personal traits? Comments like, "She seemed poised and intelligent" or, "He's a real nice guy," may be relevant but unless they are accompanied by more specific information, the postinterview analysis may show that the dyad was a waste of time. If interview information is to be used to make decisions, select an employee, implement a policy, or form a conclusion, it should be supplemented and compared with other kinds of information, like written materials, direct observations, and personal experience.

General Suggestions

Interviews vary widely; even job interviews differ greatly from one organization to the next. However, we can generalize about some problems to avoid.

In many interviews, the questioner *talks more* than the respondent. The questions are long and involved, and he or she makes elaborate replies to the interviewee's responses. Unless the interview is clearly intended as an open dialog for sharing information, the interviewer should ask brief questions and avoid lengthy comment.

In most cases, avoid the unstructured interview. According to Mayfield (1964) and Carlson *et al* (1971), studies generally show that the more structured (planned) interview is more likely to produce the information sought and to ensure reliable interpretation of that information. Use preinterview time to develop a careful plan. Try to strike a balance, however, so that this procedure does not result in a rigid and unadaptable interview.

Avoid prejudging another person or information. The purpose of the interview should be to get more accurate information than other communication formats can provide. Prejudgment causes us to perceive selectively only that information that confirms our judgment. Though some initial impressions are inevitable, we need to get the information *first* and then evaluate it.

Avoid the communication barriers of rank, status, and power. We communicate more freely and accurately with peers than we do with superiors because our equals do not pose a threat. If the interviewee fears punishment for inappropriate messages, the interview may become a series of less-than-authentic messages designed to please a superior. The individual in the superior role therefore should try to foster the relaxed climate that will encourage candor. He or she should be cordial and cooperative, recognizing that in addition to playing particular roles in the interview setting, the participants are also *people* with many similarities, people who can share not only information but an interpersonal relationship as well.

Checklist for the Job Applicant

Perhaps your most immediate concern with interviewing is its role in helping you to land a good job. The following checklist utilizes some of the material in previous sections. It suggests some strategies if you are seeking employment.

Obtain Information about the Interview Process   How long will it last? What types of questions are usually asked? Can you find out the name and some details about the interviewer? Does the interview come early or late in the hiring process? If early, the interview may determine whether your application will be taken seriously. If it occurs later in the hiring process, perhaps you have already gotten favorable evaluation from your written credentials and, as one of the final candidates, you will be interviewed in depth.

Anticipate Possible Questions   Questions on previous work experience, reasons for interest in this job, and types of skills that could be brought to this job are quite common. The interviewee should perhaps be ready to answer the question, "Why should we hire you rather than someone else?" Bone up on possible substantive information that you

should know to do the job well—materials learned in a training program, a college class, or previous work experience, for example.

Develop Verbal and Nonverbal Communication Strategies

Should speech delivery be conversational or fairly formal? What will be considered appropriate dress for the occasion? Will interaction be highly structured (speak only when asked a question) or spontaneous (interact casually and openly as in a friendly conversation)? For some jobs, like receptionist, teacher, public information officer, counselor, bank teller, and others that involve frequent interaction with the public, you may be expected to exhibit the same kind of interpersonal style and competence *in the interview* that will be expected in the job itself. Thus, communication style is crucial and should be given prior thought.

Listen Carefully to Questions   Do not assume that the interviewer is a skilled communicator. The questions may be muddled and awkward. Do not answer any question that you do not fully understand. Follow a confusing question with a specific question of your own: "Are you asking me to describe what I would do if . . .?"

Answer Questions Fully but Succinctly   Though a question like, "Have you had previous experience?" could technically be answered with a simple yes, the interviewer obviously expects you to elaborate. Avoid long-winded, rambling replies, however, and keep the initial question always in mind. Interviewers become impatient with irrelevant responses.

Always Plan Three or Four Questions about the Job Opening   The interviewer may say, "Do you have anything you'd like to know about us?" The quality of your questions indicates to the interviewer the kind of employee you will become and may help determine whether you get the job. For example, do not ask, "How soon could I expect paid vacations?" or, "Are there any fringe benefits not listed in the job announcement?" Such questions may be important to you, but they also imply that you have only shallow interest in the job itself. Furthermore, you can obtain such information through other sources before or after the interview. Instead, prepare more substantive questions that indicate your interest in the actual work to be performed. "Do you provide opportunities for me to learn new types of jobs or skills?" "Do employees have any input, any participation, in determining how to get the job done?" "What will be the company's major goals and problems in the next few years?"

Be Frank about Your Strengths and Assets   Do not brag, of course, but do not let modesty prohibit you from describing fully your accomplishments and abilities. Volunteer information about important personal assets if the interviewer neglects to ask.

Have Written Support Information Available during the Interview
A neat file folder with documents like transcripts, letters of reference, and

resumes is a useful device. Never force the employer to write or phone for such documents. Comments like, "You can contact my college registrar for a transcript" or, "If you call Mrs. Thompson, she will vouch for me", will limit your chances, especially if another applicant has such information in hand. Written support materials communicate nonverbally as well as verbally. They say, "I am a thorough person who believes in careful preparation."

Clarify What Comes Next in the Application Process   Do not lose a good job because you were not aware of the company's hiring process—for example, that a final application form had to be completed before you could be hired or that letters of reference had to be received by a particular date.

Summary

The interview is a dyad of special importance, characterized by special purposes and a more formal, structured format than routine dyadic encounters. Interview types are varied, but all can profit from careful planning, from sensitive and goal-directed communication during the interview experience, and from objective postinterview analysis. The successful interview provides information exchange in a way that other communication media and formats cannot, and the development of interview skills should be an important goal for you as students of speech communication.

Questions

1. What are some verbal and nonverbal behaviors that would probably be evaluated favorably in a job interview?

2. What are some verbal and nonverbal characteristics that might prompt a negative evaluation?

3. To what extent are these factors situational—that is, dependent on the particular type of job, type of interviewer, and surrounding environment?

4. What are some of the different types of interviews? How are they similar and how do they differ in terms of communication?

5. To what extent should an interviewee "take charge" of the situation?

Suggested Readings

BOLLES, R. N. (1982). *What color is your parachute? A practical manual for job-hunters and career changers* (8th ed.). Berkeley, Calif.: Ten Speed Press.

STEWART, C. J., and W. B. CASH, JR. (1982). *Interviewing: Principles and Practices* (3rd ed.). Dubuque, Iowa: Wm. C. Brown.

Chapter Thirteen

Small Group Communication

Preview

Most of us communicate regularly in small group settings. In these groups, we try to solve problems, maintain and nourish friendships, and learn more about the world and ourselves—seeking a delicate balance between individual and group goals. Our individual personalities cause us to enact certain roles in our group interactions. If interpersonal communication in these groups is effective, our participation is highly rewarding, and the group is productive. If communication is ineffective, productivity suffers along with personal satisfaction and growth.

This chapter introduces some of the characteristics of small groups that influence and are influenced by communication. Because the small group is such a prevalent and important communication situation, an understanding of these characteristics is essential for you as a communication student.

Objectives

To identify characteristics of small group communication dynamics

To discuss role behavior in groups

To discuss potential conflicts between individual and group goals

THIRTEEN   The logical extension of one-to-one interaction is communication in the small group. A *group* may be broadly defined as a discrete or specific collection of people who interact with a common interest in making decisions, completing tasks, achieving objectives, and receiving rewards. A *small group* is one in which direct interpersonal relationships among all group members are possible. Rice (1965, 11–12) suggests that a small group may also be called "primary" or "face-to-face." While the size of small groups will vary across cultures, Rice points out that "the relationships that have to be sustained in groups with more than 12 to 15 members become so complex that the group tends to split into subgroups." He concludes that, in general, a *small* group becomes *large* at the point where "face-to-face relationships are no longer possible."

You may wonder why a separate chapter on small group communication is necessary if one understands the basic communication process and the components of and barriers to effective interpersonal communication, and if one develops skills in face-to-face interaction. If a small group is simply people talking to people, why not merely apply the same kinds of communication principles we use for analyzing everyday casual interaction? It is true that some people who have developed personal communication skills are more effective than others in small groups. However, the small group situation not only *modifies* the ways in which we interact with others but also adds *new components* that will affect the quality of communication. We examine some of these new dimensions in this chapter.

An even more important reason for studying small group communication is that our society is becoming increasingly oriented to small groups. Most of us engage in regular and extensive participation in groups in our homes, occupations, and social lives. The family is a type of small group. So is the subcommittee in a governmental organization, a management team in a business, a bridge club, a basketball team, a therapy group, a bull session, or an airline flight crew. We are members of literally hundreds of small groups throughout our lives, and the rewards we receive depend largely on the quality of interaction within those groups. When a family breaks up, a business goes bankrupt, an athletic team loses, or a friendly meeting degenerates to name calling and fighting, we become aware of how *counter*productive small group experiences can be. When small groups succeed, our participation can be enormously satisfying. When viewed in this light, small group interaction takes on a new importance—

one that justifies not only discussion in a separate chapter, as here, but entire courses and books that focus solely on small group communication.

General Characteristics of Small Groups

Several principles are common to all small group situations, characteristics that you should expect to encounter each time you engage in group communication.

Groups Have Both "Task" and "Maintenance" Functions

Two interwoven yet identifiable events occur in small group encounters. Group members exchange information designed to *move them toward a work or task objective;* and they interact in ways intended to *preserve the group as a social unit.* The former is the *task* function, and the latter, the *maintenance* function. Both functions must be fulfilled if the group is to survive and be productive. The task dimension is also termed the *content* side of a group, whereas *process* often denotes the maintenance side of the group's efforts.

The perceptive observer of small group communication can identify messages intended for either function. Progress on the task is furthered by comments like:

"I think we've identified the problem; now let's discuss some possible solutions."

"The caterer will charge us $6.50 per serving."

"Does anyone have more information on that point?"

"I think we should summarize what we've decided so far."

"That proposal just won't work, and I'll tell you why."

These remarks obviously relate to the group's substantive objectives of "getting the job done."

In contrast, maintenance messages are illustrated by the following:

"John, you haven't said anything yet. Would you like to comment?"

"It's natural for us to disagree, but I don't think we should resort to name calling."

"Hey, that was some party we had last night, wasn't it?"

"Before we begin, why don't we each introduce ourselves."

"We seem to be getting tired. Let's take a ten-minute break."

Maintenance communication thus suggests awareness of group members as unique people and of the quality of their interpersonal transactions.

You cannot ignore either dimension, and all group members should try to remain perceptive of both. People differ, however, in their own orientation. In most groups, you are likely to find some members who seem preoccupied with content—task achievement and decision-making efficiency. The more process-oriented members seem especially aware of how the group is developing as a social unit and how each person feels at any particular moment. We believe that having both types in the group is useful and that the ideal is to have people who are continuously aware of both the task and the maintenance functions.

Group Members Are Linked by Verbal and Nonverbal Communication

The verbal and nonverbal group transactions obviously may be overlooked as group members become actively involved in the content level of decision making. Yet the quality of these linkages and transactions does much to determine group productivity. Why might a group fail to meet its goals? It may be due to insufficient information, time constraints, highly complex and complicated issues, lack of participant expertise, personal animosities, and many other factors. Continually, however, we observe groups whose inherently achievable goals are never attained because the communication process is counterproductive.

Typical problems include misperception and misinterpretation, the inability to achieve shared meanings. Group members may never truly comprehend the viewpoints of others, particularly on complex and controversial topics. Instead, they may be too concerned with advocating their own ideas to really listen to and seek clarification from those with opposing positions. Nonverbally, they may become antagonized by frowns, grimaces, shaking of the head, defiant body posture, angry vocal inflections, sighs of impatience or boredom, or any other indicators of hostility or frustration. In contrast, comments or nods of agreement, smiles, enthusiasm, friendly banter, expressions of satisfaction or consensus, accurate restatement of the ideas of others, and other positive indicators of group harmony suggest a quite different communication climate. We are *not* claiming that interpersonal conflict in groups is necessarily bad; we are, rather, establishing the centrality of communication variables in determining the interaction climate and in achieving objectives.

The communication relationships in small groups remain dyadic. All the variables that operate in one-to-one communication are relevant to small groups. Every group member hears and sees verbal and nonverbal responses of every other group member, and each person takes meaning from those behaviors. For example, think of a small group in which you have recently participated. Notice how different your relationship and interaction was with each person. You may have given much importance to the comments of one person because his or her ideas made sense to you, whereas you virtually may have ignored the messages of another who appeared uninformed or foolish. You probably felt rapport with some and alienated from others. Your comments, though heard by all, may have been directed at a single participant. Thus, though you were involved in a group process, your communicative relationships were dyadic. If there were, say, six people in the group, you were simultaneously involved in five dyads.

As groups increase in size, the number of dyadic communication channels increases dramatically. To illustrate, look what happens when a three-person group acquires a fourth member (Figure 13–1).

Keep this in mind when making decisions about group membership. The presence or absence of even one group member exerts a profound influence on the potential communication dynamics of groups.

In general, the task and maintenance functions discussed earlier depend heavily on sensitive and skillful interpersonal communication. And the personal rewards to group members come not simply from achieving objectives but from sharing in a pleasant communication event.

Group Communication Often Is Controlled by Networks

Sometimes small group communication is controlled or channeled by explicit or implicit *networks* of communication channels or paths that group members utilize (Figure 13–2). For example, in some groups all comments are directed at the leader, who controls the interaction and calls on specific people to speak (Figure 13–2a). In other groups, the networks are more extensive, and a member may talk to any other member or to the group as a whole (Figure 13–2b). One dyad may dominate other parts of the communication network, as when an ar-

FIGURE 13–1

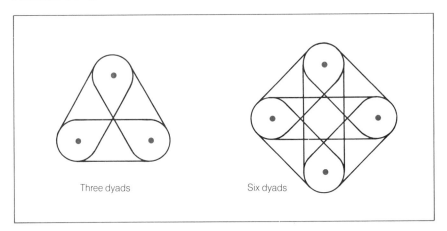

Three dyads   Six dyads

gument breaks out between two people and the other members silently observe the interchange as if they were at a tennis match (Figure 13–2c). Finally, the network sometimes excludes a particular member from active verbal (but not nonverbal) participation. That person becomes virtually isolated from the rest of the group; he or she does not speak and has no comments directed toward him or her (Figure 13–2d).

Probably the most divisive network is that resulting from the appearance of subgroups, whose members interact as much within that subgroup as with the total group. An example might be a group of seven people, five of them interacting on the task and two carrying on a side-conversation dyad (Figure 13–2e). This dyad may return periodically to the general discussion, but too often it remains passive and outside the mainstream of group communication.

Small Groups Develop a Unique Culture

As a group gradually acquires a history, collective experiences prompt the emergence of general group characteristics. These elements can be clearly identified, though they often can remain unstated.

One element of group culture is called *norms,* a set of standards or guidelines for acceptable kinds of behavior in a given situation. Every culture has its norms, and one of the objectives of educating children is to reveal these appropriate or *normative* behaviors. Similarly, group members establish norms and gradually educate each other according to their description, significance, and penalties for violation. The standards may be explicit, and some group leaders prefer a kind of *contracting* early in group development. "Let's decide on a smoking policy." "Everyone should be here on time, and we will end on time." "One person should talk at a time; I'll call on people who raise their hands." Other norms are merely implied: "We don't use profanity because several people find it offensive." "We call everyone by first name." "If someone resorts to name calling or other personal attacks, the group will side with the victim and reprimand the guilty party." In most groups, a member could, if asked, write down a fairly elaborate set of implicit group norms. Because such standards are rarely codified, however, new members in an ongoing group must spend some time trying to discern the acceptable behaviors.

Another element of group culture is *cohesiveness:* "a process in which group members are attracted to each other, motivated to remain together, and share a common perspective of the group's activity" (Applbaum et al, 1974, 161). Cohesiveness varies within and between groups. In the early development of most groups it is minimal, evolving slowly in some associations (a business conference of people with different backgrounds and interests, for example) and very rapidly in others (such as a dormitory social committee). Obviously, interpersonal communication is a key factor in building cohesion, and groups that are preoccupied with task functions may not interact enough on the maintenance level to create a common interest in meeting and sharing. Although intragroup conflict is inevitable and sometimes productive, if unresolved it may destroy whatever cohesiveness previous group interaction may have built.

Still another element of group culture is the *belief-attitude-value structure.* Beliefs are judgments about what is real or unreal, true or false. Values are beliefs about good and bad, desirable and undesirable, right and wrong, beautiful and ugly. Attitudes are systems of beliefs that apply to one central object of judgment or topic. These systems or clusters of beliefs invariably include value-type beliefs, and thus represent not just what we believe to be the facts about some topic, but our likes and dislikes about the topic as well. Together they make up assumptions or givens that guide future decisions. If a work group is to establish a new policy, for example, it must first factually identify the problem and describe the environment in which any new policy must function. The group must develop beliefs about what is real in that environment. Group members also express personal feelings about that real world and about proposed policies (attitudes), and they assess behaviors, programs, ideas,

FIGURE 13-2

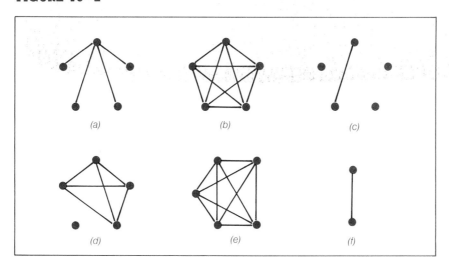

people, and objects in terms of their relative goodness, or value.

Although group agreement on a belief-attitude-value structure may not be perfect, some general consensus is necessary, for this structure becomes the basis for eventual decision making. The group culture is polarized, for example, if half the group *likes economic growth,* believes it is inevitable, and thinks it is good, while the other half *fears growth,* thinks it hurts people, and claims that it is possible to curtail it. How productive would the group process be under these polarized conditions? If you think of groups in which you regularly participate, you may begin to identify those basic assumptions that you share with all the other members.

Shared experiences make up another important group culture dimension. In-jokes, interpersonal conflicts, crisis situations, shared information, group activities, and many other elements of an "insider" perspective become part of each member's understanding of the group experience. Outsiders can only know of these events second hand, but for insiders, the feeling of "we've been through this together" is a potent unifying force. Group culture is strengthened whenever members pause to recall and rehash these events, almost as larger national or ethnic cultures develop a folklore that is regularly retold or reenacted.

Status and power frequently develop in group culture, especially if the group is continuing. *Status* is the importance of a person in the group as ascribed by other members. Some people obviously develop status as the culture develops, and the group may use overt or subtle devices to indicate that position—special titles, rights and privileges, central seating and larger chair, expanded responsibilities and authority.

Power, which is akin to influence, is the ability of a person to reward or punish others as a means of manipulating their behavior. Small group literature is filled with research that firmly establishes the importance of power in group culture (Jacobson, 1972). How might one acquire and use power in small groups? What rewards could be granted or penalties inflicted? For example, someone who has the resources (knowledge,

money, meeting facilities, equipment) necessary to sustain the group, threatens to withdraw those resources if others do not conform to his wishes. Perhaps the power source can promote the cooperative group member and fire the hostile one. Or perhaps someone is an especially adept and witty debater who can intimidate or embarrass anyone who disagrees with her. For whatever reason, power and status relationships inevitably develop, and they clearly affect the ways in which people communicate in the small group.

Overall, the term *identity* best explains the concept of group culture. We seek to identify with others on common ground. Members learn to answer the question, "Who are we?" in similar ways. "We are a team of professionals tackling a tough problem." "We are a competent staff of coaches trying to develop a winning team." "We are a group of concerned citizens trying to raise money for our candidate." Without group culture, there can be no group identity, only individual identities. Perhaps the cultural element is the key to distinguishing whether a particular event is simply "several individuals talking" or truly "small group communication."

A Group Is Characterized by Role Behavior

Roles of group members typically become a significant factor in group communication and productivity. However, this factor could just as easily be considered an important subcategory of group culture that we discussed in the previous section.

Before defining roles, we first introduce the premise that *any group participant has a potentially large and varied behavioral repertory.* That is, he or she has a *choice* of several possible actions and messages at any moment. Admittedly, some of these choices are bad ones, like walking angrily out of the room, jumping up and down, or pouring coffee on another member. But behavioral options, some appropriate and some not, nevertheless exist for every group member.

We are especially interested in *communication behavior repertories.* In developing a method for studying small group communication, Robert Bales (1950) outlined several behavioral categories that can be identified. The following summary of those message behaviors suggests a fairly complete small group communication repertory. The first six responses involve what Bales calls the "social emotional area," roughly similar to what we term the *maintenance* function:

Solidarity   Helping, rewarding, showing appreciation, raising the status of another

Antagonism   Punishing, criticizing, attacking, deflating the status of another

Tension release   Laughing, joking, showing satisfaction

Showing tension   Asking for help, expressing worry, withdrawing

Agreement   Showing acceptance, understanding, concurrence, willingness to comply

Disagreement   Rejecting, opposing, refuting

The next six responses in Bales' repertory deal more directly with the *task* function:

Giving suggestions   Directing, offering options, proposing, recommending

Seeking suggestions   Collecting information, seeking solutions or options

Giving opinions   Evaluating, analyzing, judging, expressing feelings

Seeking opinions   Collecting ideas and points of view, seeking options, assessing feelings of others

Giving orientation   Repeating, clarifying, explaining, informing, instructing

Seeking orientation   Seeking repetition, background information, instruction, clarification

It is not difficult to think of messages that illustrate each of these categories. For example, "What do you think we should do, John?" asks for an opinion. "I think we can be proud of what we accomplished today" shows solidarity. "So far, we have come up with three proposals" provides orientation. The communication choices that group members make are the most perceivable indicator of the role they are playing. *Roles* may be considered similar to parts played by actors in a drama. They are made up of a set of expected or predictable behaviors that "fit" with the general category that defines or describes the person. We can easily think of a variety of behaviors that seem typical of people whom we have seen in such roles as *tough guy, old maid, minister, villain, fashion model,* or *intellectual.*

We play many roles in our lifetime, and sometimes several each day. Because a small group quickly develops a culture, it shares with larger social groups the common trait of specific and complex role development. Group members not only identify others by their unique features—name, age, background, physical characteristics—but also by more general categories like *quiet, assertive, obnoxious, phony, intelligent, unhappy.* When this process occurs, role development has begun.

Importantly, role development is a process that will occur above and beyond prescribed or planned group behaviors—that is, it occurs naturally. In one of the best textbooks on small group communication, Bormann (1969) describes some of the characteristics of *leaderless group discussions* (LGDs) that were observed in studies at the University of Minnesota. Two important conclusions were: (1) members began specializing and acquiring status and esteem as the group got going; and (2) their role development did not take place *independently* but rather in the context of joint group consensus. Role emergence and specialization occur when key task or maintenance functions are identified (like gathering information, resolving differences, keeping the group on the track). Then, various group members are given either positive reinforcement or negative feedback as they attempt to fulfill these group functions. Role emergence is thus a trial-and-error process, often a very subtle rendering of group consensus about who should perform various tasks. An example might be two people who purport to be authorities on the discussion topic. One person is authentic; his or her comments gain immediate group approval and appreciation with reactions that say, in effect, "Tell us more." The other is a phony. His or her information does not jibe with general group knowledge; it is either disputed or ignored. Soon the group expert has emerged, and the impostor has withdrawn to a different role through group consensus.

Role development and definition occur primarily through communication. By the selection of different mixes of the message repertory discussed earlier, we gradually take our places in the group culture. The most common role in groups is *leader.* We discuss the term in Chapter Fourteen in more depth; for now, notice how we tend to ascribe traits like confidence, poise, assertiveness, knowledgeability, status, and power to that role category. We also can predict certain behaviors from people in such official roles as *recording secretary, parliamentarian, treasurer,* and *social chairman.*

Many small group roles are unofficial but still very real to group members. The effective group participant learns to watch and listen for behaviors that signal these roles. The following are only a few of the many that have been suggested in small group literature.

The Authority   People in authority roles enjoy dominating the content level of group decision making. They are opinionated, purport to be well informed, and become judgmental of others. They participate frequently and have something to say on nearly every issue. They may be dogmatic and intolerant of opposing viewpoints.

The Facilitator   Facilitators are process oriented. They are especially aware of the feelings of others and are adept at reading both nonverbal and verbal feedback of group members. Facilitators attempt to provide full participation, ensure fairness, protect group members who are attacked, perceive group tension or fatigue, and develop strategies for enhancing interpersonal relationships.

The Compromiser/Harmonizer   Closely related to facilitators, compromisers try to resolve conflict at both the substantive and interpersonal levels. They do not feel comfortable with conflicting points of view or with rigid positions; hence, they urge a give-and-take posture as a group norm and regularly suggest points of agreement and possible compromise positions.

The Efficiency Expert   Efficiency experts are task oriented. They want to ensure that the group achieves its stated objectives with acceptable results and in the allotted time. They remind the group of the topic under discussion, make lists of group conclusions or decisions, summarize key points, and keep an eye on the clock.

The Antagonist   Often in the aggressor's role, antagonists are typically judgmental, combative, and assertive. They enjoy the lively verbal game of attack and defense and view differences of opinion among participants as a win-lose situation, often turning a cooperative problem-solving venture into a competitive game. A potentially valuable antagonist role is that of the *devil's advocate,* who purposely argues a contrary position simply to assure that the group has considered all alternatives and can defend the eventual decision.

The Comedian   Some group participants view wit and humor as a fundamental part of group experience. They tell jokes, laugh, make what they believe to be humorous side comments, and generally seek an atmosphere of convivial mirth. Comedians want the group experience to be a fun time. Some people are singularly unfunny and become obnoxious, but occasional humorous communication can be a welcome release from the tension of difficult group situations.

The Socializer   Somewhat similar to comedians are the socializers, who view the group experience primarily as a chance to share casual and relaxing conversation with friends. Their messages usually express interest in what others have been doing as well as relate personal experiences and sundry gossip. Socializers are outgoing and expressive and are especially interested in perpetuating the group as a social unit, even after the group task has been achieved.

The Digressor   Digressors enjoy expounding and elaborating. They may try to tie marginally related personal experiences to discussion topics. Their messages are usually lengthy and poorly organized. Most important, their comments may evoke responses by other group members, pulling the discussion even farther off the track.

The Intellectual/Philosopher   Some group participants have a penchant for the abstract or theoretical. Their comments on relatively matter-of-fact topics often show deeper analysis or a search for meanings. They tend to generalize and try to discover new, more profound ways of phrasing group conclusions.

The Grouch   Occasionally groups are shackled with malcontents who, like the angry Muppet in the garbage can on television's *Sesame Street,* do not attempt to hide their foul mood. Their negative attitudes, their "nay-saying" responses to group decisions, often dishearten other participants and deflate group morale. Their messages are usually judgmental, clearly implying the errors of others. The skeptical, cynical verbal communication of grouches is usually accompanied by ample nonverbal cues like frowns, sighs, vocal inflections, and negative body postures.

The Quiet One   The larger the group, the greater the likelihood that some members will show minimal verbal participation. More verbal members may find these more silent members quite threatening. Although reticent members may be genuinely interested, we may interpret their silence to mean shyness, arrogance, hostility, stupidity, or disinterest. Verbal members, even if their opinions conflict with our own, still may seem more trustworthy and less suspicious, because we know where they stand. But the quiet ones may remain a mystery. They do not seem to contribute to either the task or maintenance function. Realistically, however, we all know of groups in which more constructive outcomes might have occurred had more members more frequently chosen to play the silent role!

Role development may be elaborate, varied, and subtle. The roles we have discussed are obviously the extremes, and they do not necessarily develop with such clear and uniform definition. Group members may play composites of several roles, as with a socializer who also facilitates or the digressor who philosophizes, and two or more group members may play similar roles, as with the troublesome situation of two or three task achievers having to interact with four or five socializers.

What additions to our list might be appropriate? What modifications? Which roles, if fully developed, are in inherent conflict with other roles?

Are most of these roles constructive or destructive? What situations might modify their positive or negative influence? *What communication behaviors (messages) tend to indicate particular roles?* These are just a few questions that group participants should regularly attempt to answer.

Small Groups Are Dynamic

A fairly obvious point, clearly suggested by the discussion of culture and role development, is that groups change over time. Still, we are tempted to look at familiar faces in a familiar setting with familiar tasks and procedures and assume that it is the same group we left after the previous meeting. Some cultural constants remain, of course, but the group has been modified by many intervening events. We often experience an exhilarating, meaningful group session and seek to renew that experience. Eagerly anticipating the same feelings, we may be disappointed when the next meeting fails to fulfill our expectations.

What has happened? Why can't we return to the exciting group we remember? For one thing, group membership may change. With a new member, we may be more guarded and reserved in our interaction. Or an old member may be absent, leaving us without a strong leader or tension reliever or information source. The unique blend of roles that prompted an exciting group chemistry no longer exists.

Second, the group may be affected by intragroup experiences. Perhaps the meeting begins with a comment that starts a bitter argument or insults a group member. Perhaps a usually optimistic, cheerful member expresses anger or discouragement. The communication events within the group change its basic character.

Third, extragroup experiences may affect certain members. A personal crisis or tragedy, an outside argument with another group member, or an encounter with new information that the old group did not have ("I talked to the boss, and he said he would never approve our proposal") are some of the extragroup experiences that can change the behavior of individual members. In other words, people are different because of what they have experienced since they last met.

Finally, the larger environment may change significantly. We often hear of business or government committees that try to solve problems that no longer exist. Similarly, the dynamic environment may render irrelevant the task of a small group, or environmental changes may add urgency to group deliberations or modify the kinds of things the group must do. In turn, the necessary changes in tasks, roles, and procedures will significantly alter group process.

Members of small groups are often like the college student who goes home for spring vacation and seeks out her old high school friends; because she and her companions have changed so much, however, she finds the interaction depressingly shallow and unrewarding. The perceptive group member will be alert to the internal and external factors that change group experience and will notice the verbal and nonverbal behaviors that signal basic changes in group culture. The naive group member, on the other hand, will continually search for "the way it used to be," unable to adapt to the inevitable shifts in group dynamics.

Participants Seek Both Individual and Group Goals

It would be nice to think of a small group effort in which each person contributed in a totally cooperative and selfless manner, cheerfully sacrificing personal interests and comfort for the good of the group. Athletic coaches, business executives, club presidents, and the like frequently use the team approach as an appeal to people to act unselfishly.

We believe it is naive to think that such a perfect condition is possible in group processes. The fact is that whenever we participate in a group, we bring personal objectives with us. These goals may be quite subtle or fairly obvious; they may enhance or compete with group interests and objectives. But personal goals, in some form, will always be a factor in the group experience.

What are some of those personal goals? The list below suggests only a few:

"I want to be confirmed as a human being; I want people to like me and recognize me."

"I want people to think that I'm intelligent."

"I want to convince others of my point of view; I want them to follow my advice."

"I want to avoid criticism or ridicule."

"I want to make new friends; I want to profit socially from the group experience."

"I want to acquire new information or skills that will help me in my everyday life."

"I want the group to be a sounding board for my ideas; I want reliable feedback."

"I want to tell others what I know and what I've done; I want to impress them."

"I want to get revenge against someone who criticized my ideas and embarrassed me."

"I want to criticize someone or something outside the group; I want to let off steam with the group members as my captive audience."

"I want to make this group experience as brief and painless as possible; I want to get it over with."

"I want to avoid interpersonal conflict and maintain harmony among participants at all times."

"I want the group to do what I say."

"I want to tell the group about my problems and have them give me comfort, support, and solace."

Obviously, these personal goals may impede group progress. Suppose the group goal is to obtain as much information on a public issue as is possible in a short time. The person who wants to talk about his or her problems, dominate the discussion, attack others, make new friends, or philosophize may detract from this fairly explicit goal. Sometimes a frank discussion of personal objectives—a kind of self-disclosure—can make all participants more aware of the kinds of behaviors that may destroy or disrupt a group's progress. Self-analysis of personal interests and motives by each member can also focus on potential conflicts between individual and group goals.

Group Members Are Interdependent with Each Other and with the Larger Environment

Recent interest in environmental ecology has heightened our awareness of the interrelationships of all living things. Organisms behave in relation to other organisms, not independently. We are all *interdependent*. The behavior of one affects, and is affected by, the behavior of another.

Interdependence is enormously important in relation to small group interaction. Fisher (1974) focuses heavily on this concept, suggesting that an individual behavior or *act* is not the key to understanding group behavior; rather, the crucial component is the contiguous or sequential behaviors of two or more people—the *interact*. A comment by A is the act, but B's response to A forms the interact. Then A's response to B completes the *double interact*. The focus on interaction forces us to explore the process of interaction between people and between messages rather than to concentrate simply on a single group member or message in isolation. For example, if A makes a comment that appears to be hostile and inflammatory, the statement becomes counterproductive only if B responds in equally negative ways. If B chooses to respond less antagonistically and more positively, however, the initial comment might not cause serious problems. Hence, the consequence of the single message, whether friendly or hostile, depends on subsequent messages—the interactions that result.

Another implication of interdependence is personal responsibility. Whether we decide to say something or to say nothing affects in part the eventual interaction. Because we are presumably responsible for personal decisions that affect other people, we are therefore at least partially responsible for what happens in the group. Put differently, all group members are collectively responsible for group interaction and outcomes. We argue that a person cannot realistically say, "The group has failed in its objectives because Bill and Susan are always arguing" or, "It's not my fault that the group degenerated into petty quarrels and bickering; I didn't say a word all day." Appropriate comments might have stopped either conflict and smoothed the ruffled feathers; the person who chose not to intervene was partially to blame for the negative group outcome.

In addition to the interdependence of its members, the group as a whole is interdependent with the outside environment, with the larger communication system. Group members should be aware of the effects of that system on group process, as well as aware of the effects that

group decisions could have on the environment. The failure of many well-intended programs developed in a small group is frequently due to unexpected clashes between the program and elements in the larger system.

Differences Between Small Groups

Obviously groups vary in their objectives and composition. They can nevertheless be categorized on the basis of important distinctions in terms of origin, structure, membership, and orientation.

History

Is the group *zero-history* or *continuing?* If the group is brand new—if the particular mix of people has never come together before—there is no "history" on which to base their behavior. Group members cannot recall past experiences that can guide their interaction. They must start from scratch. Hence, they begin with zero-history. The continuing group, on the other hand, does have a history of interaction. Although not all group members will have participated equally in that history in different ways, their collective past will help guide group behavior. They will tend to conform to the established procedures of the group, for they cannot arbitrarily wipe out the past or behave as if the group had never been together before.

Duration

Is the group *ad hoc* or *permanent? Ad hoc* means "for this special purpose." The term implies that the group was formed to achieve a specific, usually short-range, objective and should disband as soon as that objective is achieved or when it is obvious that it cannot be achieved. In contrast, the permanent group remains operative regardless of the types of problems or tasks that will confront it. This does not mean that the permanent group has no specific purpose. However, when the group achieves a particular goal or finishes a task, it continues to function by taking on new but related work.

A common problem with permanent groups is that they may outlive their usefulness. Because of a rapidly changing environment, the kinds of problems they were set up to solve no longer exist. Hence, the group members may struggle to find new tasks to accomplish, not because such work is necessary, but because the group does not want to disband! Such groups are typical in large bureaucracies, but most of us have been in permanent groups that should not have continued to exist.

A related problem is the ad hoc group that tries to become permanent because the members enjoy the interaction. They feel a sense of accomplishment in completing their "one-time-only" task, so they try to convince outsiders that the group should continue. As a result, the real advantage of the *ad hoc* group—specific and adaptive focus on a unique problem—may be lost to a formality or rigidity that makes the group inappropriate to deal with new and quite different problems. Further, the membership mix may no longer include people with skills needed for the new problem. Hence, new tasks should be handled by new ad hoc groups.

Structure

Is the group *structured* or *unstructured?* In the structured group, the roles of each member, the procedures by which the group moves through its business, and group goals and tasks are all well developed and formalized. Members know specifically what is expected of them as well as what topics will be discussed. Examples of the structured group are a corporate board of directors, a student council meeting, or a military court-martial.

An unstructured group flows freely from topic to topic, procedures are only vaguely and indirectly defined, and personal roles vary as the interaction progresses. Unlike a more structured group, the unstructured group may have only casual awareness of a task or objective. Time constraints are fairly unimportant. When participants tire of the interaction, they simply adjourn. An example might be a group of students who meet in the coffee shop after every class to relax, converse, and simply enjoy the company of peers.

Obviously, *structure* is a relative term. Structured groups always are somewhat spontaneous, and unstructured ones inevitably develop various stated or implicit group rules and expectations. But relative structure is nonetheless an important dimension. Some people want to know precisely how the group will proceed; others feel uncomfortable and stifled by rigid group norms and procedures. Degree of structure is one of the first decisions any group must make.

A common misconception about task groups is that the more structured the group, the more efficient it will be. Actually, strict rules and procedures may impede progress toward the goals. Members must wade through rigid agendas, tight parliamentary procedure, and restricted communication patterns. They cannot move easily from less important to more crucial items because the rules do not permit it. Thus, small groups are susceptible to the same stifling red tape that paralyzes larger bureaucracies. With less structure, members can recognize when the decision-making process is lagging and can increase productivity simply by offering informal suggestions that the others accept. The group may then move quickly to a decision without procedural constraints.

Structure is not *inevitably* counterproductive, but when any structural element is proposed, group members should always ask what it is meant to achieve: "Who will be the leader?" "How long should we discuss this?" "Should we prepare an agenda?" "Should we vote on it?" "Do we want group bylaws?" Too often we adopt group procedures simply because we are accustomed to them. And we must conclude, like the familiar poster in the executive's office, "There's no reason for it; it's just our policy!"

Member Motivation

Is the group membership *voluntary* or *involuntary?* By *voluntary,* we mean that group members perceive or feel a need to assemble with others to solve a problem or complete a task. They welcome the group process because it represents a way of achieving personal objectives and receiving personal rewards. An example is a college study group, a few students who want to pool their information before a big exam.

An involuntary group is composed of people who did not initiate their own group membership; someone else (or the circumstances of the moment) required that they participate. This does not suggest that involuntary participants are dragged, kicking and screaming, into the group or that they remain resentful and uncooperative during group interaction. It does suggest, however, that members may have to work harder to sustain enthusiasm and build commitment to the group task. Examples of involuntary groups include a management team assigned by top management to make policy recommendations, a subcommittee appointed by a club president to plan a fund-raising project, or speech fundamentals students whose instructor divides them into small groups and assigns a specific project.

Our relative voluntariness fluctuates through time. Sometimes we are motivated to meet and participate; at other times we would rather abandon the group. The perceptive group member is not only aware of personal motives but regularly assesses the temperament of the group. The leader of an involuntary group should always supply members with good reasons for participating.

Orientation

Is the small group *externally* or *internally* oriented? If a group tends toward external orientation, tasks or objectives relate primarily to achieving some impact on the outside environment. This does not mean that group members will be personally unaffected by their decisions. It means that their reasons for meeting are based on outside needs. For example, an externally oriented group might be concerned with developing a new product for a company, organizing a political campaign, or preparing a convention program. Most of our group affiliations, although they may provide significant personal rewards, are based on external factors.

In contrast, an *internally* oriented group focuses on personal rewards, development, or change for group participants. Such groups are usually termed *learning, growth,* or *therapeutic* groups. Members want to learn more about themselves, develop greater awareness of the world around them by sharing group experiences, or even try to solve personal problems through the supportiveness of other group members. Internal groups may also complete specific tasks, however, as six students who meet and plan a fishing expedition in which only they will participate. Internal groups may be called self-centered because outsiders are linked only indirectly to group outcomes.

The inherent conflict between individual and group goals is examined in Chapter Fourteen. For now, you should note that in externally oriented groups, problems may arise when a participant is preoccupied with an internal justification for meeting and impedes progress on the group task. In general, groups should remain aware of their relative internal or external objectives.

Summary

If you have a deep interest in small group interaction, you should eventually take an entire course in the area. In this chapter, we have introduced some of the key concepts that would be studied in such a course.

A small group is a collection of people who interact to achieve specific objectives. Direct, face-to-face interaction between and among all members is possible. Small groups vary widely in their objectives and composition. Perhaps the most common type is the zero-history work group, having both task and maintenance functions. Communication is the glue that holds group members together.

Small groups develop unique cultures with role development as a crucial factor. Cultural and role characteristics change over time, giving special meaning to the term *group dynamics* and suggesting that group members need to maintain awareness of the growth and development of their group. They must also be cognizant of their interdependence and mutual responsibility with other group members and with the outside environment.

Questions

1. How do the following concepts affect group process or interaction?
   Zero-history
   Involuntary group
   Maintenance functions
   Role behavior
   Networks
   Norms
   Individual goals

2. Why is it appropriate to study the communication process and dyadic communication before we explore group communication?

3. Discuss the behavior repertories that represent all the different ways members can participate in and contribute to group process.

4. What role or roles do you typically play in small groups?

Suggested Readings

ARDREY, R. (1970). *The social contract.* New York: Atheneum.

BRILHART, J. K. (1974). *Effective group discussion.* Dubuque, Iowa: Wm. C. Brown.

BURGOON, M. ET AL. (1974). *Small group communication: A functional approach.* New York: Holt, Rinehart and Winston.

CATHCART, R., AND L. SAMOVAR. (1974). *Small group communication: A reader.* Dubuque, Iowa: Wm. C. Brown.

PETERS, T. J., AND R. H. WATERMAN. (1982). *In search of excellence: Lessons from America's best-run companies.* New York: Warner Books.

Chapter Fourteen

Small Group Leadership, Decision Making, and Participation

Preview

In the preceding chapter, we introduced some basic concepts for understanding small group communication dynamics. In this chapter, we examine three important practical aspects of small group communication—the process of decision making, and leadership and participation in groups. We identify the phases groups typically go through in reaching decisions, and the elements required for good decisions. We discuss the duties and responsibilities of group leaders, some differences in leadership style that may be observed, and some recurrent problems that confront small groups. Finally, we offer suggestions for effective group participation.

Objectives

To describe the process by which groups make decisions

To help develop practical communication skills and understanding for the improvement of leadership and participation in small groups

To identify some frequently encountered leadership problems in small groups

Decision Making in Small Groups

FOURTEEN   We have explored several characteristics of small groups. Because we are concerned primarily with work groups in this chapter, we need to examine the ways in which they typically achieve their tasks— the way they make decisions. Sometimes the decision will be a *conclusion* about what the information shows, as, for example, an interpretation of experimental data by a team of scientists. The task may involve *problem solving,* as with the strategy developed by a legislative committee to curb pollution. Such decisions are integral parts of the construction of programs to accomplish specific objectives.

Phases of Group Decision Making

Decision making is sometimes haphazard and unpredictable and, therefore, difficult to analyze. Fisher's important study (1974) of small groups helps describe a typical process of decision emergence. From an analysis of both the message acts and interacts, Fisher develops a process based on four phases: orientation, conflict, emergence, and reinforcement. Although Fisher makes no claim that the four phases apply uniformly to all groups, his study gives us confidence that we can learn to observe and understand the ways in which groups use communication to accomplish tasks in fairly predictable ways.

During the *orientation* phase, group members search for ideas, directions, and purposes. Many ambiguous comments and expressions of agreement suggest that members are still uncertain of their roles and want to feel out the situation with more tentative points of view. In the *conflict* phase, issues become identified, and people state positions that others strongly support or dispute. Dissent, controversy, and polarization are frequent. Opinions are stated frequently and without the ambiguity of phase 1. In phase 3, the *emergence* phase, conflict decreases gradually, and comments become somewhat more ambiguous and tentative, less dogmatic or absolute, as the group moves toward consensus. Phase 2 statements like, "That idea is totally unacceptable," might become, "Perhaps we shouldn't totally rule out that idea," in phase 3. Group members whose attitudes are changing slowly toward the emerging decision probably use ambiguous statements as a kind of "modified dissent." Finally, phase 4 is characterized by *reinforcement* as argument virtually disappears and comments favoring the emergent solution increase. Vague comments diminish, and specific positive reinforcement becomes a device for showing unity behind the group decision.

We are reluctant to prescribe a rigid step-by-step sequence for group decision making, though such sequences have been proposed. The basis for many of these systems is Dewey's (1910) "reflective thinking" model, which suggests how disciplined minds actually solve problems. Dewey's five steps include:

1. Feeling a difficulty, being aware that something is wrong
2. Locating and defining the problem
3. Suggesting possible solutions
4. Developing, elaborating, and finding information on the suggested solutions
5. Continued testing, observing, evaluating of solutions, leading to rejection of all solutions but one

Similar processes, usually more prescriptive than Dewey's, have been developed in current literature. For example, in a popular textbook on group discussion, Brilhart (1974, 110–111) suggests specific patterns for group problem solving, as in the following series of questions:

"What is the nature of the problem facing us?"

"What might be done to solve the problem?"

"By what specific criteria shall we judge among our possible solutions?"

"What are the relative merits of our possible solutions?"

"How shall we put our decision into effect?"

Each question—or stage in the problem-solving process—can include several subquestions, which the group leader may use as a general outline for the problem-solving effort. Ross (1974, 323) introduces a four-step agenda as paraphrased below:

1. Definition and limitation of the problem
2. Analysis of the problem, its type and causes
3. Establishment of criteria for assessing solutions
4. Evaluation and selection of the best solution

It is probably unrealistic to expect group communication to progress neatly from step to step, but it evidently is useful for both leader and participants to have a general strategy clearly in mind. We suspect that regardless of planned agendas, participants will regularly digress, overelaborate, move out of sequence, and develop ideas irrelevant to the specific discussion topic. For example, a group might become preoccupied with an intriguing new program, enthusiastically discussing its merits, until one person interjects, "Hey, wait a minute. There are other ways to solve the problem, and I think we need to look at them." Another participant might complain, "By now we should be discussing some possible solutions, but we still can't agree on our goals!" Nevertheless, we know that unsystematic groups are often just as productive as more structured ones.

Essential Elements of Group Decision Making

We explain a general set of requirements for group decision making in this section. Although these elements need not develop in sequence, they are essential for productive group achievement, and all depend on verbal communication. The group leader, discussed in the next section, is usually the most significant determinant of how these four interrelated elements are developed.

Objectives   Though groups sometimes flounder aimlessly on a variety of topics, eventually they must answer the questions, "What do we want to happen? What are we trying to do or achieve? Why are we here?" Goal setting may become the most difficult and lengthy decision the group must reach or it may be brief and perfunctory. Objectives may not even be stated openly if, for example, the group meets regularly and its purpose is patently obvious. Without some general sense of objectives, however, good decisions are unlikely.

Procedure   Admittedly, many groups or committees become prisoners of procedure. They get bogged down in strict agendas and rigid parliamentary rules when spontaneous group interaction might lead to a quicker and better solution. Some structuring of group interaction is necessary, however, if only in the form of a simple statement: "Today let's decide what kinds of information we need; then we'll discuss how we can get it." Or the procedure may involve a carefully structured set of rules, like those that govern such arenas of decision as courtrooms or legislatures. A middle ground might be the step-by-step guidance provided by a meeting agenda.

The more specific and rigid the procedures, the more limited the appropriate content of any message. "I think we should still be discussing our objectives; your comments about the problem can be presented later." Although less rigidity may allow group members wider latitude in the kinds of messages they may communicate, it may also create uncertainties about how they should contribute. "May I tell you what I think we should decide or should that wait until later?" Even leaderless groups will develop some procedural guidelines, in part because such guidelines suggest appropriate kinds of input.

Information Processing   Good decision making depends on good information. A crucial advantage of group over individual decision making is the potential for pooling information and submitting it to group evaluation. The group must seek, gather, sort, combine, modify, and evaluate information. While insufficient information may lead to faulty decisions, an excess of information can cause difficulties as well. An individual may experience *information overload*—too much data to process neatly and meaningfully. The same problem may develop in groups, suggesting that one of the most important decisions the group must make is to answer these questions: "When do we have enough good information? When will further input simply confuse the issues and delay a decision?"

The Decision   The group must arrive at a decision. An obvious point? Yes, but one that is sometimes forgotten. I, Gordon, once sat on a university committee that had met several times annually for several years. We had a title and a purpose, a chairman and recording secretary, regular meeting times, and a rough agenda. But we never *decided* any thing substantive. We shared an enormous amount of information, analyzed and evaluated it, wrote and distributed reports on our deliberations, commiserated about the difficulty and complexity of the issues involved, argued about potential policies we might suggest, and regularly revised our discussion topics, focus, and procedures. But we never decided on any new policies or alteration of old ones. The committee still exists, continues to meet, and has not decided anything yet, except perhaps deciding not to decide!

Work groups meet because they want to accomplish something. The constraints of time or the urgency of the moment may force the emergence of decisions. With complex tasks and ample time, however, we may forget our ultimate purpose—to arrive at a conclusion, to achieve an objective, to make a decision. In a courtroom, when a jury cannot decide after a reasonable time, it becomes a hung jury and ceases deliberations. In some cases, when indecisive groups flounder, members may not admit their inability to get closure on their ascribed tasks, and they continue to wallow in uncertainty.

Leadership in Small Groups

How does a person become a leader of a group? What are the objectives and duties of leadership? What styles of leadership generally emerge? What suggestions can improve group leadership? These are some of the questions we answer in this section.

Group Leaders

Any group leader should ask, "How did I get here? What is my legitimacy? How will the selection process affect my relationship with the group?" Groups usually acquire leaders in one of three ways. First, the leader is assigned or elected by outsiders or is self-appointed. Examples might be a supervisor who asks an employee to head a management team or a legislature that elects someone to chair a subcommittee. In such cases, the group members have no say as to who will lead them. They also have no doubt as to who has the right to lead, for legitimacy is established immediately. However, the appointed leader must maintain that legitimacy through effective performance of leadership tasks.

Second, the leader is selected through formal group procedures as the group begins its discussions. Perhaps annual elections determine the group moderator or perhaps a casual suggestion that someone would make a good leader prompts a show of support to establish legitimacy. Thus, the group quickly assures that someone will assume responsibility for coordinating group effort, and the person chosen is secure in knowing that the role resulted from group confidence in his or her abilities. If the selected leader fails, of course the group must face the awkward task of replacing someone whom they initially supported.

Third, the leader emerges. From the Minnesota Studies on group discussion, Bormann (1969, 207–216) notes that leaderless groups usually develop structure and roles spontaneously. Through the "method of residues," the group eliminates various people from consideration until only one person remains as the emergent leader. Sometimes groups have to select from two or three contenders for the leadership role. Although the eventual leader may know that his or her special skills, knowledge, or interpersonal style may be deemed effective by the group, he or she should also recognize that some group members, especially any who also wanted to be leader, may be uncooperative and may continue to harbor bad feelings.

Leadership Goals

Leadership objectives vary with the type of group and task involved. Nevertheless, there are several goals, listed next, that are commonly suggested as relevant in work groups. Notice that some are task or content oriented, whereas others focus on group maintenance and interpersonal process. While reading each goal, try to think of the kinds of messages a group would use to achieve it.

To initiate discussion of the topic at hand

To help structure the group decision-making process, as through setting an agenda

To regulate participation, assuring that all can provide input and preventing some from monopolizing

To establish an appropriate physical environment through room preparation, chair and table arrangements, and provision of supplies

To develop appropriate communication climates: positive, cordial, relaxed, task oriented, cooperative

To help manage or resolve interpersonal conflict

To restate and clarify ideas of participants

To keep the discussion relevant and productive

To provide summaries and closure on group conclusions

To bring the group to productive achievement of overall objectives

To develop plans and objectives for future meetings

To stimulate development of group culture: build rapport, commitment, cooperation

To distribute rewards and punishments, confirming positive contributions and criticizing negative ones

To integrate oneself into full-fledged group membership; to assure personal as well as leadership input

To foster group morale and enthusiasm for the task

To provide liaison between the group and the outside environment by representing group consensus and decisions to outsiders

What other objectives might be added to this list? Are some of these goals inappropriate for certain situations? How might goal setting vary according to particular types of group experience? In general, we believe that it is useful for the leader not only to think carefully about leadership objectives in advance of the meetings but also to *discuss with the group,* perhaps even negotiate with group members, the goals he or she hopes to accomplish.

Leadership Styles

The preceding goals listed depend heavily on leadership style. The communication behavior of a small group leader is also influenced by his or her leadership style.

A distinction is made among authoritarian, democratic, and laissez-faire leadership. *Authoritarians* use authority, power, rewards, and punishments to assure group compliance with their wishes. Their communication may consist of commands, opinion statements, evaluation and criticism of others, and dogmatic arguments. Interpersonal contact is distant and cold. Authoritarian motives include domination, power, and self-fulfillment. Task achievement is more important than people.

Democratic leaders attempt to distribute power more widely throughout the group, seeking greater input for each member. They stress a "we" orientation rather than the "I" approach of the authoritarian. Key terms are participation, reinforcement, persuasion, supportiveness, mutual responsibility, and trust. Communication is usually facilitative, with leader messages consisting of suggestions, questions, clarifications, and encouragement. Democratic leaders attempt to balance concern for the group tasks with concern for people in the group. Many comments are process or maintenance oriented. In essence they ask, "How are we doing?" and "How do we feel?"

Laissez-faire leaders essentially abandon their directive roles, letting the group progress as a spontaneous social unit. Their attitudes suggest indifference and nonresponsibility for group outcomes, and may be motivated out of disgust, hostility, or hurt feelings. ("It's obvious that you don't care what I think, so you all just go ahead and discuss without me.") Such passive leaders may have been appointed to their role, and because they are shy or unskilled in group processes, they may simply withdraw. The laissez-faire style may be motivated by a sincere belief that direction stifles creativity and that total spontaneity leads to the most productive group process. Whatever the reason, abdicated leadership usually leads to (1) a group that flounders aimlessly or (2) an assumption of leadership by a more dominant, task-oriented person. Passive leaders are silent most of the time, comment only when spoken to, and are noncommittal on group decisions. Fortunately, such leaders are rare.

The key element in leadership style is *control,* the degree to which the leader seeks to direct and regulate group interaction and outcomes. Ross

AUSTRALIA II

(1974, 332) suggests the continuum in Figure 14-1 as a model for the varying levels of control. We generally support the midpoint on the continuum, the democratic style, though we agree with Fiedler (1965) that the optimum style depends in part on the type of task, its relative structure, and the comparative power and influence of the leader. In some cases, a more directive strategy of control might be appropriate. Still, leaders who are willing to treat others as legitimate partners in the group process with equal rights to participate are probably the most effective leaders in most situations.

We suggest one addition to the concept of democratic leadership—a *consensus strategy*. Phillips (1966, 7–8) offers a good definition of consensus:

The word "consensus" refers to the distinguishing feature of the small group, any group of two or more people who, for a given period of time, are concerned with a mutual goal and who devote their efforts during this time to the achievement of that goal. . . . Sometimes consensus is built on agreements about minor points over a period of time. Sometimes it is a major insight that suddenly reveals a solution that all members can accept. Consensus is the result of careful interpersonal communication in which members subordinate some of their personal feelings and desires to demonstrated facts or necessity. . . . The basic idea is that some personal preferences must be surrendered to the welfare of the group. The minority must not sulk in silent opposition. It must be reconciled. The final agreement must include the ideas of all.

Thus, consensus does not mean "majority." It means *total group agreement* on decisions. If a vote is necessary, then there are winners and losers, and the consensus strategy has failed. To achieve complete agreement, the leader may need to take more time arriving at group decisions, assuring that a cooperative, problem-solving attitude has been developed, that full discussion by all members on all important issues has been encouraged, and that all points of agreement and potential compromise have been explored. The democratic leader with a consensus strategy is quick to praise members with the courage to change their opinions and is open to accepting what he or she previously opposed. Some differences are irreconcilable, and no one should be forced to join the majority simply out of group pressure. Nevertheless, the consensus style is remarkably productive and can usually be developed by the perceptive, patient leader.

Suggestions for Group Leaders

We have noted that several types of small groups and the many spontaneous ways in which individual roles and group culture develop. Because of these variations, because each situation, leader, and task is unique, we cannot develop a list of rules that applies generally to small group communication events. On the other hand, development of leadership skills is possible if one is willing to adapt general principles to the unique group situation.

Next we try to make such an adaptation to a fairly common type of small group situation—a zero-history group with an assigned leader; the group is to meet periodically to gather information and solve a problem.

FIGURE 14–1

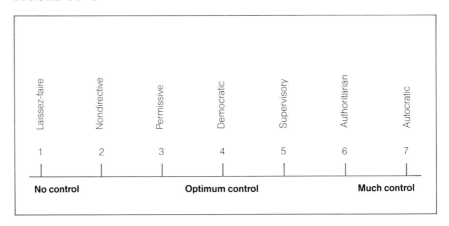

We provide general suggestions, not hard and fast rules. Feel free to dispute any suggestion and to consider situations when such behaviors would be inappropriate.

Before the first meeting

1. Review the time schedule, the topics or problems to be covered and the background materials, if any, that apply to the group task.
2. Review the roster of group members, learning their names and pertinent biographical data.
3. Visit the room or area where the group will meet, and note potential problems like lighting, seating, and noise levels.

The first meeting

1. Arrive early enough to arrange the physical environment. Use a circular seating arrangement so that each person can see everyone else. Set up any necessary equipment or supplies.
2. Remain in the meeting location to greet arriving group members.
3. Select a seat in a noncentral position to help discourage participants from directing all their comments to you. Don't isolate yourself in a special chair, and don't always sit in the same chair each meeting.
4. Explain your role as group leader and how you would like to interact with the others. They should know what to expect of you.
5. Discuss the concept of *collective responsibility* for achieving group goals, that is, no one person should bear the burden. If the group is unproductive, all should share the blame. Emphasize the active role that participants should take.
6. Negotiate ground rules for the meetings:
   a) Avoid personal attacks or innuendos
   b) Start and end on time
   c) Allow one person to speak at a time, with no side conversations
   d) Avoid tendencies to monopolize
   e) Have a smoking policy
   f) Have a policy on breaks or recesses

Whatever the ground rules, they should result from group consensus rather than from being imposed by the leader.

7. Negotiate group objectives; seek group participation in defining and limiting what the group wants to achieve.

8. Encourage an informal atmosphere. Use a casual, conversational speaking style. Suggest that the group operate on a first-name basis.

9. Do not forget the social or maintenance dimension of small groups. At this and all other meetings, encourage a few minutes of small talk on nontask topics.

All other meetings

1. In advance of each meeting, prepare at least a rough agenda, and seek agreement with the group on that agenda as the meeting begins. Be selective; it is better to discuss two or three items in depth than to be a slave to a lengthy agenda and discuss items sketchily.

2. Try to avoid defensive reactions to participants' suggestions that attempt to modify your ideas about group objectives or procedures.

3. Try to steer the group away from becoming a gripe session; suggest a more constructive problem-solving or task-oriented attitude.

4. If certain group members regularly look to you as the authority or final arbiter or ask you to clarify information and provide definitive statements on issues, try to *deflect* those questions to other group members. This may encourage participation and enhance the climate of *group* responsibility for effective results.

5. Respond selectively to group comments. Do not respond to every statement or group members will tend to direct all their remarks toward you.

6. Your substantive input (opinions, information, ideas) should be as relevant as anyone else's. Avoid dominating, but remember your dual leadership role as facilitator *and* participant. Leaders should not attempt to be neutral on all issues; nor should their points of view be communicated dogmatically.

7. Be sensitive to nonverbal cues about how well the discussion is going. Recognize, for example, people nervously shifting in their chairs, or daydreaming, or their negative facial expressions, audible sighs, and avoidance of eye contact with the speaker. Make a visual survey every couple of minutes, watching especially for people trying to get a chance to speak.

8. Be sensitive to your personal nonverbal behavior, like frowning, avoiding eye contact, or looking at your watch as another is speaking.

9. Try to observe and analyze role development in group participants.

10. Do not let the group perpetuate misunderstandings. Seek clarification and elaboration. Encourage members to restate in their own words what they understand another member to have said.

11. Try to steer long, meandering digressions back on the track, but do not adhere slavishly to the suggested topic if the group is avidly pursuing an equally relevant item. Remember that groups rarely progress in a neat, linear fashion and that group consensus often emerges at the end of a so-called digression.

12. Keep track of time; help the group modify procedures if time becomes a factor.
13. Provide occasional summaries of what has been said and about where the group is in its progress toward a solution. Note points of stated or implied agreement.
14. Avoid voting to resolve disagreements.
15. Protect the individual group member—his or her right to be heard, to finish what is being said, to be free from personal attack, and to have ideas interpreted accurately.
16. Do not discourage humor; it can relieve tension and build rapport. But do not let the group degenerate into a joke-telling session.
17. Do not permit the group to sidestep awkward or sensitive information or issues if such content is crucial to the best possible solution. For example, if the group carefully avoids any criticism of a previous policy because a group member directed that policy, the leader may have to introduce (tactfully, yet clearly) the troublesome issue and seek responses.

Closure

1. Provide *closure* with a brief summary that suggests what has been accomplished and perhaps what issues remain. Give a sense of completion. You may want to ask a competent group member to provide the summary.
2. Suggest a time for the next meeting along with possible objectives or agenda items.
3. Be the last to leave; chat casually with members about any concerns that they did not want to discuss with the entire group.

In addition to these specific suggestions, we offer some comments on knotty problems that may arise regardless of the type of small group involved.

Discussion Monopolies   If one person is monopolizing the discussion, reaffirm the ground rules. "Some of the participants haven't had a chance to speak yet." Seek responses from less vocal members. It may be necessary to talk to the monopolizer privately: "I appreciate your input, John, but I'm worried that some people aren't getting a chance to speak."

The Chronic Interrupter   In the case of chronic interruptions, reaffirm your group's ground rules. "Let's permit people to finish their comments." Interrupt the interrupter. "Just a moment, Jane; I don't think Bill was finished." If the interrupter persists, a private talk may be necessary.

Private Conversation between Subgroups of Two or More People   Stop side conversations by noting, for example, "I'm having trouble hearing. Let's try to have just one person talking at a time." If problems persist, manipulate the seating arrangement to split up the subgroup.

Silent Group Members   If the quieter members of the group appear interested, watch for nonverbal indicators that they might want to speak, and call on them occasionally. Don't embarrass them with too frequent recognition. Show interest when reticent members are talking. If silent members appear uninterested or hostile, talk to them privately to get at the cause of their negative feelings.

Extended Argument between Two People   When it is apparent that arguers are no longer giving new information but simply rehashing old data, ask for input from others. "I think Jane and Bill have given us the basis for both sides of the issue; now let's have the rest of you react to some of their ideas." Ask each disputant to rephrase the other's position. "Jane, before you reply to Bill, I'm wondering if you would tell us what you hear Bill saying. What do you think his argument is?" If more such dyadic arguments are likely, incorporate the debate format as a decision-making tool and set clear time limits.

Interpersonal Conflict   If conflict within the group is issue oriented, it can be a constructive way of getting at all aspects of the problem. In many cases, it adds interest and can be encouraged. If conflict is people or personality oriented, on the other hand, in most cases it must be stopped, or it can destroy group cohesion. Remind members of ground rules—no personal attacks. Affirm the legitimacy of conflict. "It's natural for us to disagree on controversial problems, especially when we come from such different backgrounds." Talk about the disagreement and suggest some self-disclosure on why it may have developed. *Do not try to sweep it under the rug.* Talk it out—a slow, painful, yet crucial task for group maintenance.

A Lifeless Session with Bored, Unresponsive Members   Talk out the apparent problem and make sure others share your perception. Remind the group that everyone shares responsibility for making the group a meaningful experience. Ask for suggestions. Do some self-analysis. Is part of the problem due to your own lack of enthusiasm? Analyze group members. Are the negative reactions of one or two opinion leaders casting gloom over the proceedings? Suggest a frank discussion on group goals, topics, and methods. Would other strategies, like debates or guest participants or the establishment of subgroups, enhance interest? Is this just a bad day in the life of a generally enthusiastic group? Should we adjourn early and try again next week? Has the group outlived its usefulness? These and similar questions prompt group participation in what is too often thought of as the leader's problem.

Participation in Small Groups

We conclude this chapter with some comments about productive group participation for leaders and nonleaders alike. The following suggestions may improve your constructive contribution to group goals:

1. Be aware of personal motives and objectives. Assess the extent to which those personal perspectives may either help or impede group progress.
2. Assess the expectations of other group members toward you. What role do they expect you to play? Is such a role productive? Are you willing and able to fulfill those expectations?
3. Accept equal responsibility to intervene when the group encounters problems. Recognize the interdependence of participants and that your decision *not* to intervene is still a decision affecting group outcomes.
4. Develop nondefensive, nonjudgmental communication styles. Evaluate information and ideas, not people. Remember, too, that arguments against your ideas do not necessarily signal a personal attack.
5. Actively seek clarity in communication. Ask others to rephrase comments you do not understand, and seek feedback from others regarding your messages.
6. Remain sensitive to group process. Do not place on the leader the full responsibility to monitor the interacting task and maintenance functions.
7. Develop commitment to group goals. If you cannot conscientiously do this, it may be better to drop out of the group.
8. Confront group and task problems openly and honestly. Avoid deception or evasion. Do not pretend that important group or task problems do not exist.

Summary

Effective leadership and participation in small groups requires an understanding of how groups make decisions and of what kinds of leader and member communication behaviors contribute to the quality of those decisions. In this chapter, we offer concepts useful for analysis of decision making and leadership, and give you practical suggestions for effective group participation as a leader or member of the group.

Questions

1. Suggest some pros and cons of using a structured agenda to control decision making in small groups.

2. Describe hypothetical situations in which a laissez-faire, a democratic, and an authoritarian leader might be the most productive.

3. Discuss the specific tasks for which leaders are responsible in small groups.

4. What are some common behavior problems exhibited by group participants?

Suggested Readings

BRILHART, J. K. (1974). *Effective group discussion.* Dubuque, Iowa: Wm. C. Brown.

BURGOON, M. *ET AL* (1974). *Small group communication: A functional approach.* New York: Holt, Rinehart and Winston.

FISHER, B. A. (1974). *Small group decision making.* New York: McGraw-Hill.

PETERS, T. J. and R. H. WATERMAN (1982). *In search of excellence: lessons from America's best-run companies.* New York: Warner Books.

ZELKO, HAROLD (1969). *The business conference: Leadership and participation.* New York: McGraw-Hill.

Chapter Fifteen

Listening and Responding

Preview

Most topics in interpersonal communication are approached from the speaker's point of view. This tradition is usually followed even if we adopt a "receiver-oriented" perspective. It is true, of course, that a sufficiently thorough treatment of the speaker leads inevitably to discussions of the listener, and to the dynamic interaction and interdependency of speakers and listeners. At the same time, the topic of listening encourages a look at communication processes from the listener-respondent point of view. In this chapter, we focus on the listener as an active participant with special needs, skills, and influences over the nature and quality of interpersonal communication.

Objectives

To provide a model of listening and responding

To discuss the listener in terms of his or her personal goals

To discuss the listener in terms of situational demands

To discuss listening skills and response strategies

FIFTEEN   During a social get-together of undergraduate and graduate speech majors, an undergraduate approached one of our graduate students with the comment, "You know, you graduate students act as though you are something special; you must think that you are superior or something."

The undergraduate served as an initiator and set the stage for a variety of possible responses. The graduate could have responded by trying to "deck" the undergraduate; he could have responded with an equally demeaning evaluation of undergraduates, or he could have simply turned and walked away. But the graduate student did none of these things; he simply smiled and said, "Tell me more." That response seemed to catch the undergraduate off guard and he felt compelled to "say more."

As the undergraduate continued to talk, the graduate showed considerable interest and proceeded to ask for more details. As time passed, their conversation became more relaxed and more focused upon the specific issues and concerns.

The graduate student was *listening,* and he invited the undergraduate to "say more." In so doing he was also saying, "You are a person, you count. I'm going to pay attention to you and maybe I can help." Through responding in this way, he did help. And as the conversation came to an end, the undergraduate was heard thanking the graduate for "listening to his problems."

In this chapter, the listener is viewed as an *active communicator*—a person who not only attends to speaker messages but also mediates them and reacts with responses that *make a difference.* Therefore, although we consider the traditional problems of attending and retaining, we also focus on listener *strategies* that can influence and can guide the quality of exchanges between a speaker and a listener.

A Model of Listening and Responding

A model of the communication process should recognize the *dynamic interaction* and *interdependence* that characterize all forms of human communication. An appreciation of this interaction and interdependence among speakers and listeners is more likely if we consider the *roles* of speakers and listeners—that is, if we consider what speakers and listeners *do* and how they *affect* each other (see Figure 15–1)

FIGURE 15–1

A Model of Speaker-Listener Message Activities

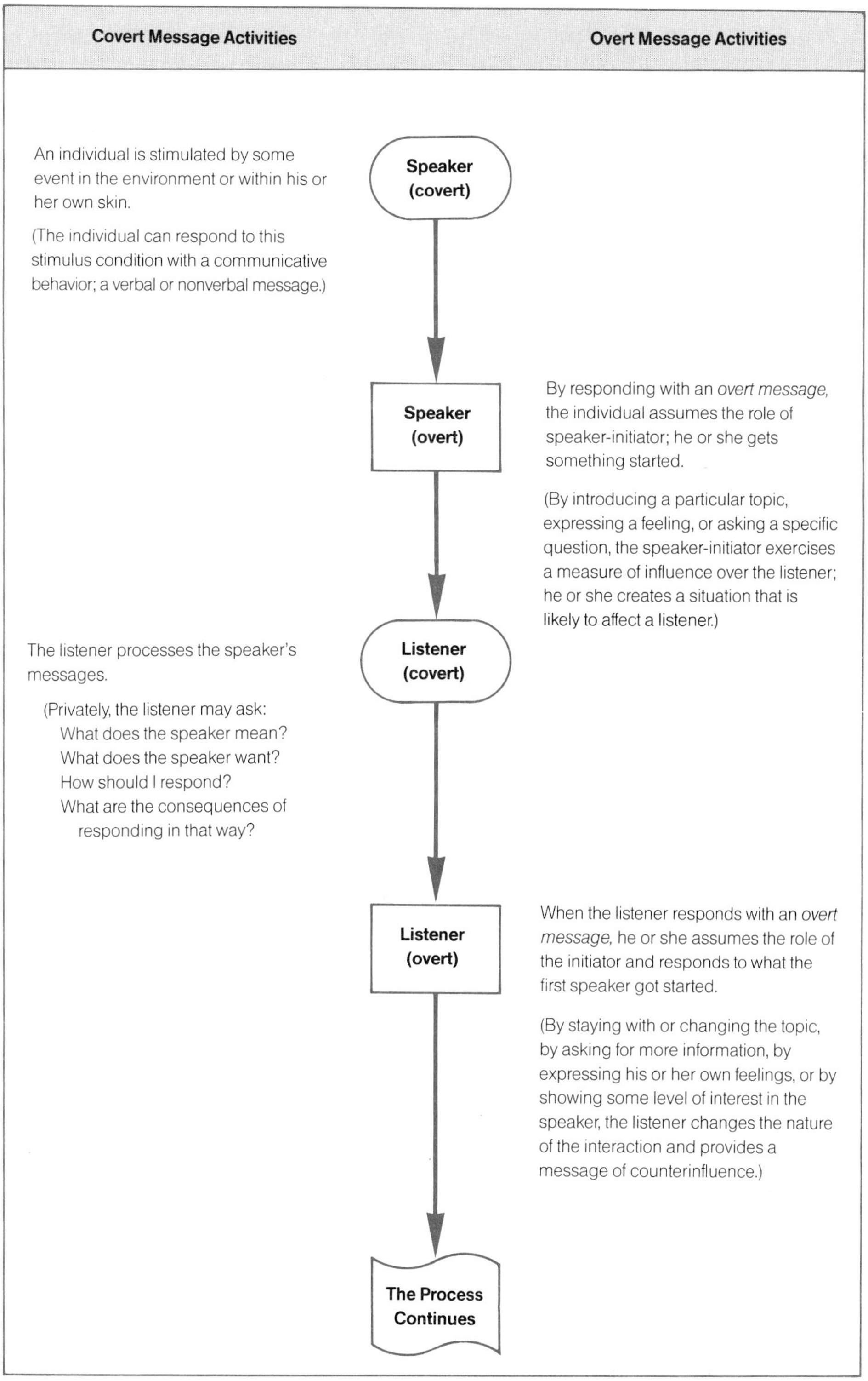

Covert Message Activities	Overt Message Activities

An individual is stimulated by some event in the environment or within his or her own skin.

(The individual can respond to this stimulus condition with a communicative behavior; a verbal or nonverbal message.)

Speaker (covert)

Speaker (overt)

By responding with an *overt message,* the individual assumes the role of speaker-initiator; he or she gets something started.

(By introducing a particular topic, expressing a feeling, or asking a specific question, the speaker-initiator exercises a measure of influence over the listener; he or she creates a situation that is likely to affect a listener.)

The listener processes the speaker's messages.

(Privately, the listener may ask:
   What does the speaker mean?
   What does the speaker want?
   How should I respond?
   What are the consequences of
      responding in that way?

Listener (covert)

Listener (overt)

When the listener responds with an *overt message,* he or she assumes the role of the initiator and responds to what the first speaker got started.

(By staying with or changing the topic, by asking for more information, by expressing his or her own feelings, or by showing some level of interest in the speaker, the listener changes the nature of the interaction and provides a message of counterinfluence.)

The Process Continues

Speaker and Listener Roles

A speaker may be viewed as one who functions as an *initiator:* A speaker introduces a given issue or topic or describes his or her feelings about something. By providing these messages, the speaker has the effect of *directing* the course of communication; that is, he or she directs the listener to particular ideas or topics. The speaker may add further direction through such statements as, "What do you think about that?" "How do you feel about that?" "Do you agree?" "Do you have any questions?"

A listener functions as a *respondent.* Some of the listener's responses are *covert* (or private), whereas others can be *overt* (or public). Covert responses include more than the traditional notions of attending and responding; they also include all phases of message processing, such as "perceiving," "interpreting," "analyzing," "synthesizing," and "evaluating." Covert responding also includes the formulation and evaluation of potential overt responses.

A listener responds *overtly* to the extent that his or her reactions are visible to the speaker. These visible responses often serve to influence and shape the course of subsequent interactions. Even a simple smile or frown might reinforce a direction taken by a speaker, might modify that direction, or might encourage a new one.

As noted in Figure 15–1, speakers and listeners affect each other by *exchanging the roles of* initiator and respondent. In the dyad, the roles of initiator and respondent move back and forth between two participants. In small groups, the roles move among several participants. In the public speaking setting—characterized by more formalized roles of speaker and audience—the dominant initiator is the public speaker, and members of the audience are temporarily cast in the role of silent respondents. Even

during a formal speech, however, an audience usually provides considerable nonverbal feedback that can influence the speaker's performance. In addition, on many occasions a formal speech is followed by a question and answer session, thus allowing for the systematic exchange of initiator and respondent roles.

In effect then, all forms of human communication are characterized by dynamic interaction and interdependence. As we have seen, the speaker-listener dichotomy is misleading if we only view the listener as passive receiver and retainer of messages. The listener is an active monitor and processor of speaker messages, and he or she frequently shifts to the role of initiator by responding with verbal and nonverbal messages that can be as influential, if not more so, than those of the original speaker. For these reasons, the *quality* or *effectiveness* of listening and responding is an essential issue in human communication.

Listening and Personal Variables

As with a speaker, a listener brings his or her own *history, motives,* and *skills* to a particular occasion for communication. These personal factors play a major role in terms of a listener's ability to deal with speaker messages as well as interest in those messages.

In important ways, *listener ability* is a function of education and training. That is, as we develop a larger vocabulary and an expanded repertory of concepts and insights, we are better prepared to deal with a broader range of speaker messages. Additionally, however, the development of specific listening skills can significantly enhance our overall listening effectiveness. Practical listening skills include (1) listening for main ideas and (2) effective note taking.

Listening for Main Ideas

Most speaker messages focus on a few main ideas, which, in turn, are clarified or developed through a larger number of supporting statements. The listener who recognizes this fact can begin to develop habits of listening for main ideas. When we can identify and understand a speaker's central ideas, we will usually find that only casual attention must be directed to the many statements used to clarify and elaborate those ideas. At the same time, when we have only a vague understanding of one of the speaker's main ideas, we can direct particular attention to the examples and other supporting materials designed to clarify or develop the implications of that idea. In any case, most of a speaker's essential meanings are usually captured in a few key statements; by learning to "zero in" on such statements, we can usually discover the essential content of a speaker's message.

Effective Note Taking

With classroom lectures or lengthly public speeches, a listener is exposed to a large quantity of messages. In cases such as these, effective note taking can help the listener retain the speaker's main ideas. Once more, effective note taking usually focuses on the speaker's key ideas, and these ideas can be captured in brief summaries. A common mistake is to try to record too much information. We can become so involved in the writing of details that we miss the speaker's main ideas. Because notes taken during an extended speech may be unorganized and sketchy, it is also helpful to rewrite and reorganize them while our recall is still fresh. We will usually do most of our forgetting during the first twenty-four hours, so notes should be rewritten and clarified as soon as possible.

Perhaps the most important factor in effective listening is *listener interest*. We all listen "selectively" and our own particular habits of *selective listening* are not only governed by our learning history but also by our current interests.

Although selective listening is a common feature of all listeners, we can become more *systematic* and *focused* in our listening activities by stating our goals as explicitly as possible. Clearly, listeners are bombarded with a multitude of speaker messages, and it is inconceivable that a listener could or should try to identify and retain a sizable percentage of them. As a matter of fact, much of what we hear is of limited or even negative value, and the more quickly discarded, the better. In any case, to gain the most from our listening experiences, it is useful to clarify our goals and to focus selectively on those messages that can make an important difference. In short, if we are highly motivated and focus our listening activities in terms of predetermined goals, our success as a listener is significantly more assured.

Listening and Situational Variables

Effective listening also requires the appropriate orientation and focus in terms of unique situational variables. It is particularly useful to distinguish

between task-oriented and people-oriented settings and the unique demands they place upon a listener.

In general, *task-oriented* settings are those in which it is appropriate to direct one's primary energies toward specific issues on topics *other than* the behaviors of participants. In contrast, *people-oriented* settings are those in which the primary focus is on the behavior of the participants—including their personal interests and problems. Quite often, the "task" of a people-oriented setting is the improvement of participants' coping skills or the quality of their interpersonal relationships.

The serving of a subpoena to appear in court is an example of a task-oriented communication event. In this case, the server's purpose is to gain the correct identity of the person to be served and to place the subpoena in his or her hand. It is doubtful that the exchange would include serious consideration for an individual's feelings about being served. On the other hand, a visit to a hospitalized friend is usually weighted toward people-oriented communication. Most likely, the central purpose of this visit is to communicate concern for the patient as a person. The messages are likely to focus on the feelings and well-being of the patient, and serious discussions about outside tasks are probably inappropriate.

In brief then, effective listening and responding requires that we recognize the primary nature of a communication setting and adapt in terms of the unique demands of that setting. In task groups, an effective listener actively evaluates speaker messages in terms of their contributions toward task achievement and responds in terms of needed information. Additionally, an effective listener keeps the exchanges moving in the direction of constructive task accomplishment. In people-oriented groups, the listener actively evaluates the needs of individual participants and attempts to respond with understanding, with support, or as a facilitator who tries to resolve personal problems or interpersonal conflicts.

Listener Response Strategies

Some still think of a listener as a relatively "passive" communicator who is simply on the receiving end of speaker messages. Accordingly, they view the listener's primary task as "attending to" and "trying to remember" speaker messages. But an active listener not only *attends* to and *retains* speaker messages, he or she also *responds* to them. These responses are a crucial aspect of the communication process.

A speaker exercises a measure of influence over a listener in the sense that his or her messages have their effects upon a listener. A speaker introduces a topic, directs attention to particular items of information, engages in persuasive tactics, and expresses judgments. But listeners are not passive victims. Through a variety of response strategies, a listener can exert considerable counterinfluence over the nature and quality of speaker-listener interactions. Effective response strategies often require skills in the use of probing language and summary language. Many settings also require the skillful use of supportive or nonsupportive messages.

Probing Strategies

A listener employs *probing language* in order to seek additional information. In general, probes include *open-ended* questions and *closed-ended* questions. *Open-ended questions provide a strategy for gaining general information* as a basis for the more specific exchanges that follow. Such questions are very general in nature and allow the respondent a considerable amount of latitude. For example, when presented with the question, "How do you feel about starting college next fall?" an individual is free to answer in a large number of ways. In effect, when a listener asks an open-ended question, he or she exercises a minimum of control over the respondent. The question might influence the general direction of the conversation through the introduction of a particular topic, but the terms of an open-ended question can be satisfied with an almost infinite number of possible answers.

Open-ended questions generate a variety of responses to a particular topic, and provide listeners with an opportunity to gain a considerable amount of information that can be utilized as a basis for further exchanges. For example, open-ended questions are frequently employed in the clinical setting to encourage an individual to talk about problems so that the therapist can better identify and deal with them. In the deliberative group, open-ended questions can be employed to gain a sense of other participants' feelings about problems and their proposed solutions. At the negotiation table or in a debate setting, a listener might employ open-ended questions to discover more about the opponent's thinking on a particular issue. A member of an audience might direct an open-ended question to a public speaker to achieve a similar purpose.

Closed-ended questions provide a strategy for gaining specific information. Closed-ended questions are very specific and tend to limit pos-

sible answers. For example, the question, "Which college will you attend next fall?" offers a person little latitude in response. In effect, when a listener asks a closed-ended question, he or she exercises considerable control over the respondent. With the closed-ended question, the listener not only introduces the topic to be discussed, but also indicates the precise nature of the response desired. In the clinical setting, a therapist might use the closed-ended question to learn of a person's precise feelings about a specific event. In a deliberative group, questions can be used to gain explicit responses on specific aspects of problems or solutions under consideration. In negotiation, debate, and public address settings, closed-ended questions can be employed to encourage a direct response to a particular issue.

The closed-ended question also provides an effective tactic for dealing with ambiguous or overly general comments. Through the skillful use of a series of closed-ended questions, a listener may direct another individual toward the more explicit expressions needed to achieve progress toward task achievement.

Summary Strategies

The listener can use summary language to achieve a number of important purposes. In both people- and task-oriented settings, for example, the use of summary statements can provide a measure of communication fidelity and can allow for the correction of errors. Through listener-provided summaries, the speaker has a chance to detect and correct for misunderstandings.

We know that different individuals assign unique meanings to a single set of speaker messages. Accordingly, the more effective listener is sensitive to the fact that *messages received* cannot be equated with *messages sent*. To avoid misunderstanding, the listener is well advised to check his or her interpretation of important messages against the intended meanings of the speaker. Clearly, the correction of errors is easier in a dyad or small group than in public speaking or larger group settings in which two-way exchange is limited. As a general rule, however, the more important the message, the more important it is for the listener to check for accurate understanding before acting on that message. Without this kind of listener effort, the listener is too often misled and the speaker is misrepresented.

The listener can also employ summary statements to identify specific points of agreement or disagreement. By summarizing different points of view, we can clarify the degree of agreement or disagreement on a given issue. Summary statements also permit a listener to identify the essential points in a participant's comments and to put those comments in perspective relative to agreed-upon tasks. Quite often, the employment of summary language provides a constructive alternative to the premature use of judgmental language.

Judgmental language includes all statements in which a communicator expresses his or her opinions concerning the "rightness" or "wrongness" of something. Unfortunately, most people rely too heavily on judgmental language and tend to introduce judgments prior to adequate understanding or sufficient deliberation. The main problem with judgmental language is that it tends to generate defensiveness and inhibits or stops the more careful deliberative processes necessary for task achievement.

Once judgmental responses are introduced, they tend to generate additional judgmental statements. For example, if a speaker is presenting ideas on a particular socioeconomic issue and the listener responds with "that sounds like a communistic point of view," the speaker will likely feel threatened and turn his attention to a defense of his own position or perhaps will counterattack the listener.

To avoid the barriers that result from the judgmental response, Carl Rogers (1961) advocates a simple technique that emphasizes the use of summary language. Rogers' technique requires the listener to repeat to the speaker's satisfaction the essence of what the speaker has said. The listener might introduce this summary with a comment like, "If I am hearing you correctly, you are saying . . ." or "What I hear you saying is that. . . ." In the listener's attempt to summarize the essence of what the speaker has said, the speaker also is provided an opportunity to detect misunderstanding and to correct errors. Through this process, much of the potential misunderstanding and breakdown that results from premature judgments can be avoided. According to Rogers, in many cases, the listener discovers that once he or she understands the speaker's comments, he or she will be in agreement.

Clearly, not all human conflict is a result of communication breakdowns. We all hold different values, and quite often the conflict can be traced to these differing points of view. Nevertheless, it is also apparent that many of our conflicts result from impulsive judgmental statements that occur prior to any real understanding, and use of Rogers' technique

can help to reduce inappropriate and unnecessary evaluative language. Eventually, of course, the nature of many communication encounters requires that we move in the direction of judgments, decisions, and the selection of a course of action. Even in these cases, however, it is likely that our tasks are more achievable if judgments are delayed until important issues and evidence have received mutual understanding and adequate consideration.

Supportive Strategies

Messages that tend to confirm our hypotheses about self, others, and our relationships may be termed *supportive messages.* Generally, supportive messages include all statements—both nonverbal and verbal—that recognize the legitimacy of a person, including his or her feelings and ideas.

At the nonverbal level, we might communicate our regard for another person through the way we manage space (finding a chair when that person enters a crowded room); or by the way we manage time (being prompt for an appointment); or through physical proximity (sitting near the other person); or by tactile contact (shaking hands).

At the verbal level, we can evidence support with a wide variety of statements. Even a routine comment such as, "Hello, how are you?" recognizes the communicator as a person and demonstrates at least moderate concern for his or her well-being. *Understanding responses* can be achieved by verbalizing the *essence* of what the other person has said; *elaboration responses* can be employed to evidence an ability to see the implications of another's statements.

Importantly, supportive communication does not require total agreement with the other person's statements or point of view. For example, when it appears that a friend is misinformed or is entertaining an ill-conceived strategy, concerned disagreement might be the most honest response and the most constructive in terms of the friend's needs and goals. The concern itself is likely to communicate regard for the communicator as a person and provide an acceptable basis for constructive disagreement.

Four Themes in Supportive Messages   In her exciting and provocative research on confirming and disconfirming communication, Evelyn Sieburg (1974, 6–9) identifies four themes that seem to describe essential aspects of supportive communication:

1. It is more confirming to be recognized as an existing human agent than to be treated as nonexistent.
2. It is more confirming to be responded to relevantly than irrelevantly or tangentially.
3. It is more confirming to have one's emotional expressions accepted than to have [them] interpreted, evaluated or denied.
4. Personal response is more confirming than impersonal response.

Sieburg's first theme underlines the notion that the initial step in supportive communication is the simple act of recognizing the existence of the other person. Although this point may seem obvious, we should consider that individuals in contemporary societies spend much of their life in relatively large, complex organizations where it is possible to remain almost completely unnoticed. Even where people have opportunities for communication, many lack the basic communication skills that facilitate contact with others. Interpersonal communication is perhaps the most rewarding of all human experiences. How human would we be without our contacts with other people?

Sieburg's second theme focuses on the *quality* of interpersonal recognition. We demonstrate supportive communication through recognition of another person, but we evidence a higher quality of support when dealing directly with the other person's feelings or ideas. When we introduce irrelevant or tangential messages, we are saying, in effect, "Your ideas and feelings do not deserve my serious consideration." It has been noted that many so-called dialogs are actually "duologs." That is, the exchange consists of each individual pursuing his or her own ideas and feelings while remaining impervious to the comments of the other person. A duolog may be compared to the "communication" between two television sets turned on and facing each other.

Sieburg's third theme suggests that there are preferred ways of *dealing directly* with another's ideas or feelings. Acceptance can be evidenced through comments such as, "I see how you feel" or "I can understand your concern." Specifically, it is more supportive to accept the other person's ideas and feelings than to interpret, evaluate, or deny them. According to Sieburg (8, 9), pseudoconfirming responses include:

> "You don't really mean that" (denial).
> "You're only saying that because you're angry—you'll get over it" (interpretation).
> "Forget it, you'll be OK tomorrow" (minimizing his feelings).
> "Everybody feels that way sometime" (discounting).

Finally, Sieburg's fourth theme suggests that communication can be more or less supportive depending on the extent to which it is *personal* as opposed to *ritualistic*. In Sieburg's words (9), "A person is more confirmed when he feels that others are willing to be involved with him as a unique person, not just as an organization role (supervisor, file clerk, executive, etc.)."

Listener Responsibility

Clearly, effective communication is more likely when the speaker's performance is communicative, and when possible, interesting and entertaining. But effective communication also places a good deal of the responsibility on the listener. Effective listening requires considerable effort when dealing with difficult topics or considerable tolerance when topics are unpopular or controversial.

We can gain a better perspective about the demands and responsibilities of listening in interpersonal settings by contrasting them with the minimal demands and responsibilities associated with television listening.

Because survival of the television industry requires a large number of willing listeners, major efforts are directed toward meeting listeners on their terms—catering to listener interests, values, and concerns in every conceivable way. To achieve listener *satisfaction,* important compromises are common. For example, substantive thought is frequently sacrificed for programming that provides popular interest and entertainment. In many speech situations, however, listener satisfaction is not the primary goal. In many cases, a speaker cannot act with responsibility unless he or she explores complex ideas that some listeners will find difficult. In other cases, a speaker may have to advocate a position that some listeners will find unacceptable.

Additionally, listening to television does not require the active participation associated with interpersonal activities. An impatient television listener can quickly change stations. In interpersonal settings, however a listener must consider the needs of others and his or her responsibilities toward them. Although interpersonal communication includes a variety of social dimensions and at times provides considerable entertainment value, many interpersonal settings primarily serve to inform or to persuade. And, to the extent that relevant information may be difficult, or that issues may be demanding, a greater burden is necessarily placed upon the listener. In effect then, listener responsibility requires an understanding of the alternative goals and tasks of interpersonal communication and a willingness to contribute to their achievement. Listening to television is usually low-demand, low-responsibility listening. Listening in the context of interpersonal settings can be far more demanding, frustrating, or anxiety producing. Fortunately, however, responsible interpersonal listening can also be far more provocative and enlightening and, in the long run, more substantive and rewarding.

Summary

A speaker functions as an initiator; through the introduction of specific topics or issues the speaker influences the initial direction of interpersonal communication. A listener functions as a respondent; through a variety of response alternatives the listener provides counterinfluences over the nature and quality of interpersonal communication.

Effective listening is a function of both personal and situational variables. It requires motivation and skills, such as (1) listening for main ideas and (2) effective note taking. Effective listening also requires a sensitivity to task versus people problems. Task-oriented settings are those in which it is appropriate to direct our primary energies toward specific issues or topics other than the behavior of participants. People-oriented settings are those in which the primary focus is on the *behavior of participants,* including their personal interests and problems.

An active listener not only attends to and retains speaker messages but also responds to them. Effective and responsible listening is facilitated through the appropriate use of probing language, summary language, and when appropriate, the use of supportive comments, both verbal and nonverbal.

Questions

1. In what sense is listening more than just attending and remembering?

2. How does goal-directed listening differ from other forms of listening?

3. Under what circumstances can probing strategies facilitate a communicator's listening goals?

4. What are the similarities and differences between people-oriented and task-oriented communication?

5. What are the differences between supportive and nonsupportive messages? Give examples of each.

Suggested Readings

HEWES, D. E., M. L. GRAHAM, J. DOELGEA, and C. PAVITT. (1985). Second-guessing: Message interpretation in social networks. *Human communication Research, 11,* 299–334.

SIEBURG, E. (1976). Confirming and disconforming organizational communication. In J. Owen, P. Page, and G. Zimmerman, (Eds.), *Communication in organizations.* St. Paul, Minn.: West.

STAUFFER, J., R. FROST, and W. RYBOLT. (1983). The attention factor in recalling network television news. *Journal of Communication, 33,* 29–37.

STEIL, L. K., L. L. BARKER, and K. W WATSON. (1983). *Effective listening.* Reading, Mass.: Addison-Wesley.

References

ABELSON, R., AND M. ROSENBERG. Symbolic psycho-logic: A model of attitudinal cognition. *Behavioral Science*, 3, (1958), 1–13.

BARNLUND, DEAN C. Toward a meaning centered philosophy of communication. *Journal of Communication 12* (December 1962), 197–211.

BEM, D. J. *Beliefs, attitudes, and human affairs.* Belmont, Calif.: Brooks/Cole, 1970.

BOHR, N. *Atomic Physics and human knowledge.* New York: Science Editions, Wiley, 1961.

BORMANN, ERNEST G. *Discussion and group methods.* New York: Harper & Row, 1969.

BRILHART, JOHN. *Effective group discussion.* Dubuque, Iowa: Wm. C. Brown, 1974.

BROOKS, WILLIAM. *Speech communication, 2d ed.* Dubuque, Iowa: Wm. C. Brown, 1974.

CARLSON, R. E., *ET AL.* Improvements in the selection interview. *Personnel Journal 50* (April 1971), 268–75, 317.

CHOMSKY, N. *Syntactic structures.* The Hague: Mouton and Co., 1957.

DANCE, FRANK E. X., AND CARL LARSON. *The functions of human communication.* New York: Holt, 1976.

DAVITZ, J. P. *The communication of emotional meaning.* New York: McGraw-Hill, 1964.

DEWEY, JOHN. *How we think.* Chicago: Heath, 1910.

FESTINGER, LEON. *A theory of cognitive dissonance.* Evanston, Ill.: Row-Peterson, 1957.

FIEDLER, FRED. The contingency model: A theory of leadership effectiveness. In L. Berkowitz (ed.), *Advances in experimental social psychology, I.* New York: Holt, 1965, 538–51.

–––. *Small group decision making.* New York: McGraw-Hill, 1974.

FOULKE, EMERSON. Listening comprehension as a function of word rate. *Journal of Communication 18* (September 1968), 198–206.

FREELEY, AUSTIN. *Argumentation and debate, 3d ed.* Belmont, Calif.: Wadsworth, 1971.

HALL, EDWARD. *The silent language.* Garden City, N.Y.: Doubleday, 1959.

HAYAKAWA, S. I. *Language in thought and action.* New York: Harcourt-Brace, 1964.

HUSEMAN, RICHARD, JAMES LAHIFF, AND JOHN HATFIELD. *Interpersonal communication in organizations.* Boston: Holbrook, 1976.

283

JENSEN, J. VERNON. Communicative functions of silence. *ETC: A Review of General Semantics 30* (September 1973), 259–63.

KNAPP, MARK. *Nonverbal communication in human interaction.* New York: Holt, 1972.

LAING, R. D., H. PHILLIPSON, AND A. R. LEE. *Interpersonal preception: A theory and a method of research.* New York: Springer, 1966.

LUFT, J., AND H. INGHAM. *The johari window: A graphic model for interpersonal relations.* Los Angeles, Calif.: Western Training Laboratory for Group Development, UCLA Extension Office, 1955.

MASLOW, ABRAHAM. *Motivation and personality.* New York: Harper & Row, 1954.

MAYFIELD, EUGENE. The section interview—A re-evaluation of published research. *Personnel Psychology 17* (Autumn 1964), 239–60.

MC GUIRE, W. J. A syllogistic analysis of cognitive relationships. In C. I. Hovland, M. J. Rosenberg (eds), *Attitude, organization and change.* New Haven, Conn.: Yale University Press, 1960, 65–111.

MEHRABIAN, ALBERT. Communication without words. *Psychology Today 2* (September 1968), 52–5.

Mental Maps. *Newsweek,* Mar. 15, 1976, 71.

MORRIS C. W. *Signs, language, and behavior.* Englewood Cliffs, N.J.: Prentice-Hall, 1946.
–––. *Varieties of human value.* Chicago: The University of Chicago Press, 1956.

OSGOOD, C. E., G. J. SUCI, AND PH. H. TANNENBAUM. *The measurement of meaning.* Urbana, Ill.: University of Illinois Press, 1957.

PHILLIPS, GERALD. *Communication and the small group.* Indianapolis: Bobbs-Merrill, 1966.

POWELL, JOHN. *Why am I afraid to tell you who I am?* Chicago: Argus Communications, 1969.

ROGERS, CARL. *On becoming a person.* Boston: Houghton Mifflin, 1961.

ROGERS, EVERETT, AND F. FLOYD SHOEMAKER. *Communications of innovations.* New York: Free Press, 1971.

ROKEACH, MILTON. *Beliefs, attitudes, and values.* San Francisco: Jossey-Bass, 1968.

ROSS, RAYMOND. *Speech communication: Fundamentals and practice.* Englewood Cliffs, N.J.: Prentice-Hall, 1974.

SAPIR, E. *Language: An introduction to the study of speech.* New York: Harcourt, Brace & World, Inc., 1921.

SIEBURG, EVELYN. Confirming and disconfirming communication in an organizational context. *The Personnel Woman 18* (February 1974), 4–11.

SOMMER, ROBERT. *Personal space.* Englewood Cliffs, N.J.: Prentice-Hall, 1969.

STEWART, JOHN (ED.). *Bridges, not walls.* Reading, Mass.: Addison-Wesley, 1973.

STICHT, THOMAS, AND DOUGLAS GLASNAPP. Effects of speech rate, selection of difficulty, association strength and mental aptitude on learning by listening. *Journal of Communication 22* (June 1974), 174–88.

TOULMIN, STEPHEN. *The uses of argument.* Cambridge: Cambridge University Press, 1958.

WATZLAWICK, PAUL, JANET BEAVIN, AND DON JACKSON. *Pragmatics of human communication.* New York: W. W. Norton, 1967.

WHORF, B. L. *Language, thought, and reality.* New York: Wiley, 1956.

Index